# Virtue's Reasons

"This interesting collection is packed with creative and interesting papers that promise to open up new debates about the connections between virtue, reason, and moral development."

—Bradford Cokelet, University of Miami

Virtues and reasons are two of the most fruitful and important concepts in contemporary moral philosophy. Many writers have commented upon the close connection between virtues and reasons, but no one has done full justice to the complexity of this connection. It is generally recognized that the virtues not only depend upon reasons, but also sometimes provide them. The essays in this volume shed light on precisely how virtues and reasons are related to each other and what can be learned by exploring this relationship.

*Virtue's Reasons* is divided into three sections, each of them devoted to a general issue regarding the relationship between virtues and reasons. The first section analyzes how the virtues may be related to, or linked with, normative reasons in ways that improve our understanding of what constitutes virtuous character and ethical agency. The second section explores the reasons moral agents have for cultivating the virtues and how the virtues impact moral responsiveness or development. The final section examines how reasons can be employed in understanding the nature of virtue, and how specific virtues, like modesty and practical wisdom, interact with reasons. This book will be of major interest to scholars working on virtue theory, the nature of moral character, and normative ethics.

**Noell Birondo** is Associate Professor of Philosophy at Wichita State University, USA. His primary interests lie at the intersection of contemporary ethical theory and ancient Greek philosophy. His articles have appeared in *The Monist, Ancient Philosophy, Ratio*, the *Journal of Philosophical Research*, the *Southwest Philosophy Review*, and the *International Encyclopedia of Ethics*.

**S. Stewart Braun** is Lecturer in the School of Philosophy and a member of the Institute of Religion and Critical Inquiry at Australian Catholic University. He specializes in social and political philosophy and also in normative and applied ethics. His articles have appeared in the *Journal of Applied Philosophy* and *Law and Philosophy*, among others.

# Routledge Studies in Ethics and Moral Theory

For a full list of titles in this series, please visit www.routledge.com

29 **Moral Responsibility and the Problem of Many Hands**
   *Ibo van de Poel, Lambèr Royakkers, and Sjoerd D. Zwart*

30 **Environmental Skill**
   Motivation, Knowledge, and the Possibility of a Non-Romantic Environmental Ethics
   *Mark Coeckelbergh*

31 **Developing Moral Sensitivity**
   *Edited by Deborah S. Mower, Phyllis Vandenberg, and Wade L. Robison*

32 **Duties Regarding Nature**
   A Kantian Environmental Ethic
   *Toby Svoboda*

33 **The Limits of Moral Obligation**
   Moral Demandingess and 'Ought Implies Can'
   *Edited by Marcel van Ackeren and Michael Kühler*

34 **The Intrinsic Value of Endangered Species**
   *Ian A. Smith*

35 **Ethics and Social Survival**
   *Milton Fisk*

36 **Love, Reason and Morality**
   *Edited by Esther Engels Kroeker and Katrien Scaubroeck*

37 **Virtue's Reasons**
   New Essays on Virtue, Character, and Reasons
   *Edited by Noell Birondo and S. Stewart Braun*

# Virtue's Reasons
New Essays on Virtue, Character, and Reasons

Edited by Noell Birondo and
S. Stewart Braun

LONDON AND NEW YORK

First published 2017 by Routledge

2 Park Square, Milton Park, Abingdon, Oxfordshire OX14 4RN
52 Vanderbilt Avenue, New York, NY 10017

*Routledge is an imprint of the Taylor & Francis Group, an informa business*

First issued in paperback 2019

Copyright © 2017 Taylor & Francis

The right of the editors to be identified as the authors of the editorial material, and of the authors for their individual chapters, has been asserted in accordance with sections 77 and 78 of the Copyright, Designs and Patents Act 1988.

All rights reserved. No part of this book may be reprinted or reproduced or utilised in any form or by any electronic, mechanical, or other means, now known or hereafter invented, including photocopying and recording, or in any information storage or retrieval system, without permission in writing from the publishers.

Notice:
Product or corporate names may be trademarks or registered trademarks, and are used only for identification and explanation without intent to infringe.

*Library of Congress Cataloging-in-Publication Data*
Names: Birondo, Noell, editor.
Title: Virtue's reasons : new essays on virtue, character, and reasons / edited by Noell Birondo and S. Stewart Braun.
Description: 1 [edition]. | New York : Routledge, 2017. | Series: Routledge studies in ethics and moral theory ; 37 | Includes bibliographical references and index.
Identifiers: LCCN 2016047701 | ISBN 9781138231733 (hardback : alk. paper)
Subjects: LCSH: Virtue. | Character. | Virtues.
Classification: LCC BJ1521 .V587 2017 | DDC 179/.9—dc23
LC record available at https://lccn.loc.gov/2016047701

ISBN: 978-1-138-23173-3 (hbk)
ISBN: 978-0-367-25844-3 (pbk)

Typeset in Sabon
by Apex CoVantage, LLC

*For Elizabeth Anne Signorelli*

*and*

*For Thomas Henry Braun*

# Contents

Introduction: Virtue's Reasons   1
NOELL BIRONDO AND S. STEWART BRAUN

## PART I
## Reasons, Character, and Agency   9

1   Moral Virtues and Responsiveness for Reasons   11
GARRETT CULLITY

2   Remote Scenarios and Warranted Virtue Attributions   32
JUSTIN OAKLEY

3   Vice, Reasons, and Wrongdoing   49
DAMIAN COX

4   Can Virtue Be Codified? An Inquiry on the Basis of Four Conceptions of Virtue   65
PETER SHIU-HWA TSU

## PART II
## Reasons and Virtues in Development   89

5   Virtue, Reason, and Will   91
RAMON DAS

6   Self-Knowledge and the Development of Virtue   107
EMER O'HAGAN

7   Aretaic Role Modeling, Justificatory Reasons, and the Diversity of the Virtues   126
ROBERT AUDI

## PART III
## Specific Virtues for Finite Rational Agents    145

8    Practical Wisdom: A Virtue for Resolving Conflicts
among Practical Reasons    147
ANDRÉS LUCO

9    The Virtue of Modesty and the Egalitarian Ethos    168
S. STEWART BRAUN

10    Virtue and Prejudice: Giving and Taking Reasons    189
NOELL BIRONDO

*Contributors*    203
*Index*    205

# Introduction
Virtue's Reasons

*Noell Birondo and S. Stewart Braun*

## I. Background to the Volume

Over the past thirty years or so, virtues and reasons have emerged as two of the most fruitful and important concepts in contemporary moral philosophy. Virtue theory and moral psychology, for instance, are currently two burgeoning areas of philosophical investigation that involve different, but clearly related, focuses on individual agents' responsiveness to reasons. The virtues themselves are major components of current ethical theories whose approaches to substantive or normative issues remain remarkably divergent in other respects. The virtues are also increasingly important in a variety of new approaches to epistemology.

Many writers have commented on the close connections between virtues and reasons: for instance between the ethical virtues—justice, courage, temperance, honesty, and so on—and the different ranges of morally relevant reasons that seem to be intimately, or even conceptually, tied to them.[1] Even so, the relationship is complicated, and it seems safe to say that no one has yet done justice to the complexity of the interconnections between virtues and reasons. To compound matters, the more recent growth of virtue epistemology, with its focus on the intellectual virtues, only makes the interconnections between virtues and reasons that much more challenging for anyone attempting to understand their relationship.

Virtues and reasons are, of course, by now widely recognized as major concepts that figure in almost any kind of serious moral thinking. They also inform philosophical work in ethics from a variety of theoretical perspectives, whether Aristotelian (or eudaimonist, or more broadly 'virtue-ethical'), Kantian, consequentialist, or intuitionist. A better appreciation for the interconnections between virtues and reasons still seems to be needed, however, since most contemporary discussions have focused on how the virtues enable

---

1 Here one might think, especially, of the work of Robert Audi (1995, 2009), Philippa Foot (1978), Rosalind Hursthouse (1995, 1999), John McDowell (1979, 1980), Martha Nussbaum (1988), and Bernard Williams (1995).

their possessors to appreciate and respond to reasons for acting in certain ways, or to the reasons for holding certain attitudes—ethically relevant attitudes, like admiration or regret, but also epistemic attitudes such as belief, which need not be of any particular ethical interest. Virtues and reasons seem to have interconnections that are not limited to the specific reasons made available to the individual practical intelligence of a deliberating (or inquiring) agent, as such contemporary discussions might suggest. Instead, virtues and reasons seem to exist in a network of mutually influential relationships, in which specific assessments of a person's character, or the specific facts that constitute (possibly unnoticed) normative reasons for her, are impacted by the nature of these relationships. It seems natural to include the wider set of issues that emerges from these relationships under the heading of 'virtue's reasons.'

In exploring such reasons, there are many interesting questions to confront. For instance, we might ask whether there actually are adequate reasons—as some recent philosophical situationists seem to suggest—for withholding the attribution of virtuous traits based on what someone would do in remote hypothetical scenarios. Perhaps such scenarios remain, in fact, irrelevant to the proper attribution of the virtues (or other stable traits) to specific individuals. There are, moreover, developmental issues regarding what normative reasons there might be for aiming, in general and in specific cases, to cultivate the virtues of character in the first place. Do such reasons have a different nature than, say, reasons for action? Are there different sorts of reasons here, not just reasons to *do* certain things, but also reasons to *be* a certain kind of person overall? Addressing such questions could presumably shed light on what it means for someone to be a good ethical role model. Connected with those developmental issues are questions concerning the reasons there might be for cultivating such seemingly admirable traits as practical wisdom, open-mindedness, and modesty—not only as ethical agents, but also as ethical theorists. By addressing a diverse set of questions on the connections between virtues and reasons, the papers here do not offer a sustained treatment of one or two core issues; instead, the papers that we have collected here form, together, a kind of kaleidoscope of issues surrounding the notion of *virtue's* reasons.[2] By appearing together in this one volume, the essays below will hopefully allow previously unnoticed patterns to come into view, enabling further research on the multiple interconnections between virtues and reasons.

The main aims of this book are therefore to foster a greater appreciation for the multiplicity of reasons surrounding the concept of the virtues and to

---

2 Highly focused collections are, of course, valuable for their own and for obvious reasons. Three recent collections along these lines are especially worth mentioning here, Lord and Maguire (2016), Peters (2013), and Snow (2015), since they contain valuable additional discussions of some of the key themes taken up in the essays presented here.

shed light on what is presumably the paradigm case, of an individual agent responding to an array of potential reasons, often in diverse circumstances and contexts. The book contains substantive contributions to a major topic that still remains underexplored, and it presents novel discussions that should enhance philosophical understanding of reasons and their interconnections with the virtues—especially the virtues of character, but also, in a more modest way, the intellectual virtues as well. Below we outline the structure of the book and preview some of the core issues discussed by the contributors.

## II. The Chapters

The volume is divided into three sections. Part I, "Reasons, Character, and Agency," contains contributions regarding the paradigm connection between virtues and reasons. The essays in this section analyze how the virtues are tied to, or linked with, normative reasons, in ways that improve our understanding of virtuous character and ethical agency. Garrett Cullity argues, in his chapter "Moral Virtues and Responsiveness for Reasons," that our rich vocabulary of 'aretaic' terms is used in an evaluative manner to assess the quality of our responsiveness to morally relevant reasons. According to Cullity, to be virtuous is to be well oriented to morally relevant reasons and to respond appropriately *for* those reasons. In other words, what makes a response virtuous is the *nature of the response* to the relevant reasons. Since any such response seems to include three main elements, namely, the reason for the response, the object of the response, and the characteristics of the response itself, Cullity sorts the virtues into a three-tiered taxonomy based on their place in this overall structure.

In "Remote Scenarios and Warranted Virtue Attributions," Justin Oakley provides an analysis of the extent to which remote hypothetical scenarios should play a role in assessing whether someone possesses a particular virtue. Oakley examines Kant's restrictive account, according to which remote scenarios are entirely instructive in assessing someone's virtue, as well as Robert Adams's looser probabilistic account (Adams 2006). Differentiating his position from both accounts, Oakley argues that in order for remote scenarios to be useful in assessing someone's virtue, we need to look beyond the actual or dispositional behavior of an agent to the larger set of *reasons* the agent has for acting, or for being disposed to act, in a particular manner in a remote scenario. For Oakley, remote scenarios are diagnostically useful only if we are sensitive to the agent's overall reasons for action.

Damian Cox argues, in his chapter "Vice, Reasons, and Wrongdoing," that aretaic judgments can be helpfully mapped onto deontic judgments in order to formulate a theory of right action that he calls 'vice ethics.' Cox identifies an asymmetry between virtues and vices, insofar as the virtues supply only *prima facie* reasons for action, whereas vices seem to supply *pro tanto* reasons. This distinction implies that if an action is vicious, then we have decisive reason not to engage in that action; but virtuous action seems to be optional, since it represents a type of moral excellence. Cox argues, then, that while reasons of virtue are supererogatory, reasons of vice introduce moral obligations, so that the right action is the "least vicious of available actions." Cox defends this account of 'vice ethics' by arguing that the account possesses distinct advantages over a near competitor: Michael Slote's 'direct virtue ethics' (Slote 2001).

The final chapter in this section is Peter Shiu-Hwa Tsu's essay, "Can Virtue be Codified? An Inquiry on the Basis of Four Conceptions of Virtue." The aim of Tsu's paper is to challenge John McDowell's well-known 'uncodifiability' thesis (McDowell 1979). Tsu identifies four ways to conceptualize virtue, depending on how virtue is thought to interact with moral rules in the reasoning process of a virtuous person. These are (1) the 'absolute' conception, (2) the '*pro tanto*' conception, (3) the '*prima facie*' conception, and (4) the 'particularist' conception. According to Tsu, McDowell's account of virtue is *only* consistent with either the '*prima facie*' conception or the 'particularist' conception. Consequently, because McDowell is not working with either the 'absolute' or '*pro tanto*' conception of virtue, these two conceptions remain unaffected by the uncodfiability thesis. Tsu believes that the 'absolute' and '*pro tanto*' conceptions of virtue remain plausible, and that therefore virtue might be achieved through some kind of rule-following after all.

Part II, "Reasons and Virtues in Development," contains essays that explore how the virtues might be developed or cultivated, so that one acts from virtue and in line with good reasons. In his chapter "Virtue, Reason, and Will," Ramon Das reformulates a dilemma for virtue ethics that he has pressed in previous work. Das argues that someone's acting *as she should* in a certain situation might require that she "transcend" the fixed aspects of character that are given such importance in virtue ethics. Das contends that theorists such as Audi (1995), McDowell (1979), and Tiberius (2006) tend to run together *motivational* and *normative* reasons, so that acting "from a virtuous motive" and acting "for a good reason" cannot be properly distinguished from one another. Das argues that when the latter two notions are clearly distinguished, we can see how someone might rightly determine, "at will" and out of character, the reasons for which she acts. Given this diagnosis, Das provides a new formulation of the dilemma facing virtue ethicists. He maintains that virtue ethics "remains plausible roughly to the extent that it construes *acting for a good reason* in a way that is not distinctively virtue-ethical."

In her chapter "Self-Knowledge and the Development of Virtue," Emer O'Hagan examines what the development of virtue requires and how agents can ensure that they are acting from virtue. This leads her to a critique of Robert Audi's perspective. O'Hagan is largely in agreement with Audi that virtue requires a relatively stable character and a sensitivity to the right reasons. But she worries about how virtue is developed within

Audi's framework. In particular, she disagrees with Audi's claim that virtue cannot be attained "at will," that is, directly through an act of self-control. O'Hagan argues that there are techniques of self-reflection and self-regulation that agents can use to improve their characters. These techniques may vary, but they aim at achieving, in O'Hagan's words, "a morally refined self-conception," one that enables people to understand themselves better so as to act in a more virtuous manner.

The section concludes with Audi's wide-ranging chapter, "Aretaic Role Modeling, Justificatory Reasons, and the Diversity of the Virtues." Drawing on an analysis of the ways that virtues are modeled and developed, Audi argues for the fundamental importance of responsiveness to appropriate reasons. Audi maintains that reasons are more basic than virtues. However, he rejects the idea that specific rules can serve as guides to virtue, given the diversity of the virtues and the diversity of goods pursued by virtuous action. This view does not imply that the virtues are subjective or somehow reducible to normative reasons, nor that people lack stable dispositions of character. The point is rather that the virtues cannot be understood in isolation from reasons, and that sensitivity to reasons is fundamental to understanding the nature of virtue and how virtue can be modeled and developed.

Part III, "Specific Virtues for Finite Rational Agents," contains essays with a more practical focus. These essays examine how specific virtues interact with reasons. Andrés Luco, in his chapter "Practical Wisdom: A Virtue for Resolving Conflicts among Practical Reasons," develops an account of how an agent endowed with the virtue of practical wisdom can decide between the rationally incomparable reasons that sometimes confront an agent's choice. Luco contends that the virtuous agent should follow what he calls the 'Override Principle.' This principle directs someone to choose the course of action that secures some good corresponding to one type of reason, when doing so does not result in the loss of any goods corresponding to another type of reason. Luco defends the Override Principle against objections and concludes that it can serve to assist the practically wise agent in deliberating among rationally incomparable normative reasons.

In "The Virtue of Modesty and the Egalitarian Ethos," S. Stewart Braun develops a novel account of modesty. After analyzing recent approaches to understanding the virtue of modesty, Braun argues that, despite the shortcomings of these approaches, they all show a modest agent to be responsive to egalitarian reasons. According to Braun's analysis, a modest agent is disposed to act in a manner that attempts to avoid establishing or endorsing distinctions in social status or respect because the agent accepts the value of social equality. This 'Egalitarian Account' of modesty explains why modesty manifests itself in people's characters and dispositions in diverse ways, and why modest agents may act in the ways described by the competing theories. Braun contends that his Egalitarian Account of modesty provides a unified account of the virtue that helps to dissolve the debate about its nature and also to explain why modesty is admirable.

In the final chapter of this volume, "Virtue and Prejudice: Giving and Taking Reasons," Noell Birondo discusses what he calls the 'long-standing' criticism of Aristotelian virtue ethics. The target of the long-standing criticism is a foundational appeal to nature that purports to validate certain traits of character as *virtues* of character. Birondo argues that this criticism only properly targets what he calls an 'external' validation of the virtues and that it fails to appreciate the resources available to an 'internal' validation of the virtues. An internal validation would require, he says, an open-ended form of reflective scrutiny, a "giving and taking" of reasons with others, even those whose ethical outlooks differ radically from our own. Birondo's account advocates a widening of cultural perspectives in order to overcome a regrettable form of prejudice: an illiberal form of prejudice that can impede the rational revision of our own evaluative outlook.

Overall, this book collects valuable new essays that we believe will influence the course of further research on virtue ethics and moral psychology. However, we recognize that this collection is far from representative of all the excellent work being done throughout the philosophical community and that the volume is particularly unrepresentative of female philosophers. For several reasons, many female philosophers whose work we strongly admire were unable to contribute. This fact is, of course, unfortunate; and it points to some regrettable structural challenges facing the discipline. Nevertheless, we do not believe that it detracts from the quality, creativity, and insightfulness of the essays collected here.

We would like to acknowledge several people whose collective efforts enabled this book to come into being. We thank the authors for their timely contributions and for working to strengthen the essays into their present form. We thank the anonymous referees whose insightful and conscientious comments led to refinements in the overall structure and presentation of the book and to improvements in the individual essays. We would also like to express our gratitude to Andrew Weckenmann, our editor at Routledge, for his patience, direction, and good will. Most of all, we are grateful to Robert Audi for his generous advice, which was indispensable to the completion of the book, and even to its inception.[3]

## References

Adams, Robert Merrihew. 2006. *A Theory of Virtue: Excellence in Being for the Good*. Oxford: Oxford University Press.
Audi, Robert. 1995. "Acting from Virtue." *Mind* 104: 449–71.

---

3 Noell Birondo also gratefully acknowledges the support of an URCA grant from the Office of Research at Wichita State University, which assisted in the final stages of production. For their help in these stages, we thank Allie Simmons, at Routledge, and two current philosophy students at WSU: Charley Cleaver, for her help compiling the index, and Daniel Saunders, for his help with proofreading.

———. 2009. "Moral Virtue and Reasons for Action." *Philosophical Issues* 19: 1–20.
Foot, Philippa. 1978. "Virtues and Vices." In her *Virtues and Vices and Other Essays in Moral Philosophy*, 1–18. Berkeley: University of California Press.
Hursthouse, Rosalind. 1995. "The Virtuous Agent's Reasons: A Reply to Bernard Williams." In *Aristotle and Moral Realism*, edited by Robert Heinaman, 24–33. Boulder: Westview Press.
———. 1999. *On Virtue Ethics*. Oxford: Oxford University Press.
Lord, Errol and Barry Maguire, eds. 2016. *Weighing Reasons*. New York: Oxford University Press.
McDowell, John. 1979. "Virtue and Reason." *The Monist* 62 (3): 331–50.
———. 1980. "The Role of *Eudaimonia* in Aristotle's Ethics." In *Essays on Aristotle's Ethics*, edited by Amélie O. Rorty, 359–76. Berkeley: University of California Press.
Nussbaum, Martha C. 1988. "Non-Relative Virtues: An Aristotelian Approach." *Midwest Studies in Philosophy* 13 (1): 32–53.
Peters, Julia, ed. 2013. *Aristotelian Ethics in Contemporary Perspective*. New York: Routledge.
Slote, Michael. 2001. *Morals from Motives*. Oxford: Oxford University Press.
Snow, Nancy E., ed. 2015. *Cultivating Virtue: Perspectives from Philosophy, Theology, and Psychology*. New York: Oxford University Press.
Tiberius, Valerie. 2006. "How to Think about Virtue and Right." *Philosophical Papers* 35: 247–65.
Williams, Bernard. 1995. "Acting as the Virtuous Person Acts." In *Aristotle and Moral Realism*, edited by Robert Heinaman, 13–23. Boulder: Westview Press.

# Part I
# Reasons, Character, and Agency

# 1 Moral Virtues and Responsiveness for Reasons

*Garrett Cullity*

Moral discourse contains judgements of two prominent kinds. It contains deontic judgements about rightness and wrongness, obligation and duty, and what a person ought to do. As I understand them, these deontic judgements are normative: they express conclusions about the bearing of normative reasons on the actions and other responses that are available to us. And it contains evaluative judgements about goodness and badness. Prominent among these are the judgements that evaluate the quality of our responsiveness to morally relevant reasons. We have a rich vocabulary for making such evaluations—our vocabulary of aretaic terms. Aretaic terms are those which can be used to attribute virtues: terms such as "kind," "honest," "fair," "tolerant," and "reliable." However, while they can be used to attribute virtues, they have other uses, too; and they can be applied not only to persons but also to various states of persons, to actions and other responses, and to patterns of response.[1] In this paper, I offer an account of the relationship between some of the principal uses of aretaic terms; and I show how a useful taxonomy of moral virtues can be generated from the thought that these are ways of being well oriented to morally relevant reasons.[2]

## 1. Dimensions of Evaluation

When we judge that a response, or the person who makes it, is virtuous, we are making an evaluative judgement, not a normative one. A misreading of Aristotle might seem to encourage the contrary view. Here is the famous passage in the *Nicomachean Ethics* in which he presents his doctrine of the mean:

> We can be afraid, for instance, or be confident, or have appetites, or get angry, or feel pity, and in general have pleasure or pain, both too much

---

1 "Response" will be my catch-all term for types of action, thought, and feeling, and "object" for that to which a response responds.
2 For this thought, compare Audi (2009).

and too little, and in both ways not well. But having these feelings at the right times, about the right things, toward the right people, for the right end, and in the right way, is the intermediate and best condition, and this is proper to virtue. Similarly, actions also admit of excess, deficiency, and an intermediate condition.

(1106b19–24)

In this translation (Irwin's), "right" surely cannot have the deontic sense of "permissible." Aristotle is surely not saying that what is proper to virtue is having these feelings at the permissible times, etc. Questions of permissibility do not arise for feelings. Nor should we read "the right times" as "the times there is sufficient reason to have them" or "the times there is decisive reason to have them." Whether a normative reason does count in favor of a feeling or other response is independent of whether you should think it does; but whether your response is virtuous is not. If you are credibly told that your friend has died, then feeling sad is proper to virtue, but if he has not actually died, then there is no fact about his death that actually counts in favor of sadness.

"Right," then, should not be interpreted in this passage as expressing a verdict about objective normative reasons. Instead, we should read it evaluatively—in one of two available ways. If our interest is in identifying a state of perfect, unimprovable virtue, then we need to read "right" as meaning perfect or unimprovable. But if we are looking for an account of the kinds of virtue-attributions we ordinarily make, it must mean instead: good enough. The responses that are proper to virtue are the ones that are good enough, in the dimensions Aristotle mentions.[3] He mentions five such dimensions for feelings. However, when the response in question is an action, there are two other dimensions of evaluation which it is important to distinguish.

### Aim and Motive

It sounds odd to talk of having feelings "for the right end." That makes it sound as though Aristotle thinks we choose to have feelings like anger and pity because there is some further aim we are seeking to achieve by doing so—but the relationship most of us have to our feelings (trained actors aside) is not like that. It also sounds a bit odd to have Aristotle talking

---

3 "Good enough for what?" The correct answer to this question is the frustrating-sounding one: for virtue. Compare: "sloppy" means insufficiently attentive—we specify how much attentiveness is insufficient through the instances of behavior that we censure as sloppy in our evaluative practice. In the same way, we specify standards for morally adequate responses through our practices of aretaic evaluation. This allows that when I fall below such a standard, my circumstances might make it unreasonable to criticize me for doing so—resulting in blameless vice.

instead of having a feeling "with the right motive" (as Ross's (1961) translation does).[4] We do have feelings because of our recognition of the normative reasons that count in their favor—I can feel pity because of my awareness of someone's misfortune—but describing this as my "motive" for pity makes the response sound more deliberate than it is.

However that may be, when we turn to actions, we find that every intentional action has an aim, most have a motive, and that the distinction between them is important. The aim of an action is the goal towards which it is directed. In order for something you do to be an intentional action, there must be some such goal—something that makes it successful or unsuccessful, towards which you exercise control in performing it. Otherwise, it would not qualify as an intentional action, only a bit of behavior.

When aims are understood in this broad way—as embracing all the criteria of success for intentional actions—they include the further states of affairs that some actions are directed towards producing, but that is not the only kind of aim an action can have. What you are aiming to do might be expressive rather than productive. Actions, broadly speaking, may have two sorts of aims: they may be productive (of a state of affairs) or expressive (of a "meaning"), or both.[5]

So: when you perform an intentional action, it has an aim. Normally, when you pursue an aim, your doing so is explained by an attitude of yours towards it—an attitude we can indicate by completing sentences of the form "She F-d out of . . ." or "from . . ." or "for the sake of . . ." or "in order to . . ."—where what is supplied in the first two cases is the name of the attitude and in the other two its content. When an attitude plays this explanatory role, it is your motive for acting.[6] And normally, the attitude that explains why I pursue an aim includes the acceptance of some consideration as a reason for pursuing it. The two "normally"s are included to allow for exceptions. The first "normally" allows for intentional actions that lack a motive. I might idly pick up a crumb from the table without my adoption of this aim being explained by any further attitude towards it (not even "that I felt like it").[7] The second "normally" allows for cases of radical akrasia: cases

---

4 Reeve's (2014) "for the sake of what we should" is better. But even that carries the misleading suggestion that there is some further state *towards* which we form our feelings.
5 Actions can have expressive aims, but they can also be expressive in other ways—as is illustrated in what Hursthouse (1991) calls "Arational Actions." When spontaneously hugging someone expresses affection, the affection can be part of the *manner* in which one acts rather than an aim of the action.
6 This covers the motives for which we do things. But there are also motives we do not act on: these cannot be attitudes that explain any actions.
7 Compare Anscombe (1957, sects. 16–17). On Anscombe's view, what makes an action intentional is that the question "Why?" has application in a sense in which a positive answer gives a reason for action. Here, she maintains, the question *applies*, even though the answer to it is, "For no reason," so the action is intentional. However, we can ask: in virtue of what does that question have application? The answer, I think, is that the action is directed towards an aim. Actions are intentional in virtue of their aim, not their motive.

which involve not only deciding to do what I think I ought not to do, but deciding to do what I think there is *no* reason at all to do. There might still be something for the sake of which I am doing it. I might be acting for the sake of revenge, despite knowing that revenge is not a normative reason for action. My action would then have a motive, but the motive would not be a state of reason-acceptance.

But in the normal cases, a motive is a state the content of which includes accepting some consideration as a reason in favor of my action. Someone who hinders you out of malice is treating the annoyance to you as a reason for hindering you; someone who helps you from compassion treats the relief of your distress as a reason for helping; and someone who attends your lectures for the sake of learning about philosophy is treating that as a reason for attending. Notice how this gives us two different ways of referring to agents' motives. One is by giving the content of the consideration which is accepted by the agent as reason-providing ("He is motivated by the prospect of personal advancement"); another is by naming the agent's state of acceptance of that consideration ("He is motivated by ambition"). It is important not to confuse the two. When we say that the motive of your action is ambition, we are not saying that what explains it is your accepting your own ambition as a reason for what you do. Rather, "ambition" names a state which includes the acceptance of another consideration—the prospect of personal advancement—as a reason for action. Seeing this is important in order not to misunderstand the other-regarding motives of morally virtuous action. To ascribe motives of kindness to an agent is to say that her action is performed for the sake of someone else's welfare, not for the sake of her own kindness.

The plausibility of these claims about motivated intentional action relies on not adopting an overly intellectualist conception of what it is for one's action to be explained by accepting some consideration as a reason for acting. Take, for example, the actions that psychologists explain as being performed unreflectively under the control of the brain's "System 1": actions like that of the experienced fire-fighter who responds immediately to subliminal cues by getting out of a dangerous building.[8] There, the fire-fighter's action is intentional—it is directed towards the aim of getting out of the building. It is performed for the sake of safety: it has that motive. And here, too, we can say that there is a consideration—the fact that the building is unsafe—to which the fire-fighter is responsive, as a reason for getting out. Neither the fact itself, nor the acceptance of it as a reason, is tokened in an episode of conscious occurrent thought. But it is the fire-fighter's sensitivity to the fact that the building is unsafe, and acceptance that there is a reason to get out, that explains the action of getting out. To cover all cases

---

8 On Systems 1 and 2, see Kahneman (2011, pt. I). For the fire-fighting example, see Klein (1998, ch. 2).

of motivated intentional action, "accepting a consideration as a reason for action" has to be interpreted broadly enough to include such cases.[9]

The distinction between aim and motive is important because two actions can have the same aim but different motives, and this can affect how morally virtuous they are. In the *Groundwork*, Kant (1996) describes a shopkeeper who scrupulously gives his customers the correct change from motives of commercial prudence (4:397). Another shopkeeper might act with the same aim—to give his customers the correct change—but from a motive of respect: out of respect for their rights. Only the latter is morally virtuous. However, notice that Kant is correct that when the first shopkeeper gives his customers the correct change, "[p]eople are thus served honestly": his action is honest. The applicability of the aretaic term "honest" to an action is settled solely by reference to its aim. If an action has the aim of open dealing, then it is an honest action, whatever the quality of the motive from which it has been performed. The motive, however, is relevant to whether an action expresses the *virtue* of honesty.

However, with other aretaic terms, matters are not so simple. Consider the aim of helping someone to get what he needs. That aim, too, can be pursued from various different motives. Your motive might be to promote the person's welfare, or to demonstrate your superiority, or to hurt his pride, or to enhance your moral reputation, or (often?) some mixture of these. However, only to the extent that your action has the first of these motives could it qualify as *kind*. Moreover, having this aim and motive does not suffice. Your action must be performed with the right manner as well. Helping in a cold, rough or overbearing manner, even if for the right reasons, could disqualify your action from being kind.

Thus, different aretaic terms are defined by reference to different dimensions of evaluation. For an action to be honest, it is enough that it has a certain aim: that of open dealing with others. Another aim-specific aretaic term is "generosity." To act generously is to act with the aim of sharing one's resources with others. It does not matter what one's motive is: you might give me an ostentatiously generous gift in order to humiliate me, out of revenge for some perceived slight. Then you would still have performed a generous action, from a reprehensible motive.[10] But "kindness" is defined by reference to three dimensions of evaluation, not one. To qualify as kind, an action must have a particular aim (procuring a good for someone), a particular motive (furthering his welfare), and a particular manner (a gentle one).[11]

---

9 An interesting and important question is what further account to give of "accepting a consideration as a reason for action." Exploring this would take us too far afield here. But for a more detailed attempt to provide an account of reason-acceptance, and reasons-responsiveness more generally, see my "Stupid Goodness" (forthcoming, sect. III).
10 Compare Swanton (2015, 47).
11 I fail to acknowledge this point sufficiently in Cullity (1994).

Why the difference? This evidently depends on the interests we have in making these attributions. A prominent interest we have in distinguishing between different kinds of shopkeeper is to identify those with an aim of open dealing, whatever their motives. But the kindness it makes sense to encourage and care about is a way of interacting with others that has all three qualities, because all three are relevant to the conferring of fellowship-benefits, through receiving the assurance that we matter to others.

I should add a qualification to these remarks. Is it true that kind action *must* have a gentle manner? If I abruptly grab you, alarmed that you are about to be run over, might that not be kind? Perhaps so. Here, I agree with those who say that aretaic concepts are ones we possess in seeing the relationship of an instance to a prototype, rather than through the possession of a sharply bounded set of necessary and sufficient conditions.[12] So my remarks are intended to apply to the prototypical cases. Roughly grabbing you could qualify as kind, then, because of the relationship it bears to those cases. It could be an expression of the same dispositions that issue in prototypically kind action, motivated in the same way.

## 2. Virtue and the Aretaic

Aretaic terms are those—like "honesty"—that *can* be used to attribute virtues. But they do not always do so: Kant's shopkeeper just showed us that. If we say that "an aretaic property" is what something has when an aretaic term applies to it, then the relationship between virtue and the possession of aretaic properties needs to be handled with care. The case of honesty above shows us that this relationship is not straightforward. Kant's shopkeeper performs honest actions. Indeed, he is an honest shopkeeper, since it is characteristic of him that he performs such actions. But he lacks the virtue of honesty.[13] And the corresponding possibility exists for kindness. An action could possess the aim, motive and manner distinctive of kindness, and therefore be a kind action, without expressing the virtue of kindness. An example of this would be an act of kindness to a perpetrator in front of his victim: kindness needs to be properly discriminating in order to be virtuous. Having the three properties that are distinctive of kindness is not a guarantee of that.[14]

---

12 See Swanton (2003, ch. 13). On prototype concepts, see Ramsey (1998).
13 "Honesty" is an aretaic term, because it can be used to attribute a virtue and a virtue is a form of excellence. The properties named by aretaic terms are aretaic properties. But bearing an aretaic property need not be a way of being excellent, as Kant's shopkeeper illustrates.
14 Most aretaic properties are such that a response or a person can possess them without being virtuous. But "wise," "just," and "tactful" are different. Being properly discriminating is necessary for the possession of these properties.

How, then, can we explain the relationship between virtue and the possession of aretaic properties? I have a two-part proposal. The first part concerns the evaluative use of aretaic terms. They also have a non-evaluative use: that will be the second part, which we will get to shortly.

To state the first part, we need to introduce some terminology. When a pair of aretaic terms $V_n$ (a noun such as "honesty") and $V_a$ (the associated adjective, "honest") is defined by reference to one or more dimensions of assessment, let us call those the $V_n$-defining dimensions, and the properties that something must have in those dimensions in order to qualify as $V_a$ the $V_n$-defining properties. There is then one honesty-defining property: the aim of open dealing with others. But there are three kindness-defining properties: the aim of procuring a good for someone, the motive of furthering his welfare, and a gentle manner.

Here, then, is the first part of my proposal. An action, or any other response, is prototypically $V_a$ when it has the $V_n$-defining properties. A response is $V_a$ when it has enough in common with prototypically $V_a$ responses.[15] A person is $V_a$ when she characteristically makes $V_a$ responses. A response is virtuous (according to the standards we ordinarily employ) when, for some virtue $V_n$, the response is $V_a$ and is good enough in all dimensions. And a person has the virtue of $V_n$ (according to the standards we ordinarily employ) when she characteristically makes responses that are $V_a$ and are good enough in all dimensions.[16]

The application to kindness and honesty is this: The actions of Kant's shopkeeper are honest because they have the honesty-defining property (the right aim), and he is honest because he characteristically performs those actions. But his motive is morally indiscriminate: he is honest only for the sake of commercial gain. So his actions are not virtuous, and he lacks the virtue of honesty. Likewise, the indiscriminately kind person performs actions with the kindness-defining properties (the right aim, motive and manner), but is insensitive to the circumstances in which he performs them. It is because his action is bad in that dimension that it is not virtuous, and if this insensitivity is characteristic of him, he lacks the virtue of kindness.

---

15 Enough, that is, for our interest in identifying $V_a$ responses to be served by classifying the cases together.
16 This proposal leaves it open what further account to give of what it is for responses to be "characteristic." My own preferred view is that this requires that they are non-accidental manifestations of stable dispositions, so that the expression of these dispositions in Va responses has a degree of modal robustness: were the circumstances to change somewhat, the Va response would still be made. What degree of modal robustness? A degree that is good enough—see note 3. But this supplementation of the proposal in the text is independent of it: if there is a better account of "characteristic" responses, it can be substituted for this one. This does not close off the possibility that "situationists" could succeed in showing that no unqualified attributions of virtue to persons are defensible: see note 26.

Notice that this does not derive the aretaic assessment of action from that of character. Whether a particular action is honest depends only on the aim of that action: it is independent of whether the action is characteristic of the agent. There is no commitment to the view sometimes made definitive of "virtue ethics" that the rightness of an action is determined by whether it would be performed by a virtuous person (acting in character).[17] On the contrary, this treatment makes it easy to see how an action (or other response) could be virtuous but wrong. "Wrong," like other important parts of our moral vocabulary, is a word with different uses; but on one prominent use, wrong action is action that there is a set of one or more serious other-regarding reasons not to perform, with no adequate countervailing reason in its favor.[18] On that use, wrongness is settled by the bearing that those reasons do have, whether we appreciate it or not. Virtue is a matter of the goodness or badness of our responses in all the dimensions in which that can be assessed, and this depends on what we accept as the reasons bearing on those responses, and why.

With this in mind, a more accurate statement can be given of the reasons-responsiveness view of virtue I am advocating. When a person makes a response because she accepts that consideration C is a reason for making it, let us call C "the reason for which she is responding."[19] One's virtue, we can then say, is a matter of the overall goodness or badness of one's responsiveness *for* (rather than to) morally relevant reasons—where this includes cases of mistakenly accepting that C is a reason as well as cases where there is no mistake.[20] The virtuousness of a particular response is the goodness or badness of *its* responsiveness for such reasons.

This proposal allows that a response can be virtuous even though the person who makes it is not. That might seem incoherent: how can a response express a virtue that the responder does not have? But this is not incoherent: the phenomenon is ubiquitous, because of the patchiness of our proficiencies. I might be tactful with my parents but not my students. With my parents, I am sensitive to what will potentially upset them and perceptive about how to head off the disturbances; but my arrogance and self-consciousness around my students results in a pattern of clumsy, tactless behavior. Given

---

17 E.g., by Hursthouse (1991, 28–29).
18 This way of thinking about wrongness—an "inadequate reasons" conception—is actually a family of different views. Members of the family differ concerning the "others" whose relationships to me generate "other-regarding" reasons. And they offer different accounts of what it for an other-regarding reason to be "serious" and a countervailing reason to be "adequate."
19 This is a stipulation, not a claim about the meaning of this phrase in ordinary English. It is hard not to hear "C is the reason for which she is responding" as factive—as implying that C. For "acceptance," see note 9.
20 Mistakes in what one accepts as a reason can themselves be morally evaluable, so they can bear on the virtuousness of one's response.

how common the latter pattern of behavior is, I cannot be described as characteristically displaying the kind of sensitivity that is constitutive of tact. But in some contexts I do, and on those occasions my action does not just possess the aretaic property of tact; it is virtuous.

## Aretaic Advice

Some of the words we deploy in moral discourse (and practical discourse more broadly) have two prominent uses. We can use them either to give prospective advice, or to make a retrospective evaluation. In the first use, we can draw people's attention to reasons they are not aware of.[21] In the second, we can evaluate the quality of their responses for the reasons they thought or should have thought they had.[22]

One prominent word with these two uses is "ought." Suppose Arthur receives a suspicious-looking parcel. You think it is a bomb; I know it is not. If you are about to destroy it out of a concern to protect him, I can advise you by saying, "You ought not to destroy it." In doing so, I need not be negatively evaluating your intended response. On the contrary: if you thought Arthur's parcel was a bomb, but failed to do anything, I could then express my *criticism* of you by complaining, "You ought to have destroyed it." The first "ought"-remark advises you by expressing a verdict about the objective reasons bearing on your action. (Notice that it does not identify those reasons—it just says that there are good ones.) The second "ought"-remark evaluates something you have done, in the light of the evidence available to you.

Aretaic terms can be used in the same two ways. So far, we have been looking at their evaluative use. But they can also be used to give advice, by drawing the advisee's attention to the existence of objective reasons. A psychologist could advise you, "The kind thing to do is to explain to the children how their parents died." Experience of situations like this indicates that that would be better for them. In giving you this advice, the psychologist need not be negatively evaluating your intention to spare them the details. That intention may have been good, if it was motivated by a concern for their welfare and you were blamelessly mistaken about what is in their interests, not having experienced such situations before. Indeed, if (in the absence of this advice) you spared them the details through justifiably (but mistakenly) believing that this would be better for them, then we could properly evaluate your response as both kind and virtuous. This evaluative use of the aretaic term would be explained in the way I indicated above. Your response is both kind and virtuous as long as it has the kindness-defining properties and is good enough in all other dimensions.

---

21 We can also advise them about the relative strengths of the reasons they are aware of.
22 We can also evaluate the quality of their awareness.

So what account can be given of the use of aretaic terms in advising, rather than evaluating? This is the second part of my proposal. In advising, we are drawing the advisee's attention to the objective reasons that bear on her choices.[23] When I advise you that "F-ing is the $V_a$ thing to do (or feel, or think, or say)," or advise you "to F because it is $V_a$," I am saying that it is because it is $V_a$ that there are good reasons to F.

In giving aretaic advice in this way, we point to the existence of the reasons supporting F. However, that is not to say that we are spelling out what those reasons are. There are three cases to consider. Some aretaic terms, like "honesty," are not motive-specific: there is no honesty-defining motive. So if I say that giving the correct change is the honest thing to do, I am saying that there are good reasons for acting honestly, and that those reasons support giving the correct change, but I have not said what they are. Secondly, there are aretaic terms, like "kindness," which describe actions that are motivated for a distinctive reason, but without spelling out that reason directly. The psychologist who advises you that informing the children is the kind thing to do has told you that this action is given overall support by the reasons distinctive of kindness. But those reasons are *that this is in the children's interests* and not *that this is the kind thing to do*. The latter is not the reason for which a kind person is motivated: it is too self-regarding.[24] The third sort of aretaic term is one that does not just refer to a reason but states it. If I say that returning the stolen goods is the just thing to do, I *have* spelled out the reason for doing so. The just person's reason for F-ing is *that F-ing is just*.

The use of aretaic terms to give advice is another respect in which the relationship between virtue and the attribution of aretaic properties is not straightforward. Virtue attributions are always evaluative: to judge that a response or a person is virtuous is to make a judgement of goodness. However, aretaic judgements are not always evaluative.

## 3. A Taxonomy of Moral Virtues

Aretaic language, then, has a range of uses that extend beyond the attribution of virtue. But the best way to present a taxonomy of aretaic categories is as a taxonomy of virtues.

Moral virtues are ways of being well oriented to morally relevant reasons—of responding well for such reasons. We have seen how, when evaluating the quality of this responsiveness, different dimensions of evaluation

---

23 Not all responses are subject to choice. But only the responses that are subject to choice are candidates for advice. It makes no sense to offer someone advice about the kind way to feel—even though there are reasons for feelings, and our feeling-responses to those reasons are properly subject to aretaic evaluation.
24 This point has often been made (e.g., by Ewin (1981, 195); Foot (1972, 165); Wallace (1978, 128); and Williams (1985, 10)); but it is sometimes contested—for example (on Kant's behalf) by Baron (1985).

are relevant to the application of different aretaic terms. We should, I think, be suspicious of attempts to systematize the variety of our aretaic vocabulary too neatly: the purposes that our aretaic evaluations serve are likely to be multifarious and to some degree haphazard. Some languages happen to lack words for qualities that are clearly morally admirable: English contains no word for "Mitfreude," for example—the sympathetic sharing of others' joy—and many languages lack a much-needed word for responding well to the prospect of one's own death. One might speculate on the cultural peculiarities that explain such linguistic facts, but that would not be relevant to a consideration of which qualities really are virtues. It should not surprise us if our actual aretaic vocabulary is to some degree a miscellaneous and accidental assortment of items. Some of the aretaic terms we happen to have do double duty, applying to more than one distinguishable virtue; some important virtues happen to lack names.

But having said that, I think the following classificatory scheme is helpful. When you make a response (of action, thought, or feeling) to an object for a reason, there are three items in this relationship: the reason, the object, and the response.[25] An illuminating way of organizing a taxonomy of moral virtues is to classify them into three corresponding categories. Some virtues are reason-categoric: they are virtues of good responsiveness for particular reasons. Some are object-categoric: they are virtues of responding well to particular objects, for a variety of different reasons. And some are response-categoric: they are virtues of making particular types of response well, towards a variety of different objects and for a variety of different reasons.

In the three sections that follow, I discuss each of these categories in turn. The structure of the first category—the reason-categoric virtues—can be understood by reference to the relationships between the reasons for which these virtues are responsive. If some of those reasons are fundamental to morality and others derive their importance from those more fundamental ones, this will give us a way of understanding the relationship between the virtues of good responsiveness for those reasons.

However, not all virtues can be identified with good forms of responsiveness for particular reasons. Courage is a prominent example. Courage can be required in acting for reasons of concern, respect or cooperation, to protect someone's rights or to stand up for justice, or for many other reasons. The courage-defining properties do not include being motivated by responsiveness for a particular kind of reason. Rather, to have the virtue of courage is to respond well to a particular kind of object: namely, the prospect of harm or humiliation. There are many reasons why that can be

---

25 This classificatory scheme is consistent with the point that all reasons for responses can be cast as references to response-types. Whenever the question, "Why make response $R$?" has the answer, "Because $X$ is true," that answer can be rephrased in the form, "Because $R$ belongs to the type: responses of which $X$ is true."

morally important; but because it is difficult to respond well when it carries the risk of harm or humiliation, it makes sense for us to have a name for the quality of doing so, in order to encourage and support it. Courage, then, belongs to our second category of virtues: those that are object-categoric, not reason-categoric. Object-categoric virtues are defined by reference to objects that warrant special attention in moral discourse, because of the special difficulty of responding to those objects well.

The third, counterpart category contains response-categoric virtues. These are defined by reference to particular types of response that it can be important to make towards many different objects, for many different reasons. Fairness will be my main example of a virtue of this category. As I see it, what the many forms of fairness have in common is that they are forms of fitting impartiality. There are many proper objects of responses of this type. Fairness can concern the distribution of goods of various kinds, the following of regulative procedures, the contribution one makes to collective enterprises, the response one makes to transgressions, the refusal to exploit others' trust, and the judgements one makes about other people. What connects these various objects is that responding well in each case requires a form of impartiality. The feature that instances of fairness have in common—the fairness-defining property—is a property of the response, and not the objects of that response, nor the reason for making it.

The taxonomy that follows is intended as a contribution to moral theory, not psychology. I do not claim that the aretaic categories we use in attributions of virtue map onto the structures in terms of which we can best understand our psychological functioning. Instead, my interest here is in the relationships between the categories we use in evaluating persons and their responses. The extent to which there is a mapping of that kind is relevant to whether we take virtue-discourse to be referring to stable psychological dispositions by reference to which we can identify right action.[26] But that is not my project; and the absence of such stable dispositions does not threaten the defensibility of our use of aretaic terms to evaluate either a person or her actions: it just means that moral generalizations about a person are difficult.[27]

## 4. Reason-Categoric Virtues

One important dimension of evaluation of our responses concerns the reasons for which we make them. When one acts for a reason, one's motive for

---

26 So I do not see the following discussion as joining the debate initiated by the situationist critics of virtue theory, such as Doris (2002) and Harman (2000, 2009). (This response to the situationists is labeled "the dodge" by Alfano (2013, 62–64).) However, it is true that if the facts of human psychology are such that there is no sense in which the making of good responses is "characteristic" of a person, then the unqualified attribution of virtues to persons of the form, "She has the virtue of $Vn$" will be indefensible—they will need to be replaced by judgements of the form, "She acts with the virtue of $Vn$ in situations of type $T$."

27 Here I am in sympathy with Adams (2006, ch. 9).

acting can be described by specifying that reason. And motives for acting are morally important: the motives of agents determine the quality of their will.[28] Whether they are maliciously, arrogantly, respectfully or cravenly motivated in their actions towards us constitutes a large part of the "meaning" of what they do, and the relationships in which we stand to them.

The corresponding point applies to responses other than action. Thoughts and feelings need not have *motives*, and need not be the product of any act of will; but we often make these responses through the acceptance of reasons for them. This, again, is an important dimension of evaluation for the non-active responses. The reasons one accepts for one's responses largely constitute the meanings that those responses have in interpersonal relationships.[29]

Consequently, we have an extensive aretaic vocabulary that treats the reasons for which responses are made as $V_n$-defining properties. *Reason-categoric virtues* are those for which there is a positive answer to the question, "In order for a response to express virtue $V_n$, does it have to be made for a particular reason?" When a virtue requires responding for a particular reason, we can then ask "What is the source of that reason?" The structure of the class of reason-categoric moral virtues is generated by the answers to that question. We can answer it by tracing the derivational relationships between morally relevant reasons.

When one reason derives from another, the relation of derivation is a relation of making the case: R's being a reason for A derives from S's being a reason for B when S's being a reason for B is part of what makes it the case that R is a reason for A. Making-the-case is a linear, one-way relationship. So unless chains of derivation go on forever, there are foundational, underived reasons.[30] Good forms of responsiveness for those foundational reasons can be classified as fundamental reason-categoric virtues.

To make this more concrete, we can consider three good candidates for foundational reasons, and examine how others can derive from them. Three candidates for underived, morally relevant reasons are the reasons we have to promote others' welfare, not to interfere with their self-asserting activity, and to join in worthwhile collective action.[31] If we accept this, it gives us three broad groups of reason-categoric virtues: virtues of concern, respect and cooperation. To the reasons that derive from these three foundational sources, there will then correspond more specific reason-categoric virtues belonging to these three groups: virtues of responding well for those reasons.

---

28 Compare the quality-of-will theory of moral worth develop in Arpaly (2002, 2003, ch. 3).
29 See Scanlon (2008, 54).
30 This is not to say that the *epistemology* of judgements about reasons or their derivation is foundationalist rather than coherentist.
31 I hope this at least has some prima facie plausibility. A defense of this large claim requires showing how it helps us to make the best sense of the overall structure of morality. I attempt that much larger task in my *Concern, Respect, and Cooperation* (forthcoming).

Perhaps the most obvious way in which one reason can derive from another is by subsumption, where making response A for reason R is a specification or a part of making response B for reason S. For example, considerateness—anticipating others' needs and acting preemptively to meet or forestall them—is a particular way of promoting others' welfare. So considerateness qualifies as a derivative reason-categoric virtue of concern. However, there are other, non-subsumptive ways in which one reason can derive from another. The derivation can involve a relationship of enabling, where making response A for reason R is an enabling condition for making B for reason S. For example, developing a moral vocabulary can be morally valuable in enabling us to treat others respectfully by giving them reasons for the way we treat them. To the extent that this is what motivates you to acquire that vocabulary, your articulacy can itself be morally virtuous: it can be a subsidiary virtue of respect. A third sort of derivation is neither subsumptive nor enabling but rather responsive: here, making response A for reason R is itself a response to someone else's making the further response B for reason S. For an example of this third kind, consider the form that patriotism and other kinds of group loyalty can take when they express an appreciation of one's place in a shared history. Here, what one is responsive to is others' having acted cooperatively—that is, their having responded for reasons of cooperation—in sustaining the group to which one belongs. The reasons there are to be appreciative of that are reasons of responsiveness to others' having acted for other, more fundamental reasons. So this kind of virtuous loyalty is a subsidiary virtue of (proper appreciation for) cooperation.

In these ways, we can explain the relationship between different reason-categoric virtues by reference to the relationship between the reasons for which the virtues respond. They can be classified as virtues of concern, respect, or cooperation, according to the source of the reasons for which they respond. However, a reason-categoric virtue can also respond for a reason which derives from more than one foundational source. Justice is a prominent example of this. The virtue of justice is a virtue of responsiveness for a particular reason: namely, facts about justice. But facts about justice, on one prominent view, are facts about whether a social structure is regulated by an authority as it morally ought, all things considered, to be. If so, justice is a reason-categoric virtue, but its derivational sources lie in all of the foundations of morality, not one alone.

## 5. Object-Categoric Virtues

Reason-categoric virtues are those whose exercise requires responsiveness for a particular kind of reason. But not all virtues are like that. The most obvious exceptions are the so-called "executive virtues"—virtues like courage, which are virtues of responding well to a particular object: in this case, the prospect of harm or humiliation. Given the strength of our aversion to that prospect, it can deflect us from doing what, all things (including that prospect) considered, we ought. The reasons for behaving courageously are reasons for not being deflected in that way, and they can come from anywhere. So there is no particular kind of reason for which a courageous person acts. Someone with the virtue of courage responds well to a certain kind of object, for whatever reasons may require doing so.

## Virtues of Self-Control

Courage belongs to the most prominent class of object-categoric virtues—the virtues of self-control.[32] There are two generic virtues of self-control: temperance, which is control over our natural appetites, and fortitude—control over our natural aversions. The point of calling these "executive" virtues is that they do not involve the pursuit of characteristic aims. Nor do they involve characteristic motives for pursuing aims. When we talk of acts of fortitude and temperance, we are not drawing attention to particular aims or motives, but rather the overcoming of powerful natural obstacles to doing the right thing: obstacles that lie in our aversions and appetites. Saying this allows for two ways in which these motivational aversions or attractions can be controlled. We can resist them when they are present but we judge it inappropriate to act on them. This is overcoming-by-continence. Or, more fully, there is the kind of state which Aristotle saw as the ideal for a virtuous agent, in which we train ourselves into only having a motivational aversion or attraction when it is appropriate to act on it. This state of full Aristotelian virtue, if we could achieve it, would be a state that supersedes continence.[33]

The subsidiary virtues of self-control are all further specifications of temperance and fortitude. Thus, one form of modesty is temperance with respect to the appetite for status, which our nature as social animals endows us with; "chastity" is the only word we have for temperance with respect to the sexual appetite.[34] Equanimity and patience are names for fortitude with respect to our aversion to frustration; perseverance and industry, for fortitude with respect to our aversion to hard work; resilience, to stress; bravery and courage, to the prospect of harm or humiliation. Those are object-categoric

---

32 According to von Wright (1963, ch. 7), all virtues are specifications of *the* virtue of self-control. I think he over-generalizes.
33 We need not see this Aristotelian ideal as a state in which the natural appetites themselves are lost. For we can distinguish between an appetite—a state of experiencing something as attractive—and the motivation to satisfy it. The Aristotelian virtue of temperance should not be seen as a state in which one does not feel hungry when one has not been fed; but it is a state in which one is not motivated to take someone else's lunch when one is hungry—there is no motivation to act that has to be resisted.
34 Chastity, of course, has acquired a bad reputation through the use of the word as an instrument of sexual repression. Perhaps our word for it needs to be retired. But we should not be led by that to doubt whether there is a virtue of self-control in relation to one's sexual appetites. As our culture becomes increasingly sexualized, our lacking a vocabulary for talking about this virtue becomes increasingly problematic.

specifications of the two generic virtues: ways of more tightly specifying the objects of appetite or aversion with respect to which self-control is exercised.[35]

### Virtues of Proficiency

Object-categoric virtues are not confined to virtues of self-control. There are also virtues of proficiency: for example, tact. Tact involves a perceptiveness about the potential for disturbance, upset or conflict, and the ability to say or do what will avert or resolve it. So it is a good form of responsiveness to a certain sort of object: difficult situations of this kind. It is not a reason-categoric virtue: the reasons why finding a tactful response is important may be reasons of concern for welfare (as when it is tactful not to mention something upsetting), but they might be reasons to preserve the harmonious functioning of a group, deriving from the importance of cooperation, or reasons to treat two people respectfully—say, by giving them both a fair hearing. And nor is tact response-categoric: there is no distinctive kind of response to difficult situations that is characteristic of tact. Not inviting two feuding friends to dinner might be tactful; but so might going ahead and inviting them, to show that one trusts them to handle their disagreement sensibly themselves.

This may invite the question: if the kinds of skill to which we give the name "tact" range so widely, should we really be prepared to say that this is the name of *one* kind of proficiency? No: we should not be prepared to say that. But in that respect, tact is no worse qualified to be a virtue than any other. We should resist the temptation to think of virtue-terms as naming categories that describe elements within the structure of the psychology of a good moral agent. They are components of our vocabulary for talking about kinds of goodness. The psychological constituents that need to be possessed in order to qualify for the attribution of such evaluative terms are another matter.

Indeed, it should by now be obvious that on the taxonomy I am recommending, when a response is virtuous, it typically expresses more than one virtue. When a particular action expresses an object-categoric virtue, it always expresses a reason-categoric virtue too: whenever an action is morally courageous, it is also kind, or just, or public spirited, or . . . To be a virtuous response to its object, it must be good in all dimensions of assessment. That includes its motive: the action must be performed for a good reason. So when one responds well to the object that specifies a virtue of

---

35 Are these virtues better classified as *emotion*-categoric? I think not. Someone lacking any feelings of frustration can still have the virtue of patience, in responding well to the situations that are the object of frustration in others. The virtue is a virtue of responding well to a particular kind of object, rather than of handling one's emotions well—although the objects with respect to which we classify these virtues can be identified by reference to the emotions they do typically elicit.

self-control or proficiency, the reason for which one is responding supplies a reason-categoric aretaic property which is also possessed by the response. Indeed, as we will shortly see, there are response-categoric virtues as well, so nothing prevents the same action from expressing a virtue of that kind too.[36]

*Object-Categoric Virtues of Relationship-Responsiveness*

There is a third type of object-categoric virtue. Some virtues are good forms of responsiveness to particular kinds of relationship. These, too, are virtues of responding well to a particular object—the relationship-type—in a variety of ways, for a variety of reasons. Loyalty and trustworthiness are examples of this type. Loyalty is the virtue of responding well to the history of a relationship of special connection with some other individual or group. Relationships of special connection need not have a history in order to be important, of course—the relationship of a parent to a newborn child is an obvious example of that—but then it ceases to be appropriate to think of them in terms of loyalty. The virtuous forms of loyalty are those that show a proper appreciation of the history of one's relationship to an individual or group, and how the meaning of that temporally extended relationship bestows upon my responses to it the significance of forms of fidelity or betrayal.[37]

Trustworthiness is the virtue of good responsiveness to the relationships of reliance through which others are vulnerable to us. The variety of expressions that this virtue has, and reasons for its importance, come from the many ways in which we are vulnerable to each other—ranging from the general vulnerability we have to being deceived by someone we have never met, to our special vulnerability to being hurt by those we have shared our lives with most intimately.

## 6. Response-Categoric Virtues

Response-categoric virtues are forms of goodness whose defining characteristic is the making of some particular type of response. The response can be made to a variety of different objects, and for a variety of different reasons. The virtues in this category seem to me more miscellaneous, so I shall not attempt to structure it further by organizing it into subtypes. Instead, I give three examples: fairness, honesty, and generosity.

---

36 An example: in a case where reasons of respect require you to treat someone impartially although you will be vilified for doing so, your action could express the object-categoric virtue of courage, the reason-categoric virtue of respect, and the response-categoric virtue of fairness, all at once.

37 For discerning treatments that distinguish virtuous from unvirtuous forms of loyalty, see Kleinig (2014) and Keller (2007)—with Kleinig tending to emphasize the former and Keller the latter. For the view that there is no virtue of loyalty, see Ewin (1992).

Fairness has a kind of generality that makes it comparable to the executive virtues just discussed. It, too, is not a sensitivity to one particular kind of reason. But it is response-categoric, not object-categoric.[38] To say that a person, motive, action, institution, distribution or judgement is fair is to say that it exhibits a kind of impartiality which is fitting, given the context. That is not to say that it picks out one particular way of being impartial and tells us to exhibit that. Rather, there are many kinds of impartiality: judgements about fairness and unfairness concern actions for which one particular way of being impartial is fitting. What fair distributions, regulations, judgements, punishments and so on have in common is not that deliberation about them is directed towards a single common object. What is common to them is that they are fitting, in a field of deliberation where finding what is fitting requires a form of impartiality. An obvious reason for our having this aretaic term comes from the strength of our motives of attachment and the need to exercise self-control in contexts in which we ought to oppose those motives. If that exhausted the content of fairness, then it would belong above, with the object-categoric virtues of self-control: it would be a form of temperance with respect to personal attachments. But fairness extends beyond such cases. The capricious judge who does not like the attire of one of the litigants or decides the case by tossing a coin is acting unfairly, but the unfairness there is not a failure to exercise self-control with respect to a personal attachment. The same is true of a lazy-minded person who criticizes someone unfairly on flimsy evidence. Personal attachment is only one of a range of different obstacles to exercising the impartiality that is contextually fitting: the virtue of fairness is the quality of doing so well.[39]

A response can be fitting without being all things considered appropriate or right. So this explanation of fairness allows that there is a gap between the possession of the aretaic property and virtue.[40] If, as the ship goes down, I waste time by insisting on organizing a lottery for the lifeboats, my action could be fair but would not be virtuous. The situation is one in which important interests generate equal claims to a scarce good, and that makes it lottery-worthy. But whether a lottery ought, all things considered, to be conducted depends on more than that—including, obviously, whether more lives will be lost as a result. This is another illustration of the earlier point: whether an action possesses the aretaic property of fairness depends only on whether it possesses the fairness-defining property: fitting impartiality.

---

38 "Why aren't *all* virtues 'response-categoric'? Aren't 'kindness' and 'courage' the names of the *responses* characteristically made by people with those virtues?" Yes, but in order for a response to qualify as kind, it must be made for a particular sort of reason; in order for a response to qualify as courageous, it must be made to a particular sort of object. The response-categoric virtues are those for which no corresponding claim is true.
39 I discuss fairness and its relationship to the morality of cooperation more fully in Cullity (2008).
40 This is a point I fail to make in Cullity (2008).

Whether it is virtuous depends on its being good enough in *all* dimensions of assessment. Fair action that is insufficiently sensitive to the loss of life is not virtuously fair.

The aretaic property of honesty was discussed earlier. I pointed out that there is one honesty-defining property: the aim of open dealing with others. An action performed from any motive can be honest; but in order to express the virtue of honesty, its motive (along with every other dimension in which it can be assessed) must be good enough. However, the defining property of an honest action is its aim. That makes it a response-categoric virtue, since the aim of an action is a property of the response one is making to an object, and not of the object to which one is responding in performing that action. And while the reason for which one performs a virtuously honest action must be good enough, it does not have to come from any particular source. Kant's shopkeeper, who acts honestly only because it keeps him in business, lacks the virtue of honesty, but a shopkeeper could have that virtue by treating his customers honestly for the sake of their welfare, or out of a respect for their rights, or from an appreciation that this is what we each must do if society is to function harmoniously—that is, for reasons of concern, respect or cooperation. So honesty is a response-categoric virtue, along with fairness.

Generosity was the other aim-specific aretaic property I mentioned in Section 1. This has the aim of sharing one's possessions with others; when it is a virtue, it is a response-categoric virtue, in the same way as honesty. Typically, generosity is a response to others' needs, in order to benefit them. When that is true, generosity is a form of beneficence; but it is not always true. I might be generous in forgoing some of my allocated speaking time in order to accord your views a hearing: then I am acting for reasons of respect. And if I generously volunteer more than my fair share in contributing to a joint cause, I might be acting for reasons of cooperation. So generosity can have various objects and be bestowed for various reasons. It is response-categoric.

## 7. The Moral Virtues

This short discussion has left many moral virtues undiscussed. I cannot claim, therefore, to have demonstrated the adequacy of the taxonomy I am proposing, since if there are any moral virtues it cannot accommodate, it has to be rejected. However, it would be a mistake to ask whether it can generate a complete list of "the" moral virtues: that would be to misunderstand the nature of moral evaluation. Our evaluative vocabulary does not itself exhaust the respects in which we and our responses can be good and bad. Some terms are finer-grained specifications of others; many apply in overlapping ways. No doubt, our vocabulary will continue to evolve, drawing our attention to particular morally important reasons, objects, and responses, and sometimes duplicating terms we have already. And a glance at any thesaurus will supply a vaguely bounded list of further words we already possess for making aretaic evaluations. So, is love a moral virtue? Flexibility? They appear on some lists; and "loving" and "flexible" are certainly terms that we use to make positive evaluations of a person or a response. If we did count them as moral virtues, they would both be response-categoric.

Moreover, providing a taxonomy like this one does not preclude the provision of others, structured to serve other theoretical purposes. The point of the taxonomy outlined here is to show how we can understand the relationships between the aretaic members of our evaluative vocabulary on a view of virtue as good responsiveness for morally relevant reasons. As I have emphasized, the vagaries of our evaluative vocabulary and the variety of purposes it serves should make us wary of an overly neat taxonomy of this domain. The one I have provided does at least allow us to understand some of the overlaps and provides a structure for seeing how further extensions of our aretaic vocabulary could be possible.[41]

# References

Adams, Robert Merrihew. 2006. *A Theory of Virtue: Excellence in Being for the Good*. Oxford: Clarendon Press.

Alfano, Mark. 2013. *Character as Moral Fiction*. Cambridge: Cambridge University Press.

Anscombe, G. E. M. 1957. *Intention*. Oxford: Blackwell.

Aristotle. 1961. *Nicomachean Ethics*. Translated by W. D. Ross. Oxford: Oxford University Press.

———. 1999. *Nicomachean Ethics*. Translated by Terence Irwin. Indianapolis: Hackett.

———. 2014. *Nicomachean Ethics*. Translated by C. D. C. Reeve. Indianapolis: Hackett.

Arpaly, Nomy. 2002. "Moral Worth." *Journal of Philosophy* 99: 223–45.

———. 2003. *Unprincipled Virtue*. New York: Oxford University Press.

Audi, Robert. 2009. "Moral Virtue and Reasons for Action." *Philosophical Issues* 19: 1–20.

Baron, Marcia. 1985. "Varieties of Ethics of Virtue." *American Philosophical Quarterly* 22: 47–53.

Cullity, Garrett. 1994. "International Aid and the Scope of Kindness." *Ethics* 105: 99–127.

———. 2008. "Public Goods and Fairness." *Australasian Journal of Philosophy* 86: 1–21.

———. Forthcoming. *Concern, Respect and Cooperation*. Oxford: Oxford University Press.

---

41 For insightful comments on previous drafts of this essay, I am grateful to Damian Cox, Christine Swanton, Justin Oakley, Glen Pettigrove, Nic Southwood, Robert Audi and an anonymous referee.

———. Forthcoming. "Stupid Goodness." In *The Many Moral Rationalisms*, edited by Francois Schroeter. Oxford: Oxford University Press.
Doris, John. 2002. *Lack of Character: Personality and Moral Behavior*. Cambridge: Cambridge University Press.
Ewin, R. E. 1981. *Co-Operation and Human Values*. Brighton: Harvester Wheatsheaf.
———. 1992. "Loyalty and Virtues." *Philosophical Quarterly* 42: 403–19.
Foot, Philippa. 1972. "Morality as a System of Hypothetical Imperatives." *Philosophical Review* 81: 305–16.
Harman, Gilbert. 2000. "The Nonexistence of Character Traits." *Proceedings of the Aristotelian Society* 100: 223–26.
———. 2009. "Scepticism about Character Traits." *Journal of Ethics* 13: 235–42.
Hursthouse, Rosalind. 1991. "Arational Actions." *Journal of Philosophy* 88: 57–68.
———. 1999. *On Virtue Ethics*. Oxford: Oxford University Press.
Kahneman, Daniel. 2011. *Thinking, Fast and Slow*. London: Penguin.
Kant, Immanuel. 1996. *Groundwork of the Metaphysics of Morals*. Translated by Mary Gregor. Cambridge: Cambridge University Press.
Keller, Simon. 2007. *The Limits of Loyalty*. Cambridge: Cambridge University Press.
Klein, Gary. 1998. *Sources of Power: How People Make Decisions*. Cambridge: MIT Press.
Kleinig, John. 2014. *On Loyalty and Loyalties: The Contours of a Problematic Virtue*. Oxford: Oxford University Press.
Ramsey, William. 1998. "Prototypes and Conceptual Analysis." In *Rethinking Intuition: The Psychology of Intuition and Its Role in Philosophical Inquiry*, edited by Michael DePaul and William Ramsey, 161–77. Lanham: Rowman and Littlefield.
Scanlon, T. M. 2008. *Moral Dimensions: Meaning, Permissibility, Blame*. Cambridge: Harvard University Press.
Swanton, Christine. 2003. *Virtue Ethics: A Pluralistic View*. Oxford: Oxford University Press.
———. 2015. "A Particularist but Codifiable Virtue Ethics." *Oxford Studies in Normative Ethics* 5: 38–63.
von Wright, G. H. 1963. *The Varieties of Goodness*. London: Routledge and Kegan Paul.
Wallace, J. D. 1978. *Virtues and Vices*. Ithaca: Cornell University Press.
Williams, Bernard. 1985. *Ethics and the Limits of Philosophy*. London: Collins.

# 2 Remote Scenarios and Warranted Virtue Attributions

*Justin Oakley*

## 1. Introduction

A virtue ethics criterion of right action has often been initially formulated as stating that an action is right if and only if it is what a virtuous agent, acting in character, would do in the circumstances.[1] An important question arising from such a formulation concerns the proper scope of such a criterion when applied to the actions of actual agents. If, when applying such a criterion, we consider whether an actual agent has a particular character-trait, or has such a trait to the level expected of virtue, should we take speculations about what she might do in remote and improbable scenarios as relevant to epistemically warranted attributions of this trait to her, and to accurate judgements of her praiseworthiness and blameworthiness on account of this? The use of various forms of testing and screening by the military and certain other employers, who observe the behavior of applicants in extreme and unfamiliar circumstances, seems to rely heavily on the assumption that our behavior in remote scenarios is highly relevant to determining whether we have the trait(s) under investigation. And many of the philosophers who have developed situationist critiques of virtue ethics take the view that the behavior of the experimental subjects in, for example, the Good Samaritan experiment at Princeton, and the Milgram experiments at Yale, revealed that the subjects' character traits were less admirable, or even more concerning, than might initially have been supposed.[2] But we sometimes instead describe behavior observed in remote and improbable scenarios as 'not in character' for the agent in question, and we may even subsequently exclude such behavior in extraordinary circumstances from the evidence we take as instructive for informing warranted character-trait attributions to the agent in question.

On one approach, the relevance of behavior in remote scenarios to warranted attributions of the virtuous character trait in question depends on

---

1 See, for example, Hursthouse (1999, 28–31).
2 See, for example, Doris (2002).

how probable such behavior would be, given the agent's behavior thus far. That is, the less likely you are to bring about a particular outcome in some set of extraordinary circumstances, the less relevant is that outcome/behavior in those circumstances to warranted attributions of the particular trait to you. In what follows, I examine the plausibility of this probability-based approach to determining the epistemic relevance of an agent's predicted behavior in various hypothetical scenarios. I argue that while such an approach can help us to determine when virtue attributions are warranted, basing virtue attributions only on such probabilities is not sufficiently sensitive to considerations of credit and fault. These considerations become apparent when considering scenarios where agents have developed certain protective strategies and skills against their responding poorly to particular eventualities. I also consider the dispositions involved in friendship, in seeking to develop a principled way of determining when remote scenarios can be diagnostic of, or at least informative about, genuine friendship and genuine virtue. I argue that even where there is only a remote probability of a certain disposition being acted on—such as a disposition to abandon one's partner if consequentialist considerations require this act—these dispositions can nevertheless help to reveal whether a relationship counts as a genuine friendship when they express values that the agent so disposed explicitly endorses, or at least, does not repudiate. Friendship cases also help to demonstrate that warranted attributions of friendship and virtue must look beyond mere behavioral dispositions, and must also consider an agent's *reasons* for their being disposed to perform certain actions in remote scenarios, and whether the agent does not repudiate—and perhaps even endorses—that behavior and their reasons for it.

## 2. Epistemically Warranted Attributions, and Improbable Outcomes in Remote Scenarios

In arguing that morality must be founded on reason rather than experience, Kant suggests that actions which appear to be done from pure duty (or for that matter, true virtue, or genuine friendship) may well upon closer inspection turn out not to be so, because (for one thing) self-love might well be our "secret incentive" for performing the action in question.[3] Kant goes on to express similar doubts about the possibility of finding true virtue, and true friendship, in the world:

> One need not be an enemy of virtue, but only a cool observer who does not confuse even the liveliest aspiration for the good with its reality, to be doubtful sometimes whether true virtue can really be found

---

3 Kant (1959, Ak 407) says "we everywhere come upon the dear self." Indeed, Kant seems to think that our true motives and virtues are ultimately *inscrutable*.

anywhere in the world. This is especially true as one's years increase and one's power of judgment is made wiser by experience and more acute in observation ... Our concern is with actions of which perhaps the world has never had an example ... For example, pure sincerity in friendship can be demanded of every man, and this demand is not in the least diminished if a sincere friend has never existed....

(1959, Ak 407–8)[4]

Indeed, Kant urges us to be on guard about what our friends might do, as their self-interested motivations might lead them to betray our trust in them: "a restraint on trust in the mutual confidence of even the best friends is reckoned a universal maxim of prudence in social dealings" (1996, 80–81). Kant seems not only to be making a point about the difficulty of discerning, in any given case, whether an action was genuinely motivated by duty, virtue, or friendship. He is also doubting whether true virtue, and true friendship, really exist at all, given what the person in question might do if circumstances were different. Thus, Kant seems to be assuming here (among other things) that remote scenarios cannot be ruled out as irrelevant to proper virtue attributions, or to warranted friendship attributions.

It is important to distinguish here between two sorts of claims about the possible relevance of remote scenarios to virtue: a claim about the *nature* of virtue, and a claim about the conditions under which attributing a particular virtue to a given agent is *epistemically warranted*. That is, it might be claimed that: (i) An agent has a particular virtue V only if the agent is disposed to perform particular sorts of actions in remote scenarios. And it might also be claimed that: (ii) Attributing virtue V to the agent in question is epistemically warranted only if the agent has demonstrated this virtue in various remote scenarios. For example, one might hold that true courage requires the confronting of extraordinary as well as ordinary dangers; and one might additionally hold that a particular agent's failure to display courage in such extreme scenarios indicates that attributing courage to this agent is epistemically unwarranted. According to this second claim, then, failing to show courage *in extremis* would 'silence' a claim made by an agent that courage is justifiably attributed to them, and so such failures help us to determine whether we are epistemically justified in attributing the virtue in question to the agent.[5] Both claims (i) and (ii) seem to be consistent with the

---

4 In "Religion within the Boundaries of Mere Reason," Kant (1996, 81) suggests that there is a certain disingenuousness between even the best of friends, and (in arguing that humans are naturally disposed towards corruption) he endorses the sentiment that, secretly, "in the misfortunes of our best friends there is something that does not altogether displease us."

5 See also Vranas (2005, 27–28), who asks: "why is deplorable (or admirable) behavior in 'extraordinary' situations not supposed to count? ... the idea that only everyday-life behavior is relevant to character evaluations seems misguided." Vranas subsequently concludes that "most people are indeterminate ... character evaluations are epistemically unwarranted:

views expressed by Kant in his discussion of duty, virtue, and friendship—so in what follows I will refer to these as 'Kantian' claims. But in any case, my ultimate concern here is with the plausibility of the claim in (ii); that is, the *epistemic* claim above about the relevance of remote scenarios to warranted virtue attributions, even if it remains uncertain whether Kant himself was committed to such a view.

According to (what I am calling) the Kantian epistemic claim in (ii), the failure to exhibit virtue V in remote scenarios indicates that attributing virtue V to the agent in question is epistemically unwarranted. Kant's concerns about such failures in humans generally also raise doubts about whether (as Kant also wonders) any genuine virtues exist at all. If genuinely virtuous character traits and actions can never be justifiably attributed to individuals, or indeed have never existed at all, this would seem to be very problematic for virtue ethics, and for applying a virtue ethics criterion of right action to the actions of agents in the real world. (In what follows, I will focus primarily on the epistemic question of whether remote scenarios are plausibly thought to be instructive for making warranted attributions of particular virtues to individual agents.)

However, the standard for warranted virtue attributions that appears to be assumed in the Kantian view seems to be overly demanding. Should such a demanding standard be accepted? In contrast to Kant, Robert Adams (2006) argues that, where virtue is concerned, we ought to give credit where credit is due. Adams provides an account of virtues which emphasizes their social dependence, whereby our social environments play a crucial role in supporting or undermining our virtuous character traits. He argues that "Our appreciation and commitment may have a significant measure of excellence even if we do not have the will power and social creativity to sustain them in those relations without the supportive context provided by other people"(2006, 161). Adams' account of the virtues is a nice expression of the way that both the 'robustness'—to use Philip Pettit's (2015) term—and the fragility of virtue are functions of our social vulnerability. Adams argues that virtues can be real if they endure over time, even if they would not be manifested across all situations: "If there are moral excellences that we have reason to admire in actual human lives, it can hardly be on the assumption that they are invincible or not situationally conditioned" (2006, 156).[6] For example, it seems plausible to think that courage need not be tested in extreme wartime situations before it qualifies as genuine courage. After all, courage can still be modally somewhat robust without needing to withstand

---

we almost never have adequate evidence to evaluate with confidence particular people as good, bad, or intermediate" (2005, 29).

6 See also Adams (2006, 119–20): "there are real moral virtues that are not extremely rare and that play a part in a wide variety of human lives ... there are qualities with respect to which it is empirically allowable to suppose that people are commonly consistent over time, and which are promising candidates for recognition as virtues or potential parts of virtues."

*extreme* circumstances.[7] In discussing warranted virtue attributions, Adams cautions against worrying about what one might do in remote scenarios: "in thinking about the moral excellences and deficiencies of people who will never experience anything like Auschwitz, there is little moral illumination to be gained by speculating about how they would have responded to an extremely malignant environment of that sort" (2006, 161).[8] Indeed, there would presumably be conceivable circumstances where even the *exemplars* which we take as providing aspirational role models might themselves fail in their virtue due to the exigencies of some remote scenario, yet it would seem overly restrictive to thereby deny that they could properly qualify as exemplars for us in the first place.

It is important to recognize that an agent's failure in an extreme scenario does not entail that they would fail in a near-extreme scenario. When interviewed many years later, one of the subjects in the Milgram experiments, Bill Menold, who gave the 'learner' what Menold believed to be a lethal electric shock said, touching his heart, "there's a little evil in there . . ." (quoted in Perry 2012, 68). And an undergraduate psychology student who also administered what she thought was a lethal electric shock when participating in an attempted replication of the Milgram experiments at La Trobe University in the 1970s said, "I had done it and for the rest of my life I knew that, to use the words of the man in America, that black evil part was my core" (Australian Broadcasting Corporation 2012).[9] But why should an agent's action in such extreme scenarios be regarded as more relevant for

---

7  See also the discussion in Doris (2002, 160–64), of Conrad's *Lord Jim*. Despite having shown courage in a variety of difficult situations, First Mate Jim is haunted by what he sees as his cowardice in abandoning the apparently sinking *Patna* before the passengers, and he takes this as overriding any claims he may previously have had to genuine courage. Doris argues, "The misproportion is that Jim reached a conclusion about himself more global than a single behavior warrants; despite the *Patna* debacle, there was much about Jim 'worth having'." The failure to act virtuously in a 'perfect storm' need not at all impugn one's claim that one would act on the relevant virtue in a less-than-perfect storm. Elsewhere in the book, Doris (66) says he is willing to accept that there can be character traits, but only highly specific and localized traits, such as "'witnessing-paper-dropping-after-finding-a-dime-in-payphone-altruism', or 'office-party-sociability'." Pettit (2015, 11) provides a familiar example of what he calls a 'non-robust' disposition: In Oscar Wilde's *The Importance of Being Ernest*, Jack Worthing uses the pseudonym 'Ernest', and this unexpectedly attracts Gwendolen (his friend's cousin): "'My ideal has always been to love some one of the name of Ernest. There is something in that name that inspires absolute confidence' . . . 'It suits you perfectly. It is a divine name. It has a music of its own. It produces vibrations'." But one can reject Kant's skepticism about genuine real-world virtue without resorting to belief only in such highly specific, localized character traits.
8  It should be noted that we are in a different epistemic position with regard to agents where we do not have data about them in the relevant counterfactual context, compared with the epistemic position we are in when we do have data about how the agent has acted in contexts which are out of the ordinary for them. Thanks to an anonymous referee here.
9  Diana Backwell, quoted in ABC, *All In The Mind*. See Milgram (2010).

the purposes of making warranted character-trait attributions to them, than is their likely action in a somewhat less extreme (though perhaps still rather remote) scenario? Even if giving a stranger what appears to be a severe electric shock at the behest of a perceived authority figure counts as an evil action, it seems something of a leap for this to qualify one as an evil person. Indeed, even if we conceded that an evil action performed by a person in an extreme scenario provides some evidential warrant for attributing a reprehensible character trait to this person, it would not necessarily follow that such a trait forms this person's "core," to the exclusion of any positive or admirable character traits whose attribution to this person may be evidentially warranted.

Of course, we *can* correctly take repeated displays of courage in an extreme or extraordinary situation as indicating *something* important about the agent—namely, that they have 'battle-courage'. So, I am not arguing that behavior displayed in extraordinary circumstances can *never* provide us with any information which would be relevant to virtuous character-trait attributions to the agent in question.[10] Rather, my claim here is that, contrary to the Kantian view, an agent's failure to display courage in such circumstances need not make attributions of courage to this agent epistemically unwarranted—nor need this silence their claim to have *genuine* courage—as they may well display courage in many *less* extreme circumstances. Failures in remote scenarios need not be diagnostic of true virtue, in the way the Kantian view in question seems to be suggesting. Therefore, we need to find some other principled way, apart from simply relying on the scenario's remoteness (or otherwise) *per se*, for determining which hypothetical scenarios are relevant to epistemically warranted virtue attributions, and might be diagnostic of genuine virtue.

If we think Kant goes too far in his reluctance to make any virtuous character-trait attributions in the real world, what principled approach might be developed to help us determine which counterfactual scenarios where an agent acts are properly treated as relevant to our being warranted in attributing a particular virtue to that agent? In other words, *when* might an agent's counterfactual failures silence that agent's claim to have the virtue in question? How might the scope for warranted character-trait attributions be broadened beyond Kant's overly demanding standard for this?[11] One natural way to answer this question is in terms of *probability*. On such an approach, the relevance of an agent's behavior in remote counterfactual scenarios to

---

10 Likewise, Vranas (2005) argues that remote and extraordinary circumstances cannot be ruled out as irrelevant to warranted virtue attributions simply because such circumstances are remote and extraordinary; but unlike Kant, Vranas does not seem to think that such circumstances by themselves provide *definitive* evidence of the presence or absence of the virtue in the agent in question.
11 One might think here that it is no wonder that Kant rejected virtue as a basis for right action, given his (epistemic) doubts about the purity of agents' character traits.

warranted attributions of, say, courage, might be thought to depend on how probable it is that the agent would encounter such a scenario, along with how probable the behavior in question would seem to be, given the agent's behavior thus far. That is, suppose we take a set of circumstances which are improbable and extraordinary for a given agent. The suggestion here would be that the agent's predicted behavior there is less relevant to warranted attribution of courage than would the agent's behavior be in more probable (less extraordinary) circumstances where courage was called for. This suggested probability-based account could also focus on outcomes. That is, it could hold that the less likely you are to bring about a particular outcome in, let us suppose, some set of extraordinary circumstances, the less relevant is that outcome to reaching warranted attributions of courage to you now. Adams offers a probabilistic account of virtues, in arguing against the view that to qualify as (for example) a generous person requires that one shows notable generosity on *every* occasion. Adams (2006, 124) argues that it is "enough" for a theory of virtue if the associated dispositions "amount to significant probabilities of relevant behavior."[12] John Doris (2002, 19) also provides a probabilistic approach here, suggesting that "*If a person possesses a trait, that person will engage in trait-relevant behaviors in trait-relevant-eliciting conditions with* markedly above chance *probability p.*"

Let me clarify such probabilistic accounts of the relevant counterfactuals. There are two locations at which these probabilistic accounts can be applied:

(1) We can ask, how (objectively) likely is it that I would find myself in a certain novel situation? The less likely the situation, such accounts hold, the less relevant is my predicted behavior in it to a warranted attribution of the relevant virtue.
(2) We can also ask: *given* a particular situation (whether likely or not for the agent/s), what are the comparative probabilities of the behavior/outcomes brought about by (say) the two agents involved? If one agent is more likely to bring about the relevant behavior/outcomes than the other, this is evidence that the virtue in question is more justifiably attributed to the former agent than to the latter. For example, if in a given scenario, I am more likely to act courageously than you, this counts as evidence that courage is more justifiably attributed to me than it is to you.

This sort of probabilistic approach gains some plausibility when we consider cases involving other sorts of dispositions, where the differential credit

---

12 Another reason why Adams (2006) says he provides a *probabilistic* account of virtues is because he says that a person's past behavior does not predict their future behavior with *certainty*.

or blame we are inclined to allocate to different agents in two scenarios with the same outcome seems due to the presence of a particular disposition in one agent (rather than the other agent) affecting the probability of that outcome occurring. For example, suppose that you have learned various defensive driving techniques, whereas I have not learned such techniques, and that we both narrowly miss sliding off an unforeseeably slippery road and crashing into an empty parked car. If your defensive driving capacities were a significant factor in explaining why you managed to avoid crashing into the parked car, whereas my avoiding the parked car was simply due to luck, it seems plausible to think that you are more deserving of credit for this outcome than I am (if indeed, I deserve any credit for this at all), because your defensive driving skills made this outcome less likely than it would have been, had you lacked such skills.

## 3. Problems with Probabilistic Accounts of Counterfactuals Relevant for Warranted Virtue Attributions

But while a probabilistic approach to warranted virtue attributions might initially seem to be plausible, further investigation suggests that it does not seem to be adequate, at least as a *sole* criterion for determining which counterfactuals are relevant for such attributions. For a probability-based approach to determining the relevance of an agent's predicted behavior in various hypothetical scenarios is insufficiently sensitive to considerations of credit and fault, which emerge when considering scenarios involving agents who have developed various insurance strategies and protective capacities against their responding poorly to particular eventualities. Consider a variation of the defensive driving example given above. These two drivers both have the same age and experience, but Driver A has successfully completed a defensive driving course, while Driver B has developed no such skills. Suppose both drivers unforeseeably encounter particularly slippery black ice on a foggy night, and that both drivers have, say, a 60 percent probability of crashing into a parked car, but that Driver A's probability of crashing here is lower than 100 percent due to his learned defensive driving skills, while Driver B's identical probability of crashing here is due to his having an involuntary tic which he is aware of but has done nothing to protect himself against.[13] Suppose that both drivers crash into the parked car. It seems plausible to hold Driver A to be less blameworthy than Driver B for the damage to the parked car, even though it is *equally* likely here that the black ice will lead them to swerve into the car. Focusing only on differential probabilities can lead us astray in scenarios where the chances of crashing are so high that they would equally likely overwhelm any driver, whether

---

13 This is a variant of one of Nagel's (1979) cases in his discussion of what he calls "resultant moral luck."

or not they have learned defensive driving techniques. For in these sorts of cases, differential blame/credit can still seem appropriate, despite equal probabilities.[14] To take a different example, the fact that two people would both buckle under extreme torture at Auschwitz to reveal the names of collaborators should not blind us to other potentially relevant moral differences between them that we might speculate would have emerged in slightly less dire circumstances—for example, where A has learned some sound resistance-to-torture skills, and B has not, and those skills would enable (or would have enabled) A to resist the less extreme torture, whereas B would still be unable to resist this.[15]

But how might such differential blameworthiness (or creditworthiness) judgements bear on the justifiability of attributing virtuous character traits to agents on the basis of what they do and bring about in extraordinary circumstances? Perhaps the following principle can serve as a plausible bridge here: where agent A is more creditworthy for outcome O, than is agent A* for the equivalent outcome O*, then this differential creditworthiness counts as (prima facie) evidence that A is a better agent (person) than is A*, at least in respect of those outcomes. (The same principle could also be articulated, *mutatis mutandis*, linking *blameworthiness* and being a *worse* agent or person.)[16] Thus, such differential creditworthiness judgements can serve as additional warrant for attributing *good* qualities to A, and thus for attributing qualities to A.

A probabilistic approach to warranted virtue attributions holds that the more likely an agent is to bring about the behavior/outcome relevant to the virtue in question, the more justifiable is this agent's claim to have this virtue. The problem for a solely probabilistic approach here is that fault and credit can enter at various points in counterfactual situations, in ways that do not depend in any straightforward way on probability. At the very least, we

---

14 It might also be suggested that our sense that Driver A is less blameworthy than Driver B here is due to the commendable concern for others shown by Driver A when they learned the defensive driving skills that Driver B lacks. (Thanks to an anonymous referee for this point.) I would be happy to accept that this feature of Driver A might contribute to the impression that Driver A is less blameworthy than Driver B for the damage to the parked car—such an explanation for this impression is compatible with my point here that comparing probabilities will not, by itself, always distinguish between the differential blameworthiness of two agents for a specified outcome.

15 The idea that the availability of a disposition in reserve as a sort of 'back-up' can count towards one's credit and virtue in the actual case is familiar from examples of *motives* being held in reserve (as indeed, some Kantians themselves seem to accept, in the case of the duty motive).

16 Note that 'more blameworthy' is ambiguous between 'more deserving of blame', and 'deserving of blame for more' (the same ambiguity also occurs with 'more creditworthy'). Here I am using 'more blameworthy' in the sense of 'more deserving of blame' (and likewise with 'more creditworthy'). (I will leave aside issues about whether blameworthiness is best analyzed in terms of desert.)

want to know whether an agent is at fault for being in such circumstances, and how prepared they should have been for them. For example, suppose a recent medical graduate finds that they are unable to courageously report to the relevant authorities a rare case of particularly egregious wrongdoing by a senior doctor.[17] In determining whether the medical graduate is blameworthy for failing to report this conduct, it seems plausible to consider not only the probability of their finding themselves in such a situation, but also whether they are at fault for failing to develop the requisite courage to report such conduct here. An advocate of a purely probabilistic approach to warranted virtue attribution might respond to this point by arguing that an agent who develops the requisite capacity for workplace courage thereby also makes it more probable than previously that s/he will report such problematic conduct to the authorities, and more probable that s/he will do this, compared with another medical graduate who has not developed this capacity.[18] Therefore, a more sophisticated probabilistic approach, which recalculates probabilities when there are changes in the relevant circumstances and capacities of the agent, might be thought to better track the differential blameworthiness of two agents, where one has developed the relevant capacities, and the other has not but (let us suppose) should have.

I agree that agents who develop capacities for workplace courage and for defensive driving seem indeed to alter the probabilities of their taking appropriate actions against corrupt colleagues and motoring dangers, respectively. Nevertheless, a purely probabilistic approach seems unable to account for the differential blameworthiness judgements we often make about pairs of cases—such as the black ice case mentioned above—which have equally probable outcomes, yet where the agents seem to differ in their blameworthiness due to one developing the relevant capacity, while the other agent is at fault for not developing that capacity. Similar problems arise when considering the differential creditworthiness which can apply to two agents in some pairs of cases which have equally probable good outcomes, but where one agent is more creditworthy than the other due to the former developing the relevant capacity, such as a virtuous character trait, while the other agent did not. These differential creditworthiness and blameworthiness judgements can also count towards how justified we are in attributing virtue or vice to the agent. For acting from virtues (typically) involves acting from certain sorts of reasons, but acting from those reasons will not always change the relevant probabilities, especially in extreme scenarios, where both agents who have and agents who lack the relevant virtue may be equally likely to fail, and yet we may not be inclined to judge them as equally creditworthy or equally blameworthy. It is not plausible to argue that *both* agents failed—and, say, were equally *likely* to fail—in this extreme

---

17 For further discussion of such cases, see Oakley (2016).
18 I am indebted to an anonymous referee for raising this point.

scenario, and that therefore there are no character-trait differences (relevant to these sorts of scenarios) between them at all: differences between these agents of relevance for warranted virtue attributions might well emerge in less extreme scenarios.

I want to emphasize that I am not arguing for the general claim that my counterfactual behavior in remote and improbable scenarios cannot count at all towards my true virtue or vice. Such behavior may or may not sometimes count—and in the next section I will outline a proposal about when such behavior might count. Rather, my claim has been that mere probability alone does not settle an agent's blameworthiness or creditworthiness for what they would do in a remote scenario, and so probability alone would not settle its relevance for the agent's claims to true virtue or true vice.

## 4. Remote Scenarios, Reasons, and Warranted Attributions of Friendship and Virtue

One possible way of developing a principled method of determining when remote scenarios can be diagnostic of genuine *virtue* might be through an analysis of when one's counterfactual behavior in remote scenarios can be diagnostic of the presence or absence of genuine *friendship*. Indeed, as we saw earlier, Kant himself drew parallels between genuine virtue and genuine friendship in such contexts, when he expressed doubts about the existence of true virtue, and true friendship, given how he thought agents might act in circumstances where their self-interest conflicts with the requirements of virtue or of friendship. So, consider here Peter Railton's (1984, 150–51) well-known example of the sophisticated consequentialist husband Juan, who Railton argues is able to overcome the problem of alienation from friends by making his commitment to consequentialism a regulative ideal rather than a motive for his every action. Railton (1984, 151) explains that Juan's motivational structure thus meets a counterfactual condition: while he ordinarily does not do what he does for the sake of doing what's right, he would nevertheless alter his dispositions and the course of his life if he thought they did not most promote the good. Thus, Juan is prepared to leave his wife Linda if maximizing the good requires him to do so. However, Railton argues that a fulfilling relationship like Juan and Linda's is of such value that the good will *usually* be maximized by the participants remaining involved in them rather than by abandoning them. But while Juan leaving Linda to work abroad indefinitely for Oxfam in a severely impoverished environment might be a remote scenario, Juan's counterfactual behavior in such a scenario nevertheless *does* seem to be relevant to determining whether Juan has a genuine friendship with Linda.

Indeed, Dean Cocking and I (1995) have argued that Juan's having such a disposition seems to *preclude* his relationship with Linda being one of genuine friendship. That is, the conditions under which various personal and professional relationships are commenced and terminated play a significant role in constituting and differentiating those relationships. For example, a disposition to terminate a relationship when one has helped the other party overcome a particular health problem does not seem incompatible with a good doctor-patient relationship, whereas such a disposition would seem clearly incompatible with a genuine friendship. Likewise, a disposition to end a relationship which has become deeply unfulfilling does not seem incompatible with that relationship qualifying as a genuine friendship. These sorts of dispositions can be characterized as the 'governing conditions' applied by one or both parties to the relationship in question. Cocking and I (1995) challenge Railton's claim that by making the governing conditions of the *sophisticated* consequentialist's relationships less *obtrusive* than the governing conditions of the *direct* consequentialist's relationships, the sophisticated consequentialist is thereby able to overcome the problem of alienation, which besets the direct consequentialist agent. For in various cases where one party finds the other party's governing conditions alienating and in conflict with friendship, the other party's adopting a similar strategy of making their governing conditions less obtrusive does not seem to redefine the relationship as a genuine friendship. For example, an ambitious graduate student who 'befriends' influential professors only on the condition that this helps his career prospects would not be able to transform such relationships into genuine friendships, simply by making the conditions of those relationships less apparent to those professors. After all, the governing conditions of the graduate student's relationship with the professors remain the same in both cases. If there is merit in this line of argument in the case of friendship, then, contrary to Adams's (2006, 161) suggestion that "there is little moral illumination to be gained by speculating about" how one would respond in a remote scenario, what Juan would do in (what we're here assuming is) the remote event that maximizing the good requires him to leave Linda seems to be directly relevant to determining whether Juan has a genuine friendship with Linda.

Of course, sometimes possible worlds which might *seem to us* to be remote from the actual world might be nearer than we assume. For example, we might find it inconceivable that a happily-married couple could ever become bitter enemies, yet if their mutual love is broken by some highly unlikely incident (such as unexpected news of dalliances with an ex-partner that one's spouse had withheld from one, despite previous reassurances of honesty), then the love may quickly turn to bitter hatred. So, this would make hating one's spouse a nearby possible world after all—i.e., it is precisely *because* one loves one's spouse that one's hating them is a nearby possible world.[19]

---

19 See Nat King Cole, "*Sometimes I love you, sometimes I hate you. But when I hate you, it's because I love you*" ("Sometimes I am Happy"). See also the now widely-used notion of a 'frenemy'. It is not clear how to move from general claims about a population—e.g., that lovers there often come to hate one another—to claims about particular members of that

One reason why dispositions—whether concerning relationships or virtuous character-traits—which are activated in remote scenarios can be relevant here seems to concern whether such dispositions are connected with our current *values* in the right sorts of ways. That is, Juan's disposition to leave Linda should maximizing the good require such an action cannot, it seems, be ruled out as irrelevant to defining the true nature of their relationship because this disposition is an *expression* of values that Juan explicitly endorses. It is not only that Juan would endorse his *behavior*—i.e., leaving Linda—in the hypothesized remote scenario, but that he would also endorse the *reason* that would lead him to perform this action—i.e., that leaving Linda to work abroad for Oxfam would in such circumstances be likely to maximize the good. And so, the corresponding proposal regarding virtuous character traits would be that an agent's counterfactual behavior (whether in remote or nearby scenarios) would count as relevant to our making warranted virtue attributions (or otherwise) to them when such counterfactual behavior, and the reasons for it, are things that the agent would now endorse as expressing values that they already accept and are committed to. For example, when considering what might be shown about the characters of the maximally obedient subjects who pressed the last switch marked 'XXX 450 volts' in the Milgram experiments, we would need to look not only at their *behavior* here, and whether they would *endorse* (or at least fail to repudiate) their behavior, but also at their *reasons* for pressing this switch here. And, in doing so, we would thereby need to consider whether they *believed* the shock machine was real, or instead, construed it as an elaborate fake—as some maximally obedient subjects evidently thought (see Perry 2012).[20] This seems to be a further reason for thinking that probability-based accounts of warranted virtue are insufficient for settling the relevance of agents' claims to true virtue or true vice.

So, the analogy with the case of friendship brings out that remote scenarios can provide important evidence of an individual's virtues, not simply through the behavior that this individual would exhibit in such scenarios, but also through the individual's reasons for their behavior here, and whether they would endorse (or at least not repudiate) both their action and their reasons for their behavior in the circumstances.[21] After all, there would

---

population—e.g., that a particular loving couple in that population might come to hate one another. Even if ex-lovers hating each other is a relatively common occurrence in a given population, it is not clear what this enables us to say about the probability that a particular pair of lovers will come to hate each other (or that a particular pair of ex-lovers will hate each other). After all, this couple might be outliers in the distribution of the population on this matter. Thanks again to an anonymous referee here.

20 For further discussion of the importance of considering subjects' construals here, see Sreenivasan (2002).
21 For a useful discussion of the significance of an agent endorsing, and not repudiating, their *feelings*, see Luke Russell (2014, ch. 9).

be some remote scenarios where Juan would leave Linda which would not plausibly preclude his relationship with her being a friendship—such as where doing so was prompted by her seriously betraying him, or was necessary to avert a lethal global pandemic—and here again what is crucial are Juan's reasons for doing so, and whether he endorses such reasons. As Aristotle argued in the *Nicomachean Ethics*, "a state of character is determined by its activities and its objects" (1980, IV.2, 1122a34–b2). Similarly, Angela Smith (2005) argues that in being justified in 'morally attributing' a certain attitude to an agent, "what matters in determining whether an attitude is morally attributable to a person is whether it can reasonably be taken to reflect that person's evaluative judgment(s)" (267).[22] The importance of an agent's reasons for their counterfactual behavior in remote scenarios, and of such behavior being endorsed (or at least unrepudiated) by them, also highlights a difference between what is plausibly taken as evidence for an agent's possessing a virtue, and what is plausibly taken as evidence for an agent possessing purely behavioral dispositions, such as being an excellent full forward in Australian rules football. For perhaps failures in remote scenarios with such dispositions in sporting contexts—such as missing a crucial goal in the only Grand Final one's team has competed in—can plausibly be taken as evidence that the player in question does lack the requisite goal-kicking skill, quite apart from what reasons they may have for missing the goal (assuming they were unimpeded in their attempt). However, purely *behavioral* failures in remote scenarios do not plausibly seem diagnostic or informative of virtuous character traits, because, unlike the sporting cases, we would need to understand the agent's reasons for such a failure, in order to be able to assess its relevance to warranted attribution to this agent of the virtue in question.

But even where an agent's counterfactual behavior is connected with their current values in the sense that the agent does not repudiate—and perhaps, even in some sense, actually *endorses*—that behavior and their reasons for it, questions might still be raised about the extent to which that behavior and those reasons reflect on them *personally*, and on their level of personal virtue. For the sorts of 'testing' mentioned earlier, whereby individuals are actually placed into the kinds of scenarios that would ordinarily be remote and improbable and their behavior and reasons are noted therein, could all presumably be used in the context of *role virtues*, without settling whether

---

22 As Adams (1985, 19) argues, "The beliefs ascribed to the graduate of the Hitler *Jugend* are heinous, and it is morally reprehensible to hold them (even if one has no opportunity to act on them). No matter how he came by them, his evil beliefs are a part of who he is, morally, and make him a fitting object of reproach. He may also be a victim of his education; and if he is, that gives him a particular claim to be regarded and treated with mercy—but not an exemption from blame." See also Adams (2006, 135) on the white supremacist: "These broadly cognitive states play a major part in constituting a person's character. If someone holds white-supremacist or other racist views, that is not a fact external to his character."

any such role virtues are also character traits of the person themselves, beyond their role. Consider here, for instance, *professional* roles, such as the role of a criminal defense lawyer. Suppose that a level of callousness towards complainants counted as a role virtue for criminal defense lawyers, insofar as they are expected to have a somewhat 'thick skin' towards complainants to enable vigorous cross-examination of them. It seems possible that a particular criminal defense lawyer might be willing to, for example, humiliate complainants in the witness box in a wide variety of remote scenarios, and might offer some standard legal rationales for this (such as clients having a right to effective representation), and thus, some may well see this as good evidence for being epistemically warranted in attributing to this lawyer (what we are assuming here is) the role virtue of callousness. Indeed, there seems to be a sense in which this lawyer does not repudiate—and even, perhaps, in a certain sense endorses—their counterfactual behavior in their role here, insofar as they offer the aforementioned standard legal rationales for their behavior here. And yet without further investigation, it may remain unclear to what extent such professional role behavior, and the lawyer's endorsement of that, reveals about them as a person, and about their personal virtue, beyond their role as a lawyer. For the remote scenario tests might simply indicate how well this lawyer has mastered certain legal skills, and to be epistemically warranted in attributing any particular *personal* virtues (or vices) to this lawyer it seems important to probe more deeply into the attitudes which this lawyer has about their exercising such skills. So, a further consideration here seems to be whether the agent—in this case, the lawyer—would be *proud* or *ashamed* of their having developed such modally robust skills, that would presumably be involved in a legal role virtue of (some level of) callousness-towards-complainants (see Oakley and Cocking 2001, ch. 6). Some criminal defense lawyers do indeed seem to be proud of their having and acting on such skills, while others confess to feeling somewhat ashamed at the robustness of their callousness and cross-examination skills (see, e.g., Wishman 1981). Either way, these emotions of pride and shame seem to provide a clear bridge between such professional skills and the person themselves, as pride and shame here both involve personally *identifying with* these skills. But equally, it seems possible that some criminal defense lawyers regard their robust cross-examination skills as somehow part of the role of criminal defense lawyer, and of the adversarial system of justice itself, without also personally identifying with those skills, or with the actions that those skills enable them to perform (even while being willing to advance standard legal justifications for such actions). I am not here arguing that a failure to personally identify with one's professional skills and behavior shields oneself from credit or blame for what one does in a professional capacity. My point here is rather that, contrary to what seems to be an implication of Kant's view described at the outset of this paper, what an agent is willing to do, or has done, in a remote and improbable scenario, cannot by itself be taken as conclusive evidence of whether they personally have the virtue in question here, for their behavior (and their reasons for it) may be manifestations of a role virtue here that they have become skilled at exercising, without yet telling us much at all about whether this role virtue is also a personal virtue of the agent.

## 5. Conclusion

We have seen above how the Kantian appeal to extreme scenarios as diagnostic of true virtue is implausibly stringent. In evaluating probabilistic approaches to warranted virtue attributions as an alternative to such a Kantian view, I argued that such approaches are also inadequate, as these approaches neglect to address whether or not agents are to be credited or faulted for the behavior they exhibit (or would exhibit) in remote scenarios. In closing, I suggested that examining the dispositions involved in true friendship can help to reveal why warranted attributions of friendship and virtue must look beyond behavioral dispositions, and must include an agent's reasons for their being disposed to perform certain actions in remote scenarios.[23]

## References

Adams, Robert M. 1985. "Involuntary Sins." *Philosophical Review* 94: 3–31.
———. 2006. *A Theory of Virtue: Excellence in Being for the Good*. Oxford: Clarendon Press.
Aristotle. 1980. *The Nicomachean Ethics*. Translated by W. D. Ross. Oxford: Oxford University Press.
Australian Broadcasting Corporation, Radio National. 2012. *All in the Mind: Behind the Shock Machine*, 3 June. http://www.abc.net.au/radionational/programs/allinthemind/beyond-the-shock-machine/4044812.

---

[23] Earlier versions of this paper were presented at the Australian Catholic University conference on Reasons and Virtues, Melbourne 2015, at the Australasian Association of Philosophy Annual Conference, Macquarie University, Sydney, 2015, and at a seminar at Kyoto University Centre for Applied Philosophy and Ethics. I wish to thank the audiences at each of these occasions for their very helpful comments. Special thanks to Steve Matthews, for his valuable feedback as a commentator on the paper at the ACU conference. I am also grateful to the following people for their comments on previous versions of the paper: Robert Audi, Russell Blackford, Steve Clarke, Ben Cullen, Garrett Cullity, Karen Jones, Satoshi Kodama, Cathy Legg, Luke Russell, Nic Southwood, John Thrasher, Bernadette Tobin, and Peter Shiu-Hwa Tsu. I also wish to thank an anonymous referee for Routledge for their insightful comments on the penultimate version of this paper, along with Stewart Braun and Noell Birondo for their helpful guidance. This paper draws significantly on my article "Diagnosing True Virtue? Remote Scenarios, Warranted Virtue Attributions, and Virtuous Medical Practice," *Theoretical Medicine and Bioethics* 37 (2016). I want to thank the guest editors of that issue of the journal, Steve Matthews and Bernadette Tobin, for allowing me to draw on that article here. Material from that article is used with permission of Springer: Springer Science+Business Media Dordrecht 2016.

Cocking, Dean and Justin Oakley. 1995. "Indirect Consequentialism, Friendship, and the Problem of Alienation." *Ethics* 106: 86–111.

Doris, John M. 2002. *Lack of Character: Personality and Moral Behavior*. New York: Cambridge University Press.

Hursthouse, Rosalind. 1999. *On Virtue Ethics*. Oxford: Oxford University Press.

Kant, Immanuel. 1959. *Foundations of the Metaphysics of Morals*. Translated by L. W. Beck. Indianapolis: Bobbs-Merrill.

———. 1996. "Religion within the Boundaries of Mere Reason." In *Religion and Rational Theology*, translated and edited by Allen W. Wood and George Di Giovanni, 39–217. New York: Cambridge University Press.

Milgram, Stanley. 2010. *Obedience to Authority: An Experimental View*. London: Pinter and Martin.

Nagel, Thomas. 1979. "Moral Luck." In his *Mortal Questions*, 24–38. Cambridge: Cambridge University Press.

Oakley, Justin. 2016. "Diagnosing True Virtue? Remote Scenarios, Warranted Virtue Attributions, and Virtuous Medical Practice." *Theoretical Medicine and Bioethics* 37: 85–96.

Oakley, Justin and Dean Cocking. 2001. *Virtue Ethics and Professional Roles*. Cambridge: Cambridge University Press.

Perry, Gina. 2012. *Behind the Shock Machine*. Melbourne: Scribe.

Pettit, Philip. 2015. *The Robust Demands of the Good: Ethics with Attachment, Virtue and Respect*. Oxford: Oxford University Press.

Railton, Peter. 1984. "Alienation, Consequentialism, and the Demands of Morality." *Philosophy and Public Affairs* 13: 134–71.

Russell, Luke. 2014. *Evil: A Philosophical Investigation*. Oxford: Oxford University Press.

Smith, Angela M. 2005. "Responsibility for Attitudes: Activity and Passivity in Mental Life." *Ethics* 115: 236–71.

Sreenivasan, Gopal. 2002. "Errors about Errors: Virtue Theory and Trait Attribution." *Mind* 111: 47–68.

Vranas, Peter B. M. 2005. "The Indeterminacy Paradox: Character Evaluations and Human Psychology." *Nous* 39: 1–42.

Wishman, Seymour. 1981. *Confessions of a Criminal Lawyer*. New York: Times Books.

# 3 Vice, Reasons, and Wrongdoing

*Damian Cox*

Does justified belief that acting in a certain way would be vicious furnish a reason against acting in that way? Is this a special kind of reason, distinct from other kinds of moral reason? Can it form the basis for a theory of right action? In this chapter, I explore positive answers to each of these questions.

## 1. Virtues, Vices, and the Moral Middle

Let me set out a series of assumptions that guide my answers. Aretaic judgment takes the form of both judgment of character and judgment of action. My initial assumption is that virtues and vices are broadly structured into trichotomies. An action or a trait can be virtuous or vicious or neither virtuous nor vicious. An act of helping or of not helping might be generous or selfish, or neither generous nor selfish. We may encounter situations which force a dichotomy upon us—situations where the moral middle disappears and our actions can only be virtuous or vicious—but this is not the invariable, or even ordinary, run of things. Traits may seem to invite dichotomous judgment: that a person is either considerate of others or not considerate of them; courageous or not courageous; temperate or intemperate; a dedicated and professional colleague or a lazy, distracted and unprofessional colleague. People seem either to have integrity or to lack it. Generally, however, these cases involve an implicit third term. A person may be neither especially temperate nor especially intemperate; they may be considerate to others to a substantial degree, often, but not always, and not especially so. Integrity is something we possess in degrees.[1]

A second assumption is that virtuous action is independent of virtuous character in the sense that it is possible to act virtuously in a particular way—courageously say—without possessing the relevant virtue. A habitual coward is capable of acting with true courage. The same thing goes for vices and vicious actions. A habitually courageous person can turn to jelly. An action isn't virtuous or vicious because it is reflective of an agent's character.

---

1 This view of integrity is defended in Cox, La Caze, and Levine (2003).

It is difficult to work out the precise relationship between aretaic characterizations of actions and aretaic characterizations of character and I wish to leave the question as open as possible, given the various assumptions I set out here.

A third assumption is about the relationship between virtues and excellence. Virtues are kinds of moral excellence. A virtue is an excellence of character; a virtuous action is an excellence of action. Virtuous action exhibits a robust kind of moral excellence and an action is not virtuous unless it exhibits this excellence. Consider Kant's example of the honest shopkeeper.[2] A shopkeeper may be scrupulously honest with her customers because she wants their continued business and is wary of earning their distrust. Alternatively, she may genuinely respect her customers' property. In the latter case, were she to ask herself why she routinely gives her customers the correct change, she might answer that it wouldn't occur to her to steal money from her customers, that it is not her money. Because the contrast is drawn between non-virtuously motivated honest behavior—a case of merely acting in accordance with duty—and what seems to be a wholly satisfactory motivation—a case of acting from duty—it is tempting to say that the shopkeeper's actions exhibit the virtue of honesty in the second case, but not in the first. I wish to resist this inference. It seems to me that the shopkeeper's actions are not virtuous in either case. A virtuous action is a display of moral excellence, but there is nothing excellent in the ordinary and unremarkable behavior of the honest shopkeeper. We act with virtuous honesty when it is hard be honest; for instance, when acting with honesty entails a considerable risk of harm. Exceptional individuals may find virtue easy, or may find particular acts of virtue easy, but an action does not count as virtuous—does not count as a morally excellent act—if it is something that would have been easy for just about anyone to have done. Ordinary, undemanding honesty, such as the honesty of a shopkeeper giving her customers the correct change, is not a virtuous action because it is too undemanding to qualify for the requisite moral excellence. By giving her customers the correct change, the shopkeeper has managed to avoid acting dishonestly. She does not, by this kind of act alone, demonstrate the virtue of honesty. Virtuous action, then, being a kind of moral excellence, is exceptional. It is somewhat rare. The avoidance of vice, by contrast, is common.

A fourth assumption is that the virtuous nature of action depends upon the circumstances of the agent and, in some respects, for some virtues and vices, the nature of the agent. I wish to draw together a number of ideas about virtuous action: that they need not be displays of settled character; that they are nonetheless acts of moral excellence; and that their excellence

---

2 Kant, *Groundwork of the Metaphysics of Morals*, 4:397.

depends upon circumstances and conditions of the agent. Consider the example of a shopkeeper with an inner kleptomaniac compulsion. He might display a kind of moral excellence (e.g., strength of morally good will) when he deals honestly with his customers. It would be virtuous in one respect for him to give the correct change to customers where it would not be virtuous for a person lacking his psychological debilitation to do so. I don't think the kleptomaniac shopkeeper's action is an example of virtuous honesty, however. I think it is an example of strength of will or moral courage, but not an especially virtuous act of honesty. It is virtuous in one respect, but not another.

Actions can be virtuous in some respects and not others; they can be virtuous in some respects and vicious in other respects at the same time. This leads me to my final assumption. It is that the ways in which actions are virtuous and vicious can be summed together so that we can rank actions, most importantly prospective actions, according to their degree of overall virtuousness or viciousness. I make no assumption about inter-agent comparisons of virtue and vice. Competition between people about who is most virtuous is not my concern here. Rather, I assume that it is possible to rank potential actions of individual agents in a way that facilitates moral deliberation on their part and, after the fact, assessment of whether they have acted rightly or well.

Building on these assumptions, my key claim is that attributions of virtues, vices, and what I am calling the moral middle line up with deontic judgments of action. Virtue judgment has a trichotomous structure: dividing between the virtuous, the vicious, and the neither virtuous nor vicious. Deontic judgment also has a trichotomous structure, falling into three basic classes: that of the obligatory, the supererogatory, and the merely permissible (i.e., permissible but not obligatory). Roughly speaking, virtuous actions are supererogatory, the rejection of vicious action is obligatory, and actions that are neither virtuous nor vicious are merely permissible.

## 2. Vices and Reasons

Accepting my assumptions, even if only in order to see what might follow from them, paves the way for proposing a number of asymmetries between the way virtues and vices function in moral deliberation and judgment. That an act would be virtuous constitutes a reason to do it. That an act would be vicious constitutes a reason not to do it. But these needn't be the same kind of reason. An action is not vicious because it amounts to a failure to act virtuously. It needn't be vicious to fail to act virtuously; it could be neither virtuous nor vicious. Thus, the reason constituted by an action's virtuousness doesn't automatically translate into a reason not to act viciously. Reasons of virtue and reasons of vice are distinct kinds of reason. But how distinct are they?

My suggestion is that reasons of virtue and reasons of vice generally operate in distinct ways. Reasons of vice are predominantly *pro tanto* reasons; reasons of virtue are predominantly *prima facie* reasons. For any prospective action, one can describe the action in appropriately evaluative terms such that either the action would be vicious for the agent to do in her circumstances or would not be vicious for the agent to do in her circumstances. If it would be vicious, the agent *ipso facto* has a reason not to do it. My suggestion is that such reasons are *pro tanto* reasons. These are reasons that are not erased by other features of the action, including any of its virtuous characteristics. If an action would be cruel, for example, there might be much else to be said for it. Its being cruel may be outweighed by other reasons, but the cruelty of the act tells against it no matter how these other reasons go. One of the distinguishing properties of *pro tanto* reasons is that they leave an affective trace. This is to say that, even when outweighed by other reasons, they make a certain kind of regret fitting. That I have acted cruelly towards another is something it is always fitting for me to regret, even if a set of conclusive reasons drove my decision to act as I have. (How this kind of regret works—what it is to regret an action even when I do not wish to have acted otherwise—is a nice question, but one I have not the space for here).

By contrast, reasons of virtue do not characteristically work this way. That I have forsaken an opportunity to act virtuously is something that may occasion regret, but needn't. That an action would be virtuous is a reason to perform it that can be extinguished rather than merely outweighed, which is to say reasons of virtue operate as *prima facie* reasons. For example, that an act would be a kindness to a stranger may well constitute a reason to do it, but not invariably. It may be no reason at all if it is just one of many such opportunities. Reasons of virtue are not always *prima facie*. There are circumstances in which they are *pro tanto*. These are circumstances in which the moral middle disappears: where one faces a choice between acting virtuously or viciously, with courage or cowardice, for example. In such circumstances, one's reason to act virtuously is *pro tanto*. It is a reason that can only be outweighed, not extinguished. This is because, when the moral middle disappears, failing to act virtuously entails acting viciously. In other circumstances, the prospect of failing to act virtuously furnishes only *prima facie* reasons.

Given the tripartite account of virtues, vices, and the moral middle I am assuming, it is not surprising that reasons of virtue are characteristically *prima facie* rather than *pro tanto*. In deontic terms, reasons of vice introduce—in the right circumstances—moral obligations. Reasons of virtues—except where the moral middle disappears—are supererogatory. That an act falls within the moral middle—that it is merely permissible—constitutes no reason to do it or not do it.

## 3. Vice Ethics

I began the chapter with three questions. Are there reasons of vice? Are they distinctive? Can they form the basis of a theory of right action? My answer to the second question encourages a positive answer to the third, though does not strictly require it. This is the view that right action can be defined in some way in terms of vicious action. The remainder of the paper is concerned to set out such a formulation of right action and examine its initial plausibility. Deontic judgments—that an action is right, wrong, permissible, obligatory, or prohibited—map respects in which we are amenable to others in a particular way, answerable to a particular sort of critical appraisal, deserving or not of social censure or punishment. They are regulatory moral categories, whose fundamental point seems to be to support and encourage ways of life that are necessary for cooperative human flourishing. At first blush, it seems that a vice-centered ethics, while accommodating only a limited range of moral judgments, is well suited to this regulatory role.

Virtue ethics defines right action in terms of virtue; vice ethics defines it in terms of vice. How the category of right action maps onto the deontic categories I employed earlier in the chapter—that of the obligatory, the merely permissible, and the supererogatory—is a matter of some dispute. For my present purposes, right action is best interpreted as permissible action and wrong action as impermissible action. There is at least one clear sense of the term which is captured by this interpretation and it has the advantage of establishing a dichotomy between right and wrong. The trichotomy of the obligatory, merely permissible, and supererogatory is readily defined in terms of this dichotomy.[3]

Direct forms of virtue ethics, sometimes called agent-based forms, say that actions are right if and only if they are virtuous.[4] Indirect forms, sometimes called qualified-agent forms, say that actions are right if and only if they are what a fully virtuous person would characteristically do in the circumstances.[5] However, there is another way of defining right action in aretaic terms, one that deserves close attention. Instead of attempting to define right action in terms of virtuous action, we might define it in terms of

---

[3] Much turns on this initial identification of right action with permissible action. Rosalind Hursthouse (2006) holds a contrasting view. She identifies right action with exemplary action: action about which there is no ground at all for moral complaint. I don't think that this is merely a verbal disagreement. We use the concept of rightness in moral deliberation, in framing moral guidance, and in moral assessment. It is the basic concept we appeal to when we hold ourselves to account for what we do to each other. The key question is whether accounts of rightness developed in aretaic terms can play these roles satisfactorily and, if so, which version does so more successfully. The identification of rightness with either the exemplary or the permissible is crucial here. See also my discussion of Daniel Russell's (2009) view in footnote 17.

[4] The most prominent proponent is Slote (2001).

[5] The most prominent proponent is Hursthouse (1999).

vicious action.[6] This is the approach I label vice ethics. Vice ethics mirrors virtue ethics, but does so in terms of wrong action. In its simplest direct form, an action is wrong if and only if it is vicious and in its simplest indirect form, an action is wrong if and only if it is what a fully vicious person would characteristically do in the circumstances.[7]

I wish in this chapter to sketch a direct form of vice ethics. Here is an initial formulation:

($W_0$) An action is wrong if and only if it would be vicious to do it.
($R_0$) An action is right if and only if it would not be vicious to do it.

The pleasant simplicity of this formulation does not survive close scrutiny, however. $W_0$ and $R_0$ do not make explicit the relativity to persons and circumstances implicit in them. An action is not vicious *per se*. It is vicious for a particular agent, in the particular circumstances of that agent. We can safely leave this relativity implicit, however, as long as it is not overlooked in applications.[8]

More troubling are cases in which it seems that an agent must choose between two ostensibly vicious actions. An example from Slote (2001) illustrates this situation. Slote imagines a prosecutor who is asked to prosecute a defendant who she cannot but feel malice towards. Because there are no alternative prosecutors available, she faces a choice of either dropping the prosecution or going ahead with it in spite of her feelings of malice towards the defendant. Were she to drop the prosecution, her action would be vicious. It would show insufficient regard for justice or the victims of the crime being prosecuted. Were she to take on the prosecution, but prosecute in malice, her behavior would also be vicious. So what judgment would a vice ethicist offer about the case? The obvious thing to say is that the prosecutor should choose the lesser vice. Plausibly—but contestably—the lesser vice is to prosecute. (The prosecutor is not a judge after all; prosecuting with malice is not the same thing as judging with malice). I think we should say that by choosing to prosecute, the prosecutor does the right thing, even though her action is not without vice. Choosing the lesser vice leads, in

---

6  Slote (2001, 38) comes close to this. He says that "An act is right (morally acceptable) if and only if it comes from good or virtuous motivation . . . or at least doesn't come from bad or inferior motivation . . . ." One trouble with this formulation is that it remains unclear under what conditions a lack of bad motivation may suffice for right action. According to the version of vice ethics defended here, lack of bad motivation (and other vices) always suffices for right action.
7  Van Zyl (2011) defends the indirect formulation, although she does not suggest basing an account of right action on it alone.
8  On this view, rightness of actions is a property of individual actions, not a property of types of actions. The token judgment has priority over the type judgment; we settle on the view that a type of action is wrong or impermissible because we see that the great majority of instances of the type are wrong. Self-serving lies are impermissible as a type, for instance, because nearly all self-serving lies are impermissible.

circumstances like these, to right action; it is what the agent ought to do. On this basis, let me reformulate:

> (R) An action is right if and only if it is the least vicious of available actions.
> (W) An action is wrong if and only if it is not the least vicious of available actions.[9]

This form of vice ethics amounts to an injunction to never be more vicious than we need be. Most of the time we needn't be vicious at all, in which case we shouldn't be vicious at all. Of course, there needn't be only one least vicious available action in particular circumstances. There may be many, in which case a right action is a merely permissible action. If there is only one least vicious action available, then not to perform it is to act wrongly, in which case right action is an obligatory action.

## 4. Difficult Cases

There is one obvious bullet to bite in accepting vice ethics. According to vice ethics, agents can do terrible things and yet not act wrongly. They do so when all other possible choices are worse. Say that a teenager steals a car for a joyride. When the car's brakes fail he faces a choice of driving into a large group of bystanders or turning to the left and hitting a solitary bystander. According to vice ethics, the teenager acts rightly by turning left because this is the least vicious option in the circumstances. But this appears to imply that driving a stolen car deliberately into a bystander is not wrong. This judgment sounds silly, but the silliness is dispelled by more careful parsing of the action. The act of stealing a car and driving it into a bystander is wrong because, taken as a temporally extended whole, it is much more vicious than other available actions, like not stealing the car in the first place. The viciousness of the stealing determines the wrongness of the larger sequence of events. The act of turning left, considered by itself, is the least vicious available thing to do when the brakes of the stolen car fail. So the act of turning left is not wrong when considered by itself. The part is not wrong even if the whole of which it is part is wrong. The teenager hasn't just stolen a car and he hasn't just saved a lot of lives. He has wrongfully stolen a car and killed someone with it. In judging actions—their overall rightness and wrongness, and also their blameworthiness and their fitness for punishment—we must make a judgment about the scope of the action we are judging: when it starts and when it finishes; what parts are to

---

9 It might seem that "least vicious" implies "vicious to some degree," but I am clearly denying this implication. Often the least vicious action available to us will not be vicious at all. Thus, I should specify "least vicious action" to mean "an action with the least vicious character." On this reading, an action that is not vicious at all has the least possible vicious character. It is the null case. I would like to thank an anonymous reader for this volume for pointing out to me the need to clarify this matter.

be treated together and what parts separately. In this case, it seems apt to treat the sequence of events beginning with the car theft and ending with the death of a bystander as the primary object of judgment. Vice ethics tells us that the sequence is wrong, though not wrong in all its parts.

Cases that involve doing the right thing from bad motives present a different kind of challenge for vice ethics. Ramon Das (2003, 326) discusses the case of a man who dives into swimming pool to rescue a child, solely motivated by a plan to impress the child's mother with a view to sleeping with her. His action is vicious: sleazy, manipulative, and probably dishonest. But is it wrong? Assuming that the man did not have available to him the choice of a better motive—one is rarely able to choose one's motives on the spot like this—his only alternative was to let the child drown. In doing so he would act more viciously still: at a minimum the man would be acting with callous indifference. In saving the child the man acts viciously, but less viciously than he otherwise would have, so he does not act wrongly. How plausible is this? According to the formulation of vice ethics I am offering, for the man to have acted wrongly there must have been some other course of action he should have taken, something he should have done instead. If there is none, then he did not act wrongly. Putting the case in terms of right action: the man acted rightly because, of the action choices available to him, he made the morally correct choice. It doesn't follow from this that he should review his conduct with satisfaction. He has much with which to be dissatisfied. What a judgment of rightness indicates about an action is that it is the right thing for a person to have done in the circumstances they confront. It does not, according to vice ethics, indicate that the action is morally flawless or exemplary. In this way, judgments of praiseworthiness and rightness come apart.[10] The man in this example may be morally criticized in many aretaic respects. His attitudes to the child's mother and his vile motives for the rescue are not whitewashed because we judge that he acted rightly in saving the child. Of his decision to save the child we can but say that he chose rightly and rightly acted on this choice.

Here is another challenging case for the vice ethicist. Consider a thoroughly vicious person who is under an inner compulsion to sadistic, bullying behavior. He faces what he thinks of as a choice between hurting—say mocking and chastising—one person or two people. He does not consider

---

10 Although praiseworthiness and rightness come apart in the version of vice ethics I am describing, blameworthiness and wrongness do not. Setting aside exculpatory factors and excuses, choosing a more vicious action than one needed to is blameworthy. Some philosophers, most prominently consequentialists, have argued for the existence of blameless wrongdoing, see, for example, Parfit (1984) and Tännsjö (1995). I do not see it as a significant shortcoming of vice ethics to demur. On the other hand, vice ethics readily accommodates the idea that blameless actions can nonetheless carry a moral residue. In choosing the least vicious action available to me I may nonetheless choose a vicious action. And although I may not be fairly blamed for making this choice rather than some other choice available to me, I would have still acted viciously and may indeed own the burden of this.

the possibility that he not hurt anybody to be an option: the volcano of his sarcastic temper, he thinks, needs an outlet. He thinks that it is inevitable that sooner or later—sooner—he will give in and act on his urge to verbally abuse another person. Let us assume that he is right about this; that he really is under a strong compulsion to act viciously in this way. What are we to say of such a person? Does he act rightly by choosing to abuse only the one person? We need to be careful about how we specify what count as alternative courses of action. In the case of the swimming pool man, I noted that he is unlikely to be able to choose his motive. Nonetheless, he had available to him, in some sense not yet specified, two courses of action: to save the child or not save the child. These were his two choices because they were the only things *to* do. Psychological impediments to choice may be relevant for exculpation or blame, but judgment of the rightness and wrongness of actions requires us to keep track of what a person could have done in a less psychologically constrained way. Our sarcastic bully with the temper of a volcano, even if under a compulsion, has available to him, in some sense, the action of hurting nobody.

I suggest that the sense of available action in formulations of vice ethics should exclude the psychological particularities of the agent. These come under the spotlight later on in the process of aretaic judgment so we needn't include them in setting up what counts as an option for the agent. We can avoid doing so by stipulating something along the following lines:

(A) For the purposes of judging right and wrong, an action is available to an agent if and only if it could be performed by the agent were the agent of a mind to do it.

If this is correct, we need not worry that the bully acts rightly by only bullying one person rather than two. He has available to him the act of bullying nobody; this is the least vicious act available to him and he only acts rightly if he avails himself of it. Matters are not quite this straightforward, however. Consider the case of Professor Procrastinate.[11] Professor Procrastinate is asked to review a colleague's new book. Of all potential reviewers, she is best placed to undertake the review. Other reviewers would not match her insightful treatment of the book. However, Professor Procrastinate knows only too well that she is unlikely to finish the review in good time. She knows that she almost invariably fails to complete tasks like this on time, putting them off until much too late. So what is the right thing for her to do? The chief positions in the debate are those of the actualist—who thinks the professor should decide on the basis of what is actually going to happen if she accepts the task—and the possibilist—who thinks the professor should decide on the basis of what is possible for her, roughly what she could do if she had a mind to. I think it is worth carefully comparing this case with

---

11 The example is from Jackson and Pargetter (1986, 235).

that of the sadistic bully. It might seem that the account of action availability described in the case of the sadistic bully commits me to a possibilist response to the Professor Procrastinate case. But this is not in fact the case.

In judging the sadistic bully, we compare actions available to him: bully one, bully many, bully none. I have suggested that a thin concept of availability is relevant to this task. If it is possible to perform an action were the agent to have a mind to perform it, then the action counts as an available action for the purposes of our forming a moral judgment of it. In the case of Professor Procrastinate, available actions are only two: accept the request to review the book or don't accept it. In judging the action we must decide upon the least vicious action. Is it more vicious to undertake to review a colleague's book, knowing full well that you are likely to fail to complete the task on time, or is it more vicious to refuse to undertake the review, thereby failing to act as a good colleague? When is it merely prudent to accept predictable limitations upon one's future agency and when is it viciously self-indulgent to do so? That, I think, is exactly the right question to be asking of cases like this. It sets out the best terms in which to judge Professor Procrastinate's actions and it is the best way for her to deliberate about her dilemma.[12]

I have outlined a direct form of vice ethics and demonstrated how it applies to various difficult cases. I next aim to set out the advantages this form of aretaic ethics might enjoy.

## 5. Why Vice Ethics?

What advantages might vice ethics enjoy over virtue ethics? Given limitations of space I can only introduce one comparison here. Let me compare the merits of direct vice ethics as I have formulated it with one of its closest virtue-theoretic rivals: direct virtue ethics. According to Michael Slote's version of direct virtue ethics, an action is right if and only if it comes from good or virtuous motivation.[13] In its simplest form such a theory runs into considerable difficulty (Brady 2004; Cox 2006; Das 2003; Jacobson 2002; Johnson 2003; Ransome 2010). What of a version of direct virtue ethics that mirrors the form of direct vice ethics I have outlined? In this case, an

---

12 Framing the issue between actualism and possibilism in aretaic terms like this, does not resolve the issue so much as reframe it; and reframe it in a way that makes it hard to form a general case for either actualism and possibilism. An actualist stance is right if it would be viciously unwise and shortsighted to ignore one's predictable future actions. A possibilist stance is right if it would be viciously self-indulgent to take refuge in one's bad propensities. Judgments will vary, case to case.
13 As noted in footnote 6, Slote (2001) on occasion modifies this formulation to allow for an absence of bad motivation. This creates a hybrid virtue/vice ethics, but as I pointed out it is not clear how the two component parts are meant to work together. I ignore Slote's hybrid theory for present purposes of comparison.

action would be said to be right if and only if it is the most virtuous of available actions.[14] Let me call this maximizing virtue ethics. What advantages are there for (minimizing) vice ethics over maximizing virtue ethics? I think there are three main advantages; whether or not they are decisive advantages is not entirely clear.

First, vice ethics offers a smooth way of introducing judgments of supererogation. A supererogatory action is one that is not obligatory and yet virtuous. This is readily described by the vice ethicist.

(S) An action is supererogatory if and only if it would be virtuous to do it, but not vicious not to do it.

By contrast, maximizing virtue ethicists can struggle to make sense of the supererogatory. According to maximizing virtue ethics, it is always wrong to do what is of lesser virtue. Refusing to perform a supererogatory action is to choose the lesser virtue (or to choose no virtue at all). So if a supererogatory action is among our options, it would be wrong not to do it, in which case it wouldn't be supererogatory.

The second advantage of vice ethics is that it can readily avoid a theoretical flaw I will call "strong self-effacement."[15] Maximizing virtue ethics is strongly self-effacing; vice ethics need not be. In general, a theory is self-effacing when it cannot always be used to guide action. There are a number of ways this might come about. Here are two. First, direct guidance by the theory might, in some circumstances, be ruled out by the theory. This is a weak form of self-effacement.[16] Second, guidance by the theory might sometimes take the form of recommending action that is wrong by the theory's own lights. This is a strong form of self-effacement. Vice ethics is weakly self-effacing, but, depending upon how one specifies the vices, it needn't be strongly self-effacing. On any plausible account of the virtues, by contrast, maximizing virtue ethics is both weakly and strongly self-effacing. Let me consider weak and strong self-effacement in turn.

It can be less than virtuous to be purely motivated to act virtuously. It can be vicious to be purely motivated to avoid being vicious. Acting so as

---

14 Christine Swanton (2001, 2003) offers a sophisticated alternative to this kind of direct virtue ethics. According to Swanton, an action is right if it is overall virtuous, i.e., virtuous in all relevant respects. She denies, however, that an overall virtuous action is an ideally virtuous action, i.e., an action that is as virtuous as possible. This view makes good sense given her target centered account of virtues and virtuous action. Since she thinks that virtues aim at characteristic ends or targets, meeting a target in an appropriate way will suffice for virtuous action.
15 I can only sketch out the main issues here. I elaborate on kinds of self-effacement and the theoretical problems they pose in Cox (2012).
16 Keller (2007), Martinez (2011), and Pettigrove (2011) all discuss weak self-effacement with respect to virtue ethics.

to be kind is not the same thing as being kind, and arguably it is kindness that lies at the heart of virtue, not the desire to be kind. It might well be vicious to save a drowning child merely because one is concerned not to act viciously. Such a motive seems to exemplify the vice of valuing one's moral health above what is really most important in the situation. Because of cases like these, aretaic ethics tends to be weakly self-effacing. If it is ever vicious to explicitly follow, and be motivated to follow, the rule to do what is least vicious, vice ethics won't always furnish explicit action guidance. It may specify what the right thing to do is, but it does not do so in a way that is of much direct and immediate use to a person wanting moral guidance. This is true, but it makes for less trouble than it might at first seem. Vice ethics is weakly self-effacing in the way that theories of practical action are often weakly self-effacing. Consider a theory of bicycle riding. The theory instructs riders to do various things, and one of the things it is likely to instruct them to do is to not consciously attend to all the principles of bike-riding when trying to ride a bike. To ride a bike too self-consciously, is to ride a bike badly. The theory of bike-riding thus guides action, but only indirectly. In the same way, vice ethics often guides action indirectly. It is therefore self-effacing in a largely harmless way.

Strong self-effacement represents a more substantial theoretical problem. To see how this works, consider briefly a non-aretaic theory of right action. Consider a version of utilitarianism according to which it is right to donate all of one's surplus income to life-saving charities and wrong not to do so. Recognizing that this is an extreme (if correct) demand, and that it would be counterproductive to insist upon it, utilitarians sometimes recommend that those above a particular threshold of income donate a sub-optimal percentage (say five percent) of their income to life-saving charities. Peter Singer (2009) defends such a utilitarian tactic. However, five percent donations are wrong by utilitarian lights. There is much more that moderately prosperous people could do to save lives and it is wrong of them not to do it. Utilitarians therefore sometimes advise moral agents to act in ways that conflict with a utilitarian standard of rightness. They are wise to do so. The advice to donate five percent of one's income has a much better chance of improving the plight of the poor than the advice to donate all of one's surplus income. Utilitarianism can thus be strongly self-effacing. When it is, it does more than merely guide action indirectly, it guides action to wrongness.

Does either vice ethics or maximizing virtue ethics guide agents towards wrong action? Consider the example of self-assessment. Should moral agents draw up forensically precise accounts with themselves about their own moral performance? Should they be rigorously honest in their moral self-assessment? A fully virtuous person may well thrive under such a regimen, but rigorous moral audit of the self is a debilitating condition for those who struggle to be fully good. It is sometimes better for morally fragile people—people who genuinely wish to be good, but who struggle to be so—to think better of themselves than a merciless self-accounting would reveal. It is better for them because it enables better action, better attitudes, better thoughts, better relationships; in short, it enables them to lead a better, more virtuous life than they would otherwise lead. Rigorous and fully honest moral self-assessment may be fine for the fully virtuous, but for the morally fragile it risks disenchantment and a collapse of confidence. The trait of self-pandering—thinking too well of oneself too readily, dissembling to oneself about one's venal motives, concocting self-rationalizing excuses for serious wrongdoing, and so on—is a serious vice. Neither advocate of vice ethics nor maximizing virtue ethics would recommend this sort of laxness of moral self-assessment. But what of moderately generous self-assessment? Moderately generous self-assessment may not be vicious, but it is less virtuous than fully honest self-assessment. Maximizing virtue ethics has it that right action is always the most virtuous available action, so it is hard to see how a maximizing virtue ethicist could judge less than fully honest self-assessment as right. Still, the virtue ethicist should find a way to guide morally fragile agents towards such a thing. It is, arguably, a more virtuous form of advice-giving than sticking by the official standard of right action. It is more generous and helpful. The best form of action guidance to emerge from maximizing virtue ethics might therefore be strongly self-effacing: guiding agents towards the less than virtuous (and thus wrong) in order to make their lives better and, in the end, more virtuous than they would otherwise be.

Vice ethics might suffer from the same condition, but it needn't. It depends on how the relevant vices are specified. In the case at hand, one might claim that a moderately generous form of self-assessment, though not as virtuous as rigorous self-assessment, is not vicious. When faced with the task of reviewing our conduct, we are guided by vice ethics to do so in the least vicious available way. Moderately generous self-assessment is arguably not vicious at all, so it can stand as both the recommended form of self-assessment and right. Because of its emphasis on the avoidance of vice, vice ethics appears able to offer a coherent package of moral assessment and moral guidance.[17] Maximizing virtue ethics lacks the resources to do this and so tends to become strongly self-effacing. A theory is not refuted because it is shown to be strongly self-effacing, but I think it is better to

---

17 Daniel Russell (2009, 53–59) argues that complaints such as the one I evoke here with an accusation of strong self-effacement are based on a conflation of right with ought. Rightness, he claims, is a fundamentally a property of action assessment; what one ought to do is fundamentally a property of action guidance. The two readily come apart. While it is possible to define rightness in this way, it is a conceptual misfortune to do so. It departs significantly from our ordinary way of speaking. When we deliberate about what to do, we readily frame it in terms of what would be the right thing for us to do. When I say of someone that they made the right moral choice, I mean to say that they did what they ought to do: no more, no less.

avoid strong self-effacement if one can. All else being equal, theories that are not strongly self-effacing are preferable to those that are.

The third advantage of vice ethics is that it is likely to better serve the fundamental purpose of deontic judgment: the regulation of social life. Vice ethics directs our attention to potential moral failings and the negative judgment that attends them. Virtue ethics, both in its maximizing form and, arguably, in other forms, directs our attention to potential moral excellences and the positive judgment that attends them. Avoiding doing wrong is a better regulative technique than seeking excellence. We tend to be loss averse in this matter.[18] Losing moral face generally looms larger for us than gaining moral kudos; reasons of vice-avoidance tend to be psychologically weightier than reasons of virtue-accomplishment. This is because reasons of vice-avoidance foreground the possibility of moral loss, whereas reasons of virtue-accomplishment foreground the possibility of moral gains. Unless we have already lost a great deal, we tend automatically and unconsciously to put more value on avoiding losses than on making gains. Vice ethics works with this tendency by defining our obligations in terms of the avoidance of moral loss. The task of regulating social behavior is of fundamental importance, but it faces a problem of general motivation. It is not enough that a community be liberally sprinkled with virtuously motivated people; it should be peaceful and cooperative even if many in it are not especially moved by virtue. Avoiding moral losses and the negative emotions that attend them motivates in the absence of high levels of virtue and thus motivates the many to work for peaceful and cooperative co-existence.

Quassim Cassam's (2016) work on vice epistemology suggests another possible advantage of vice ethics over maximizing virtue ethics, and perhaps over virtue ethics more generally. Cassam explores the significance of intellectual vices for epistemology. He has both a particular explanatory aim (how epistemically poor beliefs often arise) and a particular normative aim (how to reduce the pernicious influence of intellectual vices).[19] He points out that an emphasis on vices rather than virtues may well help address situationist criticism of appeals to character traits in explanations of bad epistemic behavior. What sting there is in the situationist critiques of virtue theories is, perhaps, either ameliorated or removed when our focus turns to vices rather than virtues, as I do in this chapter. Cassam (2016,

---

18 Cass Sunstein (2007) makes this observation, deriving it from the work of Kahneman and Tversky. As Sunstein argues, the sorts of heuristics and biases that involve our propensity to risk aversion in moral judgment often lead to poor decision-making, particularly when evaluating the consequences of risky action. My suggestion, however, is that in judging right action we can use our propensity to risk aversion to help regulate our moral behavior by orientating us away from vice and the moral loss that it entails.
19 This contrasts with my analytic ambition of using vice concepts to frame our understanding of right action.

171–74) cites literature which demonstrates connections between general aspects of a person's mentality and their propensity to believe in conspiracy theories (a robust example of bad epistemic practice). Cassam does not make this claim, but it might well be that vices play a more secure role, quite generally, in production of bad behavior than virtues do in the production of good behavior. If virtues and vices are asymmetric in this way, we have an additional reason to approach the task of social regulation primarily through vices and their amelioration rather than virtues and their cultivation.

One concern about doing so is that we run the risk of setting our moral sights too low. Merely aiming to avoid acting viciously seems unlikely to inspire the development of virtue. It seems to encourage aiming at getting by.[20] The virtues, by contrast, are aspirational. They define for us what it is to be the best we can be and they are indispensable features of our moral world view. What they don't do, if vice ethics is correct, is govern our conception of right action. This means there is more to our moral lives than acting rightly. A life well lived is a life in which we have aspired to excellences beyond merely acting rightly. I think this is true, but it is especially important if vice ethics is correct. The concept of right action best frames the task of regulating our social behavior; it is in terms of right action that we primarily hold each other to account for particular actions. Our conception of right action sets the standard by which we are amenable to others for what we do. The virtues, on the other hand, best frame our moral aspirations. They are the terms in which we may review a life and consider its moral merits: its conduct and its character; what is done and what is not done. My suggestion, then, is that the virtues are indispensable moral concepts, but are not the best terms in which to seek to regulate social behavior and to ensure such things as decency, cooperation, and social harmony. Vice-avoidance is better suited to this job.

## 6. Conclusion

I have argued that vice ethics has a number of significant advantages over maximizing virtue ethics as a theory of right action. It is an open question whether these advantages, or others, carry over to a comparison with other forms of virtue ethics. I hope, however, to have motivated the idea of vice ethics sufficiently to demonstrate its potential. The account of vice ethics I offer depends upon a number of claims about the nature of virtues, vices, and the reasons for action they entail—claims I set out in the first part of this chapter. That a plausible theory of right action—one that can guide both deliberation and assessment—can be built up from them I think lends the claims some credence.

---

20 I would like to thank an anonymous referee for suggesting this way of putting the worry.

# References

Brady, Michael. 2004. "Against Agent-Based Virtue Ethics." *Philosophical Papers* 33: 1–10.
Cassam, Quassim. 2016. "Vice Epistemology." *The Monist* 99: 159–80.
Cox, Damian. 2006. "Agent-Based Theories of Right Action." *Ethical Theory and Moral Practice* 9: 505–15.
———. 2012. "Judgment, Deliberation, and the Self-Effacement of Moral Theory." *Journal of Value Inquiry* 46: 289–302.
Cox, Damian, Marguerite La Caze, and Michael Levine. 2003. *Integrity and the Fragile Self.* Aldershot: Ashgate Publishing.
Das, Ramon. 2003. "Virtue Ethics and Right Action." *Australasian Journal of Philosophy* 81: 324–39.
Hursthouse, Rosalind. 1999. *On Virtue Ethics.* Oxford: Oxford University Press.
———. 2006. "Are Virtues the Proper Starting Point for Morality?" In *Contemporary Debates in Moral Theory*, edited by James Dreier, 99–112. Oxford: Blackwell Publishing.
Jackson, Frank and Robert Pargetter. 1986. "Oughts, Options, and Actualism." *Philosophical Review* 95: 233–55.
Jacobson, Daniel. 2002. "An Unsolved Problem for Slote's Agent-Based Virtue Ethics." *Philosophical Studies* 111: 53–67.
Johnson, Robert N. 2003. "Virtue and Right." *Ethics* 113: 810–834.
Kant, Immanuel. 1996. *Practical Philosophy.* Translated by Mary Gregor. Cambridge: Cambridge University Press.
Keller, Simon. 2007. "Virtue Ethics Is Self-Effacing." *Australasian Journal of Philosophy* 85: 221–31.
Martinez, Joel A. 2011. "Is Virtue Ethics Self-Effacing?" *Australasian Journal of Philosophy* 89: 277–88.
Parfit, Derek. 1984. *Reasons and Persons.* Oxford: Clarendon Press.
Pettigrove, Glen. 2011. "Is Virtue Ethics Self-Effacing?" *Journal of Ethics* 15: 191–207.
Ransome, William. 2010. "Is Agent-Based Virtue Ethics Self-undermining?" *Ethical Perspectives* 17: 41–57.
Russell, Daniel C. 2009. *Practical Intelligence and the Virtues.* Oxford: Oxford University Press.
Singer, Peter. 2009. *The Life You Can Save.* New York: Random House.
Slote, Michael. 2001. *Morals from Motives.* Oxford: Oxford University Press.
Sunstein, Cass. 2007. "Moral Heuristics and Risk." In *Risk: Philosophical Perspectives*, edited by Tim Lewens, 156–70. New York: Routledge.
Swanton, Christine. 2001. "A Virtue Ethical Account of Right Action." *Ethics* 112: 32–52.
———. 2003. *Virtue Ethics: A Pluralistic View.* Oxford: Oxford University Press.
Tännsjö, Torbjörn. 1995. "Blameless Wrongdoing." *Ethics* 106: 120–27.
van Zyl, Liezl. 2011. "Right Action and the Non-Virtuous Agent." *Journal of Applied Philosophy* 28: 80–92.

# 4 Can Virtue Be Codified?
## An Inquiry on the Basis of Four Conceptions of Virtue

*Peter Shiu-Hwa Tsu*

In this chapter, I distinguish and advance four conceptions of virtue according to how moral rules and virtue interact in a virtuous person's moral reasoning processes: (1) absolute conception, (2) pro tanto conception, (3) prima facie conception, and (4) particularist conception. The distinction helps to answer a much debated, yet still muddled, question, raised particularly by John McDowell in an influential series of papers, of whether what virtue requires can be codified into rules. While McDowell gives a negative answer, I argue that this uncodifiability conclusion only obtains under McDowell's specific conception of virtue (something that lies in the vicinity of (3) and (4)); there are, however, other significant conceptions of virtue (i.e., (1) and (2)), according to which virtue might well be codifiable. I will articulate what they are and make a *prima facie* case for them. If these other conceptions of virtue also appear prima facie plausible or even more prima facie plausible than McDowell's, as I will argue, then there is reason to doubt the uncodifiability conclusion. For presumably, our interest in the question of whether what virtue requires can be codified lies essentially in figuring out whether it can be codified on the *most plausible* conception of virtue.

### 1. McDowell on the Uncodifiabilty of Virtue

In an influential series of papers,[1] McDowell argues that the requirements of virtue cannot be codified into rules.[2] Here is McDowell:

> If one attempted to [codify] one's conception of what virtue requires [into] a set of rules, then, however subtle and thoughtful one was in drawing up the code, cases would inevitably turn up in which a mechanical application of the rules would strike one as wrong—and

---

1 Especially relevant are McDowell's (2002a, 2002b, 2002c).
2 I shall use "rule" and "principle" interchangeably in this chapter.

not necessarily because one had changed one's mind; rather, one's mind on the matter was not susceptible of capture in any universal formula.

(2002a, 58)

In this oft-quoted passage, McDowell is generally taken to argue, in effect, for an *uncodifiability thesis*: the thesis that *the requirements of virtue cannot be codified into "a set of rules."*

The chief motivation for this thesis is derived from McDowell's attempt to dislodge a moral outlook where moral rules or theories occupy center stage. According to this moral outlook, the concept of virtue, if it has any place, is only secondary. It is seen as a disposition to perform the right actions. Yet, the right actions are pre-determined by moral rules or theories. Virtue is thus seen as conceptually posterior to the concept of a moral theory or rule, which explains or determines what right actions are. That is, the nature of virtue is explained from "the outside in," to use McDowell's apt phrase.

Contrary to the above claim, McDowell (2002a) argues that a conception of right conduct must be grasped from "the inside out." To put it differently, the concept of virtue is conceptually prior to the concept of right conduct. The question of how one should live is necessarily approached via the notion of a virtuous person. Simply put, what is right is captured by the judgment of a virtuous person. Rules, at their best, according to McDowell, are merely generalizations that hold most of the time.

It has to be stressed here that McDowell is not alone in championing the uncodifiability thesis. In fact, the anti-codification sentiment is widespread. Nussbaum (1990, 95), for instance, contends that "excellent choice cannot be [codified] in general rules, because it is a matter of fitting one's choice to the complex requirements of a concrete situation, taking all of its contextual features into account." Or more recently, Valerie Tiberius (2014) comments that "what can't be codified, on my view, is the decisions that a wise person will make in different contexts." Despite some differences in details, what all these uncodifiability approaches have in common is that they are all pretty much in the grip of a specific conception of virtue, according to which, rules, being generalities, are too crude to capture what it is that virtue requires in particular circumstances. Once we are in its grip, I think it is hard not to reach the uncodifiability conclusion. Indeed, when one surveys the recent virtue ethics literature, it is hard not to form the impression that uncodifiability has virtually become the orthodox.[3]

However, the uncodifiability conclusion is not inevitable. For the very specific conception of virtue the uncodifiability conclusion is premised on

---

3 Indeed, Onora O'Neill (1998, 37) observes that "it has been tempting to think of virtue [as uncodifiable] because other approaches seem not merely unavailable but questionable in a culturally diverse world." Yet, she hastens to add, quite correctly in my view, that "there is little to be said for succumbing to [this] temptation."

is not the only viable choice; there are some other significant and at least prima facie plausible conceptions of virtue under which virtue might well be codifiable. To demonstrate this, in section 3, I will distinguish four conceptions of virtue according to how virtue and rules interact in a virtuous person's moral reasoning processes.

Why should we care about whether uncodifiability obtains or not? One reason, I submit, is that it has great implications for our moral education. In particular, it makes a great difference as to whether we teach virtue with or without rules. If virtue cannot be codified at all, then one might naturally suspect that the teaching of virtues does not and perhaps should not consist in the teaching of principles. Although this issue deserves further investigation, for the purposes of this chapter, I will set it aside. My focus in this chapter is instead on whether the uncodifiability thesis is true across the board on all of the four conceptions of virtue that I distinguish.

A few words about methodology: for the purpose of this chapter, I will focus my discussion mostly on the uncodifiability thesis advanced by McDowell, chiefly because his version is the most systematic (as far as I know), and thus constitutes a worthwhile target. But what I say about it can certainly be generalized, *mutatis mutandis*, since practically all the other uncodifiability approaches share with it in the core a specific conception of virtue. Once we see that it is not the only viable choice, we will see that the uncodifiability conclusion is not inevitable. And indeed, I will argue that we even have reason to doubt the credibility of the specific conception of virtue that the uncodifiability conclusion is premised on. If this is right, there is also reason to doubt the credibility of the uncodifiability conclusion that follows from it.

Now, before I get to the four conceptions of virtue that I plan to distinguish and advance, let me further clarify the uncodifiabilty thesis.

## 2. The Uncodifiability Thesis in Focus

According to the McDowellian uncodifiability thesis, *"one's conception of what virtue requires" cannot be codified into a set of rules*. To determine whether the uncodifiability thesis can go through, several questions immediately arise. (1) Whose conception is at stake here? (2) On this conception, what is it that virtue requires? (3) What sort of rules does McDowell have in mind?

With regard to (1), unfortunately, McDowell does not tell us specifically whose conception he has in mind. But given McDowell's overall Aristotelian moral outlook, it is not unreasonable to surmise that what he has in mind is the Aristotelian conception. In any case, this is what I will assume. With regard to (2), according to the Aristotelian conception, what virtue requires of a person is doing the right things for the right reason at the right time and in the right way (Aristotle, *Nicomachean Ethics* III.7). For instance, what courage requires of a person is not only doing the right things (courageous things in this case), but also for the right reason at the right time and in the right way. With regard to (3), again, McDowell doesn't tell us explicitly what sort of rules he has in mind. But we can glean from his (2002a) article that the rules are merely generalizations that hold *"for the most part."* And for this reason, what virtue requires of a person, being *invariably* the morally right things according to the Aristotelian conception, cannot be codified into rules. And any attempt to codify is bound to fail, according to McDowell, because there will invariably be cases where the rules give us the morally wrong answers.

Now, some comments on (3) are in order here. First, some might wonder: didn't we already codify the Aristotelian conception of what virtue requires into a rule, i.e., the rule that we should do the right things for the right reason at the right time and in the right way? In reply, the answer is "yes" and "no." Yes, because it is indeed a rule in a very trivial sense. No, because the rule is too trivial in the sense that it does not provide much specific guidance for our actions or choices, which is an important role for rules to play. By this light, it does not really count as a rule proper.

Presumably, when McDowell argues that one's conception of virtue cannot be codified into a set of rules, what he has in mind are more substantive rules such as "telling a lie is wrong," "breaking a promise is wrong," or "helping people in need is right"—rules that purportedly provide correct action guidance. We may call these guidance rules 'natural-moral rules' in that they link the natural with the moral of an action type. So the uncodifiability thesis presumably targets these natural-moral rules that purport to provide substantive action guidance. And this is for good reasons. For these rules seem to run into exceptions in some cases. For instance, it seems morally permitted to tell a lie to a Nazi guard to save the life of a Jewish girl.

Second, how about those rules that are couched in virtue-related terms, rules such as "honesty is the best policy," "be kind to people," or "don't be stingy," or what Hursthouse call the *v-rules* in general? Does McDowell resist the idea that one's conception of what virtue requires can be codified into the v-rules? Since McDowell himself doesn't address this issue directly, the answer to this question is up for grabs.

On one interpretation, McDowell does resist the v-rules. There is some textual evidence that suggests that this is the case. This resistance is mainly due to McDowell's commitment to *the unity of the virtues*—the thesis, according to McDowell, that virtue is a complex *unified sensitivity*, which invariably issues in right actions. Holding this thesis, McDowell (2002a, 58–59) maintains that the problem with equating a particular virtue with a particular sensitivity is that the particular virtue so construed might lead to wrong actions in some circumstances.

For example, a sensitivity to kindness prompts the agent to engage in kind actions. But it might be possible that kindness of the action is not the only relevant moral consideration in a situation. So the v-rule "Be kind" might well mislead people into performing the wrong actions just as the natural-moral rule "help people in need." Both rules might well run into counterexamples. For instance, just as one shouldn't help a bank robber in need of assistance, one shouldn't be kind to a torturer who is torturing an innocent. Therefore, the notion of virtue fares better, according to McDowell, if understood as a *unified sensitivity*, which, in McDowell's construal, invariably leads the agent to do the morally right action.

On the above analysis, following the v-rules does not necessarily mean that one is doing the morally right thing. One sometimes has to be unkind or even nasty, for instance, in order to do the right thing. To be more specific, if we have to break the torturer's arm to save the innocent victim, we may think we should break his arm. Following the v-rule "be kind" here can mislead one into doing the wrong action. This point, *mutatis mutandis*, can be generalized. All the v-rules will seem to run into exceptions on some occasions. And this seems to provide at least one of the motivations for McDowell to espouse the uncodifiability view.

Now, on a different interpretation of McDowell, he does not really reject the v-rules. All he wants to maintain, on this interpretation, is that in applying the v-rules, a *unified* rather than *fragmented* sensitivity is required; the v-rules, when applied with unified, rather than fragmented, sensitivity, would invariably lead us to do the morally right action.

But the trouble with this interpretation is that what virtue requires can then be codified into the v-rules. For instance, on this interpretation, what kindness requires can be codified as the v-rule "be kind," for when the v-rule is applied with unified sensitivity, it will not have exceptions, and a person following it will invariably do the right thing. To be more specific, on this interpretation, a virtuous person, due to his unified sensitivity, will know that the v-rule "be kind" simply *doesn't apply* to one's behavior to the torturer, since doing so may encourage the torturer's barbarous behavior. So the torturer case cannot really be used as a counterexample to the codified v-rule.

But if the codified v-rules, when applied with unified sensitivity, are free from the threats of exceptions, McDowell's own cherished uncodifiability view will be threatened; this is because the uncodifiability view is premised on the thought that all rules will inevitably run into exceptions, as we have seen in the quote in section 1. Moreover, the codified v-rules, unlike the trivial rule of "doing the right thing for the right reason at the right time and in the right way," seem to be pretty substantive in that they certainly provide guidance for actions. (Just think about how many times we tell our children to be honest or be generous). So McDowell cannot seem to escape by maintaining that the v-rules are not rules proper and, therefore, despite their being exceptionless, are not the real targets of the uncodifiability thesis.

So, in light of the trouble mentioned above, it seems more reasonable to attribute to McDowell the former rather than the latter interpretation. This is what I will assume in any case. That is, McDowell's uncodifiability thesis targets at not only the natural-moral rules, but the v-rules as well.

Finally, how about very complex rules? Do they count as rules proper? While it might be true that what virtue requires may not be codified into some simple rules such as "help people in need" or "be kind," they may nevertheless be codified into more sophisticated rules which incorporate the possible exceptions, some may think.[4] Does McDowell object to the idea that these rules are capable of codifying what virtue requires? Again, McDowell is silent on these issues. And I suspect people's intuitions diverge on them.

One thought is that even these complex and sophisticated rules won't be able to codify what virtue requires. While one might be able to build exceptions into the rules, there can still be further exceptions to exceptions. What it is that virtue requires may vary from context to context such that no rules, being generalities, can codify them. The other thought is that while these complex rules may codify, they can hardly count as rules proper. For their complexity might well undermine some of the major functions moral rules are expected to play in our moral life. For instance, due to their complexity, they may well be very difficult to apply, given our cognitive limitations. And for this reason, they are probably not the sort of rules we use to teach our kids. Now, for McDowell's purposes, he need not adjudicate between these two conflicting lines of thought; on either line, his uncodifiabilty thesis can still go through. For either the complex rules do not codify, or they do, but do not count as rules proper.

To take stock, the uncodifiability thesis mainly targets the natural-moral rules and the v-rules that purport to provide substantive action guidance. When it maintains that one's conception of virtue cannot be codified into a set of rules, it is mainly these two rules that McDowell has in mind.

Having clarified what McDowell means by "rules," it may seem that the uncodifiability thesis is plausible for the various reasons indicated above. Yet, we need to note that its plausibility is premised on a specific Aristotelian conception of virtue. On this conception of virtue, it only seems natural that what virtue requires, being variable from context to context, cannot be codified into general rules (be they the natural-moral rules or v-rules). However, as we have mentioned in section 1, people often seem to forget that there are other significant and plausible conceptions of virtue. This is one of the main reasons, I suspect, why people declare unconditional devotion to the uncodifiability conclusion.

However, my view is that once we are made vividly aware of the existence of other significant and plausible conceptions of virtue, we might change our attitudes to the uncodifiability conclusion in the following two ways. First, we may have a sense of liberation from the uncodifiability orthodox in virtue ethics, feeling that it is not the only viable option. Second, we may even come to prefer these other competing conceptions of virtue once their attractions are revealed. In what follows, I will lay out these different conceptions of virtue in contrast with the Aristotelian one. Furthermore, I will argue that the Aristotelian one is not as attractive as it first appears and that the other conceptions contain at least some prima facie plausibility.

---

4 This line of reasoning is, on one interpretation, endorsed by Richardson (1990).

As a note of terminology, when I speak of rules or principles, I mean henceforth general rules that are of either the natural-moral type or the v-rules, which can provide substantive guidance for actions.

## 3. Four Conceptions of Virtue in Relation to Rules

My purpose in this section is to parlay four conceptions of virtue in relation to rules. They do not exhaust all the possibilities. However, they are particularly salient. This move is a first step in loosening the stranglehold of McDowell's Aristotelian conception on us, making us vividly aware that it is not the only plausible option.

(1) Absolute Conception: a virtuous person is a person of absolute principle(s). For instance, an honest person is one who sticks to the absolute principle of honesty, whereas a benevolent person is someone who follows the absolute principle of benevolence. The requirements of virtue can be codified into the requirements of a single absolute principle or a set of them, depending on whether one takes a monistic or a pluralistic view of the number of absolute principles. On this conception of virtue, virtue is principle or rule-following. This is not to say that virtue is following a rule *blindly*. Following a rule is entirely compatible with the exercise of judgment. A rule-follower doesn't have to be a stickler.[5]

(2) Pro Tanto Conception: a virtuous person is a person who has a commitment to *pro tanto* moral principles and feels compunction about breaking them.[6] She follows the dictates of pro tanto moral principles when no conflicts between them arise. Should a conflict arise, she knows, due to her practical wisdom, how to adjudicate between them without recourse to further moral principles. Unlike the conception of virtue mentioned in (1), it is not merely rule-following. It has a substantive adjudicating role to play in a virtuous person's moral reasoning processes.

(3) Prima Facie Conception: a virtuous person is a person who subscribes to some *prima facie* moral principles. She treats principles as quick and easy rules of thumb and follows them most of the time (Sherman 1999, 39). Unlike a pro tanto virtuous person, she feels no compunction about breaking a rule when she sees that doing so is what the requirements of virtue dictate. Rules have no intrinsic value. Rather, they are useful tools to the extent that they help a virtuous person to perform what

---

5 See Herman (1993, 81–82).
6 This conception of virtue is inspired by the works of W.D. Ross (1930, 1939). Although Ross himself used the phrase "prima facie" to describe the sort of rule or duty that carries some moral weight, it is now widely agreed that it is a misnomer. The phrase Ross should have used is "pro tanto."

virtue dictates. When they cannot do their job, they should be put aside without tears. Virtue thus plays the role of discerning the occasions in which prima facie moral principles ought to be rightfully infringed to carry out the right action.

(4) Particularist Conception: a virtuous person is a person who simply "sees" the right thing to do. Principles, be they absolute, pro tanto, or prima facie, are simply useless at their best or even harmful at their worst (Dancy 2009; McNaughton 1988). Morality is not about equipping one with the right set of principles, but about the sharpening of one's moral vision (Davis 2004). In short, virtue consists in an ability to "see" the right thing to do on each occasion.[7]

Now, with the four conceptions of virtue in place, some preliminary comments are in order. First, on all of the above-mentioned four conceptions, insofar as I conceive of them, what virtue requires is what a virtuous person would do. And the four conceptions are all compatible with the Aristotelian insight that what virtue requires is doing the right thing for the right reason at the right time and in the right way. In fact, when the requirements of virtue are stated so abstractly, they are something all virtue theorists should agree on. The major difference amongst these four conceptions lies in whether a virtuous person fulfills the requirements of virtue *with* or *without* following rules, and if she does by following rules, what are the nature of the rules that she follows.

On the particularist conception, a virtuous person simply doesn't follow any rule, for what virtue requires really has nothing to do with the demands of rules, be they absolute, pro tanto, or prima facie in nature; it hinges on the particular features in the moral situation that the virtuous agent encounters.

And on the prima facie conception, the prima facie rules are merely generalizations that might hold most of the time; their demands might well diverge from what virtue requires and do not *determine* what virtue requires for that matter. They are merely reminders for the virtuous.[8] Such being the case, the prima facie and the particularist conceptions are not a million miles away from McDowell's Aristotelian conception, as we have presented it in sections 1 and 2. And indeed, McDowell's Aristotelian conception has often been interpreted as one of these two conceptions, since the natural-moral rules or the v-rules under McDowell's Aristotelian conception are typically treated as useful prima facie rules of thumb at best or dismissed altogether as detrimental at worst. Assuming that such interpretations are correct (and I think they are), it is little wonder

---

7 These four conceptions of virtue were taken from and first advanced in Tsu (2010). They are adapted and revised here for our purposes. A word of self-disclosure: I do not think the absolute conception is as vulnerable as I used to think it is. I will explain why this is so in section 4.
8 Herman (1993, ch. 4) calls them "rules of moral salience."

that McDowell espouses the uncodifiability view, maintaining that what virtue requires cannot be codified into a set of rules; for on neither conception can the requirements of virtue be codified into rules such that rule-following can invariably lead the moral agent to do the morally right thing.

However, there are at least two other significant conceptions of virtue—the absolute and the pro tanto conceptions, that are very different from McDowell's. The requirements of virtue, on these conceptions, might well be codifiable, or so I will argue anyway. In addition, I will argue that McDowell's rule-following attack as well as two other attacks on the absolute conception can be effectively parried, and that there is a good case, at least a prima facie one, we can make for the superiority of the pro tanto conception over McDowell's conception.

## 4. Comments on the Absolute Conception

### (4.1) The Absolute Conception: Background

On the absolute conception of virtue, insofar as I conceive of it, what virtue requires can clearly be codified in the sense that its requirements are determined by absolute principles or rules. The absolute conception of virtue, on some interpretations, is implicitly espoused by Kant,[9] Anscombe (1958), and perhaps even the utilitarians. Kant (2002, 24) famously contends that moral rightness is determined by the *a priori* categorical imperatives rather than general rules derived from empirical generalizations. The rule against lying, being one of those categorical imperatives, is absolute; presumably, for Kant, a virtuous moral agent is someone who would never tell a lie. In addition, Anscombe contends that a virtuous agent will not even *contemplate* torturing an innocent.[10] Finally, the utilitarians certainly regard their favored versions of the principle of utility as absolute—how else could they be utilitarians!—and the requirements of virtue, for the utilitarians, are simply those required by the utility principle (Oakley 2014, 66).

Here, I am not concerned to settle the disputes amongst these different brands of the absolute conception regarding what the substantive absolute rules are and how many of them are actually absolute in nature. What I want to stress here, is that on the absolute conception of virtue, what

---

9 On Thomas Hill's (2012) interpretation of Kant's virtue ethics, Kant would agree that "one has particular virtues insofar as one has a strong will to fulfill the various moral requirements of justice, truthfulness, self-improvement, beneficence, gratitude, respect, and so on" (140). This interpretation fits nicely with the absolute conception under which virtue is rule-following; for the absolute rules can be understood as specifying the moral requirements the virtuous have a strong will to follow.
10 Chappell (2014, 87) also comments: "The possibility remains that virtue ethics might recognize *absolute rules*; or at least, some rules which it would be inconceivable a virtuous agent could prefer to break than to die" (emphasis added).

virtue requires can certainly be codified; that is, a virtuous person, on this conception, can do the right thing for the right reason at the right time and in the right way by rule-following (More on this in (4.2) below). So, unless the absolute conception is proved wrong, we should not jump to the uncodifiability conclusion. In what follows, I address three objections against the absolute conception.

## (4.2) Objection 1: Mechanical Application

Against the absolute conception, it has been argued by McDowell, as we have seen in the quote in section 1, that a *mechanical* application of the absolute rules would inevitably strike us as wrong in some cases; so there does not appear to be any rule that is absolute in nature. By "mechanical application," I take McDowell to mean something that can be done by a computing machine or a computer. For instance, in running a program, a computer can just execute the command rules without sensitivity or judgment. In reply, two comments are necessary. First, proponents of the absolute conception could plausibly maintain that the application of the absolute rules doesn't have to be *mechanical*. It is entirely compatible with the absolute conception that judgment and sensitivity are required for the application of the rules. To use an example from Hart (1994, 125–26) to illustrate, even a simple rule such as "No vehicles allowed in the park" requires judgment and sensitivity to determine whether it applies to rollerblades. If the purpose of the rule is to ensure the safety of the pedestrians, it might well do; however, if it is to reduce noise, it might not. Admittedly, the rule in Hart's example might not be regarded as un-adulteratedly moral due to its man-made legal nature.[11] Yet, the point is that the application of any rule, be they moral or non-moral, need not be mechanical. And I think it would be slanderous to claim that the absolute conception cannot accommodate this point.

And relatedly, once judgment and sensitivity are *not* denied to the virtuous rule-followers, they, just like their Aristotelian virtuous cousins, might well do the right thing for the right reason at the right time and in the right way. That is, on the absolute conception, the absolute rules determine what the right thing to do is, whereas sensitivity and judgment help a virtuous rule-follower determine how and when they can apply.

To illustrate, let's suppose that the virtuous rule-follower, due to her sensitivity and judgment, sees that the purpose of the rule against vehicles in

---

11 I'm inclined to regard this rule as not just legal but moral in nature as well. For if its purpose is either to reduce the noises or safeguard the pedestrians, it is concerned with well-being and thus moral in nature, in my view. Well-being may not be the whole point of morality, yet it is at least one of its important points. I don't have the space to defend this view here. But I plan to do so in "Non-Reductive Welfarism" (unpublished manuscript).

the park is to ensure the safety of the pedestrians. Such being the case, it is reasonable to surmise that she, being a virtuous rule-follower, would just take off her rollerblades when going into the park (i.e., do the right thing at the right time and in the right way).

In terms of reasons for action, she need not do so for the sake of rule-following. (If she did, she might seem to be rule-worshipping rather than virtuous). This is not something that the absolute conception per se, insofar as I conceive of it, requires of her. Rather, she can do so for reasons of protecting the pedestrians' safety. That is, she can still do the right thing *for the right reason* under the absolute conception. In a nutshell, once judgment and sensitivity to the purpose of the rules and their applications are granted to the virtuous rule-follower, doing the right thing for the right reason at the right time and in the right way doesn't seem to be a patent exclusive to the Aristotelian virtuous.

Now, it might be further objected along the line run by Nussbaum that the absolute principles are generalities too crude to capture the demands of the particular situations, which might vary from case to case. For instance, there might well be a situation where an ambulance has to be admitted into the park in order to save the life of a seriously injured person; sticking to the rule that "no vehicle is allowed in the park" seems to be rule-worshipping rather than virtuous. In reply, it has to be pointed out, first of all, that the no-vehicle rule might not be absolute in terms of its status, as rightly suggested by our objector. But this doesn't mean that there aren't any such rules whatsoever. There might still be other rules that are absolute in nature. What are these rules, one might rightly wonder? This relates to my next point.

Second, although the mechanical-application point against the absolute conception may not go through, some might insist that McDowell's basic insight can be maintained; that is, all rules, even carefully formulated and sensitively applied, will inevitably run into exceptions and therefore no rules are absolute in nature. In reply, I think this is unduly pessimistic; there seem to be at least some rules that are exceptionless. According to Hursthouse (2011), rules such as "murdering is wrong" or "when you can, get informed consent before surgical operations" are likely candidates. And to these, perhaps one can also add "don't abuse your children" or "raping is wrong," and so on. It is presumably not that easy to conceive of exceptions to these rules except when one is willing to resort to extremely outlandish scenarios. But then, it is not entirely clear how much force these outlandish cases carry against the absolute force of the rules in the real world.[12]

---

12 While admitting the existence of these absolute moral principles, it is sometimes objected by moral particularists that there is just not enough of them to *cover* the moral ground (Dancy 2004, 116). In reply, it has to be pointed out, first of all, that coverage is an issue independent from that of codifiability. So long as there are these absolute moral principles

Moreover, even if no existing rules proposed by the proponent of the absolute conception are correct, this doesn't mean that there aren't such rules. As Parfit (1984, 453–54) perceptively observes, in view of the development of non-religious ethics, we are still very much at the infant stage of rigorous normative ethical theorizing. Drawing upon Parfit's insight, I think it fair to say that it is far too early to pronounce for our great-grandchildren that no absolute rules are possible.

In fact, the Hursthousean kind of v-rules, when sensitively applied, seem to be promising candidates for the title of absolute rules, too. For instance, anyone who is not completely lacking in sensitivity can see that the rule, "be kind" doesn't apply to our attitude or behavior towards a torturer who is bent on his job; instead, it requires us to be kind to the innocent victim of the torture and stop the torturer if we can. Here, to put the point in a somewhat sarcastic way suggested by Mill (1998, 155), any application of rules will give us the wrong results if it is combined with idiocy. But the v-rule followers need not be idiots.

Now, it might be objected that McDowell, when properly understood, would also embrace this line of reasoning and, thus, the codified v-rules. But I think this very much depends on how we interpret McDowell, and I shall not dwell too much on this hermeneutical issue, since, due to the rich complexities of McDowell's thoughts, I doubt the result would be very fruitful. Let me just say this: to the extent that McDowell accepts the codified v-rules, McDowell should retract his uncodifiabilty view or at least substantially qualify it, for the codified v-rules are certainly rules proper that play a substantive role in our moral life, whether in terms of action guidance or moral education.

## *(4.3) Objection 2: Moral Conflicts*

Another objection that is commonly brought up against the absolute conception is that it can't adequately deal with moral conflicts between absolute principles; since both of the conflicting principles are absolute, in choosing to follow one of them, a virtuous person, on this absolute conception, is bound to violate the other and therefore does the morally wrong thing. But presumably, the purpose of following a codified absolute principle is to do the morally right thing. (Why else should the virtuous follow it?) So it seems that the absolute conception cannot be right, for the existence of these moral conflicts reveals the real possibility that following a rule might lead to morally wrong actions.

---

that exceptionlessly determine what is morally right, what virtue requires is not uncodifiable. Second, the v-rules, if they are absolute, as they might well be, as I will argue two paragraphs later, might actually *cover* a lot of moral ground for morality not to be entirely *shapeless* as often suggested by the moral particularists (cf. Tsu (2013, 2016). In fact, Swanton (2003, 73) argues that "the moral domain of virtue ethics is particularly rich, detailed and broad-ranging." She illustrates in her book quite nicely how the v-rules can be applied on various occasions.

In reply, it ought to be noted that a supporter of the absolute conception, in principle, can admit upfront that absolute moral principles can conflict[13] and that there are therefore *irresolvable* moral dilemmas posed by such conflicts. These moral dilemmas are irresolvable in the sense that no matter how the virtuous person chooses, she is bound to do the morally wrong thing. It would be quixotic, in my view, to claim that a virtuous agent can never be faced with irresolvable moral dilemmas and thus do the morally wrong thing;[14] after all, it is a live possibility that she might just run into bad luck through no fault of her own. If I am right, it is actually a merit rather than a defect of the absolute conception that it *truthfully reflects* the fact that a virtuous person can be enmeshed in a tragic irresolvable moral quagmire.[15] Brad Hooker (2012, 39) puts it quite nicely: "To the extent that our ethical experience strongly indicates that . . . [irresolvable] dilemmas are ineliminable, then we should expect the most plausible ethical theory to admit these elements."

To put things slightly differently, if irresolvable moral dilemmas exist, as they may well do, then it is a phenomenon that needs to be accommodated by all conceptions of virtue. And on no conceptions of virtue, including McDowell's, can the virtuous agent avoid doing the morally wrong thing in such scenarios (that's why these dilemmas are irresolvable after all). If the absolute conception can be faulted on the ground that rule-following in these scenarios doesn't give the right answer, McDowell's conception can be faulted on similar grounds as well, for moral sensitivity or practical wisdom wouldn't give us the right answer in such scenarios either (remember that these dilemmas are irresolvable). So, if the existence of irresolvable moral dilemmas is a problem, it is not a problem *unique to* the absolute conception. Rather, it is a problem universal to all conceptions of virtue. Proponents of the absolute conception should not be particularly embarrassed by this fact.

## *(4.4) Objection 3: Rule-Following Considerations*

McDowell, on certain interpretations, contends that there is a decisive reason for refraining from the absolute conception of virtue (Crisp 2000, 25–26; Wallace 1991, 484). It is that the absolute conception of virtue is based on a prejudiced conception of rationality. On this conception of rationality, to be rational means to follow a rule consistently. The rules provide the rails, as it

---

13 Unless, of course, they take a monistic view of absolute moral principle, like the utilitarians, for instance. In such cases, no conflicts between absolute moral principles can arise, for it takes at least two to tango.
14 This is echoed by Hursthouse (1999, ch. 3) and Russell (2009, 69).
15 Of course, there are those who expect a principled conception of virtue such as the absolute one to come up with an *algorithm* to resolve moral conflicts. See, for instance, Kamm (2002, 337). But, I regard this expectation as unrealistic, for no one, insofar as I know, has even come close to producing such an algorithm. If it had been available, the computer, in principle, would have been able to resolve all the moral conflicts.

were, on which the train of rational thoughts proceeds. And since a virtuous agent's moral judgments about what she ought to do have to meet at the very least the minimal requirement of rational consistency, there must be a rule, let's say, a rule like "Do x!"[16], that she follows when she makes moral judgments in situations that are identical in all morally relevant aspects. That is, a virtuous person follows a rule consistently in making her moral judgment; the requirements of virtue, according to the absolute conception of virtue, are simply those rules that are followed by the virtuous.

Citing Wittgenstein, McDowell contends, however, that the rule-following conception of rationality is a prejudiced one because one might well be following a "bent" rule without meeting the demands of rationality. For instance, one might continue a series of numbers such as 2, 4, . . . 996, 998, 1000 with the number of 1004 instead of 1002 by contending that he has all along been following a rule which says that "add 2 before 1000, but add 4 after 1000." If being rational just means following a rule consistently, his behavior is perfectly rational. In fact, on the rule-following conception of rationality, he can claim to be rational by extending the series with just any number, say, 78452, by contending that he has all along been following a rule which says that "add 2 before 1000, but add 77452 after 1000." However, it is far from clear that so doing is rational at all; in fact, this seems completely arbitrary. Thus, on some interpretations, McDowell contends that rational consistency does not require the following of a rule; instead, it requires an ability to see how to go on (in our case, after 1000) (Crisp 2000, 25–26).

In my view, however, the rule-following considerations do not really militate against the absolute conception of virtue; they fail to show that a virtuous person does not have to follow a rule in order for his moral judgments to meet the requirements of rational consistency. In fact, as McDowell (2002a, 59–60) himself seems to acknowledge: the rule-following considerations are not meant to cast any doubt on our confidence that the rational move after 1000 is 1002 when we continue the series and that by so doing we are following the right rule; rather, they are merely meant to "shift the ground of our confidence" for the correctness of the rule (59–60). The rule is correct, not because any individual following it thinks it is correct,[17] but because it

---

16 Here "x" is a variable for a type of action.
17 For if it were not so, then it would not make much sense to ask whether an individual is *justified* in thinking that the rule he thinks he has all along been following, for instance "add 2," is the correct one (Kripke 1982). Yet, it *does* make sense to raise such a question, because, as we have suggested earlier, the series of numbers is consistent with an infinite number of rules, say, for instance, the rule which says: "add 2 before 1000, but add 77452 after 1000." So, the rule "add 2" cannot be the correct one followed by an individual, *just because he thinks so*. What justifies the correctness of the rule is our shared "forms of life," or our common way of seeing things, according to (my interpretation of) McDowell.

is embedded in our cultures and practices, or in our shared "forms of life," to put it in McDowell's own terms (59–60).

If there is nothing wrong with a rule-following conception of rationality, one may wonder, whence does the prejudice we mentioned earlier come from? The prejudice in the commonly espoused rule-following conception of rationality stems from, in my view, the thought that the rule we follow is independent of cultures and practices, not relative to the "form of life" we share. The prejudice to be dispensed with is therefore *not* that rational consistency requires rule-following, but rather that it requires following a rule that is *not* embedded in cultures or practices.

To put it differently, the rule-following considerations do not really pose a threat to the idea that a virtuous agent has to follow a rule consistently in order for his moral judgments to be rational. It is just that the correctness of the rule he follows might well be relative to the form of life he participates in, since what counts as rational (consistency) might well vary from one form of life to another.[18]

And this comports well with the absolute conception of virtue. For nothing in the absolute conception, *per se*, rules out the possibility that the absolute requirements or rules followed by the virtuous can be relative to forms of life, unless, of course, the absolute conception is coupled with the Kantian view that moral rules are categorical imperatives, whose validity is necessary, not contingent on, or relative to, "forms of life."[19] Yet, while the absolute conception *can* commit itself to the Kantian view, it *need not*. It is certainly not a far-fetched idea that the absolute requirements of virtue are relative to "forms of life" or "practices," as has been quite emphatically illustrated by MacIntyre (1985) and Williams (2006).[20] For instance, loyalty might require a samurai to perform "*seppuku*" (ritual suicide) in ancient Japan to honor his deceased lord, whereas it requires no such thing of an American soldier who loses his commander-in-chief in the Vietnam War. Moreover, while it is true that the rule of loyalty still holds in both ancient Japanese society and the contemporary American one, despite their different requirements in the particular societies, it may not hold at all in a future society that exists one million years later, which has a radically different form of life. In fact, on a certain interpretation of the studies of Ruth Benedict (1934), the Dobu society might already fit the bill. People who are loyal in that society are objects of ridicule rather than respect.

---

18 I do not claim any originality for this claim. It has been pointed out and effectively illustrated by Peter Winch (1964) by way of the Azande witchcraft culture.
19 Here, the idea of categorical imperatives is contrasted with that of hypothetical ones whose binding requirements are relative to our subjective ends or desires (or "forms of life" at the macro-level). See Foot (1972).
20 This is, to some extent, echoed by Chappell (2014, 86); cf. Nussbaum (1993).

## 5. Comments on the Pro Tanto Conception

On the pro tanto conception, what virtue requires can be codified into a set of rules that are pro tanto in nature. For on this conception, the pro tanto rules determine what virtue requires the moral agent to do when there is no conflict between them; rule-following can invariably lead one to do the morally right thing in such peaceful scenarios, according to the pro tanto conception.

When conflicts between these pro tanto rules arise, things become trickier. Insofar as I understand the pro tanto conception, in cases of moral conflicts, it is still the pro tanto rules that determine what virtue requires a moral agent to do and thereby what a virtuous person would do in those circumstances. It is just that it takes practical wisdom or judgment to determine which rule 'outweighs' which.

For instance, in a scenario where the pro tanto rule for keeping one's promise conflicts with the pro tanto rule for saving a life (say, the life of a seriously injured victim of a car accident), it might well be the case that it is the latter rule rather than the former that determines what is the morally right thing to do in that scenario, and a virtuous person should follow the latter rule rather than the former, but it takes practical wisdom to see this. For there can also be scenarios where if one doesn't keep one's promise, thousands of lives will perish, and there happens to be someone else who can help the seriously injured person. In those cases, it may well be the pro tanto rule for keeping one's promise that determines what is the morally right thing to do.

So, on the current construal, what virtue requires a moral agent to do can be codified in both conflict and no-conflict cases. It is just that in conflict cases, it takes good judgment or practical wisdom to see which pro tanto rule determines one's overall duty; a virtuous and practically wise person would follow the right rule on the pro tanto conception. A caveat to be noted here is that, on the current construal, pro tanto theorists need not deny that some of the moral conflicts can be constituted by a clash of absolute principles, and are, hence, irresolvable. What they want to emphasize, insofar as I understand their view, is that not all of them are.[21] There are also moral conflicts that are constituted by a clash of pro tanto rules. In such conflicts, there can be a solution, according to the pro tanto theorists, which is determined by the morally 'weightier' rule in the situations.

Although this conception of virtue has rarely received explicit endorsement in the literature,[22] as far as I know, it certainly draws its inspiration

---

21 This is why the Rossian scheme of pro tanto rules is generally regarded as a vast improvement on the Kantian one of absolute categorical imperatives; the former can accommodate the very real phenomenon of *resolvable* moral conflicts between the requirements of different rules, whereas the latter seems to lack the theoretical apparatus to do so.
22 On a certain interpretation, Audi's view comes close. See his (2005).

from the works of W. D. Ross (1930, 1939). And even if it turns out that this conception is not endorsed by Ross himself, I think it is nevertheless worthy of serious investigation in its own right, given its initial plausibility. In any case, I think that anyone concerned to address the issue of whether virtue can be codified should take this conception seriously.

Unfortunately, in considering the question of whether what virtue requires can be codified, McDowell fails to consider this salient conception. The uncodifiability conclusion he reaches is thus faulty or at the very least limited, in my view—it merely stands in the prima facie and particularist conceptions of virtue spelled out in section 2. When it comes to the pro tanto conception, it doesn't seem to sustain, at least not clearly.

Here, an obvious question to ask is: is there any reason to prefer the pro tanto conception of virtue over McDowell's? If there is, then the question of whether what virtue requires can be codified might well again be answered in the affirmative. In what follows, I will argue that there is at least a prima facie case for preferring the pro tanto conception. I have to emphasize that the case for it is merely prima facie. I do not purport to make a comprehensive case for its correctness and, practically speaking, do not have the space to do so. It will satisfy my purpose if the readers can discern some merits in it and do not dismiss it as a non-starter out of hand.

## (5.1) *A Prima Facie Case for the Pro Tanto Conception*

Let me start with a characterization of McDowell's conception of virtue that is relevant for comparison with the pro tanto conception here. To begin with, McDowell (2002a, 52) maintains that "virtue issues in nothing but right conduct." As a clarification, this should *not* be understood as claiming that a person who performs nothing but right conduct is thereby virtuous. As is widely agreed, such a person might not be virtuous; he at least has to act out of the right motive.

McDowell is fully aware of the significance of the motivational aspect of a virtuous person's moral psychology. In fact, to bring this out more clearly, McDowell contrasts the virtuous with the continent. The virtuous are motivated by nothing but what is morally right, whereas the continent feel the inclination to do otherwise but manage to keep it at bay. For the virtuous, such an inclination is completely 'silenced,' according to McDowell (2002a, 56).

While McDowell is certainly right to emphasize that the motive of the virtuous is different from that of the continent, I think the 'silencing' view does not seem to square well with the moral psychology of those who we normally regard as the *truly* virtuous, especially in cases of moral conflicts arising from a clash of pro tanto rules, or so I will argue. Let us consider an example taken from Sophocles's *Antigone*, due to Nussbaum (1986, 55–56): Creon, as the governor of the city, faces a conflict between the requirement of benevolence to bury Polynices' corpse in the Attic territory and the requirement of justice *not* to honor treachery (for it was believed that Polynices was contriving a political coup).

In his decision-making process, Creon was completely *un*moved by the requirement of the principle of benevolence. Upon making up his mind that it was only right *not* to grant the burial, Creon's inclination to follow the principle of benevolence was completely 'silenced,' to put it in McDowell's term. Such being the case, it is not unimaginable that he wouldn't in the least harbor any sense of regret about not being able to fulfill the requirement of benevolence.

Is Creon virtuous? It doesn't appear to be so. In a conflict situation like this one, it seems that we would expect to find Creon, if he were truly virtuous, enmeshed in a psychologically tormented state due to the dilemma;[23] he would have cared a bit more about the requirement of the principle of benevolence even though he couldn't have fulfilled it (given that he felt fulfilling the requirement of the principle of justice was the only right thing to do and would stick to it). And yet, as we have seen, he is stone-hearted, lacking any sense of regret for not burying Polynices' corpse. He departs greatly from our image of a virtuous person. Yet, on McDowell's silencing view, Creon can be perfectly virtuous, for he is motivated by nothing but the morally right (let's assume for the sake of the argument that his decision is indeed right) while his inclination to do otherwise (i.e., to bury Polynices' corpse) is completely silenced. But this doesn't show Creon to be *truly* virtuous. Instead, this only suggests, somewhat ironically in my view, that the Creon case really works as a *reductio* of McDowell's silencing view.

Now, how does all this connect up with McDowell's uncodifiability thesis, one may wonder? As we have clarified in section 2, according to McDowell's unified sensitivity view, the fragmented independent v-rules (including the rule of benevolence and the rule of justice) might well mislead, and thus become the target of McDowell's uncodifiability thesis. They thus do not enter into the deliberations of the McDowellian virtuous. Rather, according to McDowell, the virtuous, due to their unified sensitivities, can just *see* the morally right thing in moral conflicts. The v-rules can, at their best, merely play the role of prima facie principles, in a way that has been suggested by the prima facie conception. On this conception, when the v-rules are discerned to be misleading, they are to be put aside without tears. To use McDowell's metaphor, their voices do not get a hearing from the virtuous agent; rather, they are completely "silenced." Yet, the relegation of the v-rules to the status of prima facie principles has the sorry consequence of leaving McDowell with no resource to handle well a virtuous person's moral psychology in moral conflicts constituted by a clash of these v-rules. For even when these v-rules have to be put aside, they should only be put aside with a lot of tears and regrets.

---

23 Using a different example, Stohr (2003) makes a similar point.

By contrast, the pro tanto conception of virtue seems to square better with our ordinary conception of virtue and thus seems to be much more intuitively appealing. If Creon is a pro tanto virtuous person who has a commitment to the pro tanto principle of benevolence, a sense of regret over the violation of this principle would be in place. For on the pro tanto conception, Creon will rightly feel torn between his conflicting duties specified by the pro tanto rules. The example of Creon thus gives us at least some prima facie reason, in my view, to believe that the pro tanto conception is better equipped to capture a virtuous agent's moral psychology in moral conflicts than McDowell's.

Now, examples like this can be easily multiplied. But someone might object that there are certainly also moral conflict cases where 'silencing' is more plausible. For instance, when considering whether to lie to the Nazi guards in order to save a Jewish girl's life, it seems far more plausible to suggest that the inclination to tell the truth is completely *silenced* for the virtuous, and rightly so, because to tell the truth in a situation like this is obviously the wrong thing; and the virtuous are right in this case not to feel any regret about telling a lie to the Nazi guards.

In reply, there are at least two ways proponents of the pro tanto conception can go. First, they might well contend that no real moral conflicts arise in this case, for the requirement to tell the truth (or not to lie) is not a duty at all in this case, not even a pro tanto one. It is at its best a prima facie one (i.e., a duty merely at first glance), which really carries no moral weight with the pro tanto virtuous. To put it differently, the pro tanto duty to tell the truth doesn't even apply in this case. So, like the McDowellian virtuous, the pro tanto virtuous feel no inclination at all to tell the truth in this case. So, on this front, the McDowellian conception doesn't have an edge over the pro tanto. Second, a supporter of the pro tanto conception might take a slightly different tack and argue that there is really no pro tanto duty to tell the truth in general; instead, what we have is a pro tanto duty to be honest.[24] Since telling a lie to the Nazi guards cannot be properly evaluated as 'dishonest' without distorting the negative evaluative meaning of "dishonesty,"[25] it does not really violate the pro tanto duty to be honest (Crisp 2000; McNaughton

---

24 The pro tanto duty to be honest is different from the pro tanto duty to tell the truth, in that honesty, as I understand it *pace* Crisp (2000, 38) here, is regulated by practical wisdom, and therefore may not require us to always tell the truth. Remaining silent is consistent with the requirement of honesty.

25 A dishonest action seems to involve more than telling a lie; it involves at least telling a lie out of a malicious or self-interested motive. In addition, it has been suggested by Crisp (2000) and McNaughton and Rawling (2000) that "dishonesty" is a morally thick concept that has an in-built *negative* evaluative meaning. This explains why a person cannot be regarded as having acquired full mastery of the concept until he knows that it is derogatory (rather than positive) in meaning. But there does not appear to be anything negative at all about telling a lie to a Nazi guard to save the life of a Jew. Hence, the inapplicability.

and Rawling 2000). So in this scenario, the pro tanto virtuous would not feel any regret about telling a lie to the Nazi guards, just like the McDowellian virtuous. So again, the McDowellian conception doesn't score any points on this matter. Now, despite the replies above, some might still insist that there must be *some* other cases where 'silencing' is more plausible. But I would argue that we need clear cases first. Then we can reply to them. Otherwise, I think we can remain suspicious—the burden of proof rests with the dissenters.

To briefly take stock, we have already considered the moral conflict cases (or their likes), so to complete the picture, let's now consider cases where, clearly, no moral conflicts arise.

With regard to non-conflict normal cases, the pro tanto conception is not inferior to the McDowellian conception either. On McDowell's conception, the virtuous experience no internal conflicts when doing the morally right thing in normal cases; a virtuous agent is not tempted by an inclination to do otherwise. For instance, the McDowellian virtuous do not feel the temptation to lie, even when doing so can accrue enormous benefits for themselves. Indeed, this is how the virtuous distinguish themselves from the continent. This is a significant distinction, for there does appear to be a difference in terms of moral psychology between the virtuous and the continent and that difference is nicely captured, in my view, by McDowell's perceptive observation that the continent are enticed by an inclination to do otherwise than what morality demands, whereas the virtuous aren't.

Does this give an edge to McDowell's conception of virtue? My answer is "no," for neither are the pro tanto virtuous tempted to do otherwise than what morality demands, for they follow the dictates of the pro tanto rules, and their motivation is fueled by the demands of the pro tanto rules when no moral conflicts arise.[26] So, on the pro tanto conception, neither do the virtuous feel tempted by an immoral desire to do the wrong thing (as they are motivated to abide by the pro tanto rules in no-conflict cases).[27] Therefore the distinction between the virtuous and the continent can be fully accommodated by the pro tanto conception.

So, to sum up, we are now in a position to claim that in no-moral-conflict cases, the McDowellian conception of virtue is *not* superior to the pro tanto conception in capturing a virtuous person's moral psychology, and in moral-conflict cases, we have reason to believe that the pro tanto conception

---

26 The fact that the pro tanto virtuous are motivated by the demands of the pro tanto rules (e.g., "be honest") is entirely compatible with the fact that they have others' interests in mind (rather than the promotion of their own virtue or rule-following) when they are motivated to follow the rules. For instance, what the rule of honesty requires of the pro tanto virtuous in a particular circumstance might well be that they don't shortchange their customers; it is not impossible at all for the pro tanto virtuous to have their customers' interests in mind while being motivated to follow the rule of honesty.
27 Here, I assume that the pro tanto rules are morally correct ones.

can perhaps do even better. So overall, I think it is fair to say that, other things being equal, we have at least a prima facie reason to prefer the pro tanto conception over McDowell's.

## 6. Conclusion

In this chapter, I have been concerned to address the question of whether virtue can be codified. We have seen that virtue cannot be codified if we subscribe to the particularist or the prima facie conceptions as McDowell does. However, there are two significant conceptions of virtue according to which virtue might well be codifiable. They are the absolute and the pro tanto conceptions. With regard to them, I have argued that McDowell has not provided us with compelling arguments to rule out their plausibility. I therefore conclude that although virtue, in McDowell's specific conception of it, cannot be codified, there are at least two *prima facie plausible* conceptions of virtue under which the requirements of virtue might well be codifiable. Until more evidence shows that McDowell's conception of virtue is much more plausible than the absolute and the pro tanto conceptions, I think it is far too early to announce that 'virtue,' *simpliciter*, cannot be codified.[28]

## References

Anscombe, G. E. M. 1958. "Modern Moral Philosophy." *Philosophy* 33 (124): 1–19.
Aristotle. 2004. *Nicomachean Ethics*. Edited and translated by Roger Crisp. Cambridge: Cambridge University Press.
Audi, Robert. 2005. *The Good in the Right*. Princeton. NJ: Princeton University Press.
Benedict, Ruth. 1934. "Anthropology and the Abnormal." *Journal of General Psychology* 10: 59–82.
Chappell, Timothy. 2014. "Virtues and Rules." In *The Handbook of Virtue Ethics*, edited by Stan Van Hooft, 76–87. New York: Routledge.
Crisp, Roger. 2000. "Particularizing Particularism." In *Moral Particularism*, edited by Brad Hooker and Margaret Little, 23–47. Oxford: Oxford University Press.

---

28 The research on this chapter is funded by Taiwan's Ministry of Science and Technology (NSC 101–2410-H-038–001-MY2; MOST 104–2628-H-194–001 -MY2; MOST 105–2410-H-194–096 -MY4). The earlier version of this chapter was presented in a conference on Virtue and Reason in Australian Catholic University. I thank my commentator, Robert Audi, and the audience, Ramon Das and Nick Smith in particular, for their constructive comments. I also thank Jeanette Kennett, Michael Davis, Roger Crisp, Hsu Hahn, Kazunobu Narita, Hiroshi Miura, James Grant, Renjune Wang, Sher-Ming Hsieh, Kiki Wang, Kokyong Lee, Chih-Ching Ho, Chung-I Lin, and Cheng-Hung Lin for discussions of relevant ideas on various occasions. Finally, I thank two anonymous referees for their helpful and constructive feedback. I am indebted to the *Australasian Journal of Professional and Applied Ethics* for allowing me to use in section 3 of this chapter some of the materials in the section 4 of (Tsu 2010).

Dancy, Jonathan. 2004. *Ethics without Principles*. Oxford: Oxford University Press.
———. 2009. "Moral Particularism." In *The Stanford Encyclopedia of Philosophy*, edited by Edward N. Zalta. http://plato.stanford.edu/entries/moral-particularism//archives/spr2009/entries/moral-particularism/.
Davis, Darin. 2004. "Rules and Vision: Particularism in Contemporary Ethics." Ph.D. Diss., St. Louis University.
Foot, Philippa. 1972. "Morality as a System of Hypothetical Imperatives." *Philosophical Review* 81: 305–16.
Hart, H. L. A. 1994. *The Concept of Law*. Edited by Joseph Raz and Penelope Bulloch. Oxford: Oxford University Press.
Herman, Barbara. 1993. *The Practice of Moral Judgment*. Cambridge: Harvard University Press.
Hill, Thomas Jr. 2012. *Virtue, Rules, and Justice*. Oxford: Oxford University Press.
Hooker, Brad. 2012. "Theory versus Anti-theory in Ethics." In *Luck, Value, and Commitment: Themes from the Ethics of Bernard Williams*, edited by Ulrike Heuer and Gerald Lang, 19–40. Oxford: Oxford University Press.
Hursthouse, Rosalind. 1999. *On Virtue Ethics*. Oxford: Oxford University Press.
———. 2011. "What Does the Aristotelian Phronimos Know?" In *Perfecting Virtues: New Essays on Kantian Ethics and Virtue Ethics*, edited by Lawrence Jost and Julian Wuerth, 38–57. Cambridge: Cambridge University Press.
Kamm, Francis. 2002. "Owing, Justifying, and Rejecting." *Mind* 111: 323–54.
Kant, Immanuel. 2002. *Groundwork for the Metaphysics of Morals*. Edited and translated by Allen W. Wood. New Haven: Yale University Press.
Kripke, Saul. 1982. *Wittgenstein on Rules and Private Language*. Cambridge: Harvard University Press.
MacIntyre, Alasdair. 1985. *After Virtue*. London: Duckworth.
McDowell, John. 2002a. "Virtue and Reason." In his *Mind, Value, and Reality*, 50–73. Cambridge: Harvard University Press.
———. 2002b. "Are Moral Requirements Hypothetical Imperatives?" In his *Mind, Value, and Reality*, 77–94. Cambridge: Harvard University Press.
———. 2002c. "Non-Cognitivism and Rule-Following." In his *Mind, Value, and Reality*, 198–218. Cambridge: Harvard University Press.
McNaughton, David. 1988. *Moral Vision*. Oxford: Blackwell.
McNaughton, David and Piers Rawling. 2000. "Unprincipled Ethics." In *Moral Particularism*, edited by Brad Hooker and Margaret Little, 256–75. Oxford: Oxford University Press.
Mill, J. S. 1998. *On Liberty and Other Essays*. Edited by John Gray. New York: Oxford University Press.
Nussbaum, Martha. 1986. *The Fragility of Goodness*. Cambridge: Cambridge University Press.
———. 1990. *Love's Knowledge*. New York: Oxford University Press.
———. 1993. "Non-Relative Virtues: An Aristotelian Approach." In *The Quality of Life*, edited by Martha Nussbaum and Amartya Sen, 242–70. Oxford: Oxford University.
Oakley, Justin. 2014. "Virtue Ethics and Utilitarianism." In *The Handbook of Virtue Ethics*, edited by Stan Van Hooft, 64–75. New York: Routledge.
O'Neill, Onora. 1998. *Towards Justice and Virtue: A Constructive Account of Practical Reasoning*. Oxford: Oxford University Press.
Parfit, Derek. 1984. *Reasons and Persons*. Oxford: Oxford University Press.

Richardson, Henry. 1990. "Specifying Norms as a Way to Resolve Concrete Ethical Problems." *Philosophy & Public Affairs* 19: 279–310.
Ross, W. D. 1930. *The Right and the Good*. Oxford: Clarendon Press.
———. 1939. *Foundations of Ethics*. Oxford: Clarendon Press.
Russell, Daniel C. 2009. *Practical Intelligence and the Virtues*. Oxford: Oxford University Press.
Sherman, Nancy. 1999. "Character Development and Aristotelian Virtue." In *Virtue Ethics and Moral Education*, edited David Carr and Jan Steutel, 35–48. New York: Routledge.
Stohr, Karen. 2003. "Moral Cacophony: When Continence Is a Virtue." *Journal of Ethics* 7: 339–63.
Swanton, Christine. 2003. *Virtue Ethics: A Pluralist View*. New York: Oxford University Press.
Tiberius, Valerie. 2014. "Mostly Elephant, Ergo. . . " In *Philosophy at 3 AM: Questions and Answers with 25 Top Philosophers*, edited Richard Marshall, 111–20. Oxford: Oxford University Press.
Tsu, Peter Shiu-Hwa. 2010. "Can Morality Be Codified?" *Australian Journal of Professional and Applied Ethics* 11: 145–54.
———. 2013. "Shapelessness and Predication Supervenience—A Limited Defense of Moral Particularism." *Philosophical Studies* 166: 51–67.
———. 2016. "Can the Canberrans' Supervenience Argument Refute Shapeless Moral Particularism?" *Erkenntnis* 81: 545–60.
———. (unpublished manuscript). "Non-Reductive Welfarism."
Wallace, R. Jay. 1991. "Virtue, Reason, and Principle." *Canadian Journal of Philosophy* 21: 469–95.
Williams, Bernard. 2006. *Ethics and the Limits of Philosophy*. London and New York: Routledge.
Winch, Peter. 1964. "Understanding a Primitive Society." In *Rationality*, edited by B. R. Wilson, 78–111. Oxford: Blackwell.

# Part II
# Reasons and Virtues in Development

# 5 Virtue, Reason, and Will

*Ramon Das*

## 1. Introduction

Virtue ethics holds that an act based entirely on virtuous motives or good reasons is morally superior to the same act based (even partly) on vicious motives or bad reasons. For instance, a beneficent act done entirely from beneficent motivation and/or for some related good reason(s) is, morally speaking, more creditworthy than the same act done even partly out of self-interest. Following Audi (2009), call this the difference between *acting virtuously* and (merely) *acting in conformity with virtue*. Most virtue ethicists agree with Audi that both of these ways of acting fall short of a third and most creditworthy standard of moral rightness: acting *from* virtue. Meeting this last standard requires not only that an agent acts for a virtuous motive or good reason, but that she actually possesses—as a "firm and unchanging" element of her character—the relevant virtue(s) (Audi 2009, citing Aristotle, *Nicomachean Ethics* 1105a30–35).[1]

In this paper I argue that both *acting from virtue* and (at least on Audi's interpretation) *acting virtuously* are deeply problematic when understood as bases for a standard of moral rightness. The reason, which has received relatively little attention in the literature, is that complying with either standard appears to be *beyond the ability* of anyone not possessed of the relevant virtue(s).[2] This is perhaps clearest in the case of *acting from virtue*, since agents often do not possess the requisite (firm, unchanging) traits of character and evidently cannot acquire them at will. Arguably, the problem applies no less to *acting virtuously*, which also requires the possession of certain (desire-like) motives, such as benevolence. Again, if an agent does not possess these at the time of action, and cannot acquire them at will, it seems she is unable to act virtuously.

This way of thinking about why virtue ethics is problematic builds upon a critique I have developed in earlier work (Das 2003, 2015), which is that

---

1 See also Annas (2006), Audi (1995), Hursthouse (2006), Kawall (2009), and McDowell (1979).
2 Exceptions include Eshelman (2004), Eylon (2009), Roberts (1984), and Slote (1990).

virtue-ethical accounts of right action face a dilemma: roughly, they are plausible to the extent that they lose their distinctively virtue-ethical character.[3] I won't repeat those arguments here but rather offer a diagnosis of why virtue ethics confronts this dilemma:

*Thesis:* The implausibility of distinctively virtue-ethical accounts of right action stems largely from the negligible role they accord the exercise of *will* or *volition* in their act-evaluations.

The basic idea is that virtue ethics accords far too much importance to relatively fixed traits of character that are *beyond the agent's control at the time of action*, and not nearly enough importance to the agent's ability effectively to *transcend* relevant aspects of her character at the time of action, to act as she should. This centrally important ability is reflected in the truism that sometimes, good people do the wrong thing and bad people do the right thing. More generally, people may and sometimes do act "out of character." And it is deeply plausible that they generally retain this ability even when they act "in character."

Another and familiar way to put the problem is to say that *acting from virtue* and *acting virtuously*, understood as distinctively virtue-ethical standards of moral rightness, appear to violate the principle *ought implies can*—at least for any agent not possessed of the relevant virtues, either as stable elements of character, or as occurring motives on which she can act. In what follows, I shall understand this putative violation of "ought implies can" as equivalent to the worry that virtue ethics effectively makes acting rightly beyond the ability of many ordinary agents. I shall also consider and rebut a recent argument to the effect that "ought implies can" does not pose a problem for virtue ethics (Russell 2009).

In arguing for my thesis, I shall urge a sharp distinction between two concepts that most virtue ethicists (along with many others)[4] tend to run together: acting *from a virtuous motive* versus acting *for a good reason*. The distinction I have in mind is very close to the one commonly made in metaethics between *motivating reasons* and *normative reasons*. For present

---

3 More specifically, in order to avoid the most damaging objections to them, such theories must, and typically do, appeal to elements that are not distinctively virtue-ethical. For the argument, see particularly Das (2015). I should say that I have not argued, and do not believe, that no similar argument can be made against other ethical theories. Thus, I think that Hursthouse's (2013) *tu quoque* or "partners in crime" response to certain objections to virtue ethics has some force. I am inclined to think that this indicates a problem for systematic ethical theorizing generally, but I can't begin to make the argument here. In any case, I think the objection I develop in this paper—that virtue-ethical assessments of rightness far overestimate the importance of character and far underestimate the importance of the agent's ability effectively to transcend her character through an act of will—is especially if not uniquely pressing for virtue ethics.
4 For the classic statement of the underlying view, see Davidson (1963).

purposes, the salient difference is this: whereas the former (paradigmatically, desires) are relatively fixed psychological states that play a reasonably clear role in generating action, the latter often have a psychological status, and play a psychological role, that is very unclear. In particular, although a "virtuous motive" (motivating reason) may, in tandem with a means-end belief, constitute in Audi's words a "sufficient motivational ground," for action, a "good reason" (normative reason) does not. Having a good reason, as I shall understand it, is *never* a sufficient motivational ground for acting—nevertheless, it seems undeniable that we may and sometimes do act on our good reasons.[5]

In these terms, the dilemma for virtue ethics is that it remains plausible roughly to the extent that it construes *acting for a good* reason in a way that is not distinctively virtue-ethical. A distinctively virtue-ethical construal, in my view, holds that the ability to act for good reasons is in some way tied to the possession of relatively fixed traits of character—virtues—which many ordinary agents simply lack at the time of action. Yet, it is implausible that such agents lack the ability to act for good reasons—a claim that virtue ethicists are, in any case, understandably reluctant to embrace.[6] Their problem is that in moving toward a more plausible construal of acting for a good reason—one that respects the truism that agents typically have the ability to act *out* of character—they move away from any construal of that key notion that is distinctively virtue-ethical. So, at any rate, I shall argue.

The rest of the paper is structured as follows. In the following two sections, I approach the problem sketched above by critically discussing Audi's (2009) account of acting virtuously. I focus on his claim that we lack the ability to determine *at will* the reasons for which we act. I argue that once we distinguish *acting from a virtuous motive* from *acting for a good reason*, we can see that it is a mistake to think that we cannot, at will, determine for what reasons we act, and that this leads away from virtue-ethical accounts of evaluating action. In section 4, I consider an objection due to Daniel Russell about the relevance of "ought implies can" to virtue ethics. In section 5, I briefly conclude.

## 2. Audi on *Acting Virtuously*

I shall approach my thesis through a critical consideration of Audi's (2009) discussion of a closely related problem that he thinks arises for *acting virtuously*:

---

5 This view may commit me both to an anti-causalist position in the philosophy of action and a libertarian position on free will. I am happy to accept both positions but I cannot discuss either in any detail here.

6 An anonymous referee writes: "I don't know of any virtue ethicist who makes this claim" (that the ability to act for good reasons is dependent on the possession of relatively fixed traits of character). McDowell (1979) probably comes closest to embracing the view forthrightly.

AV: [G]iven that acting virtuously is in part a matter of acting for the right kind of reason, and that . . . we cannot at will determine for what reasons we act, we cannot act virtuously at will (Audi 2009, 1).

Audi argues that "we cannot at will determine for what reasons we act" and thinks it follows from this that we cannot act virtuously at will. It is telling, however, that his considered view regarding acting virtuously is more nuanced than *AV* suggests. Although he holds that we cannot act virtuously "at will," he thinks that we *do* have the power, "in certain ways and under certain conditions," to conduct ourselves in morally admirable ways (2009, 1). More specifically, Audi notes that we have a kind of "negative control" over our motivational tendencies: "if we cannot at will eliminate a motive, we often can at will resist acting on it" (2009, 16–17). These latter claims are evidently in tension with *AV*, and Audi (2009) may be read as an attempt to resolve the tension.

As I see it, the latter claims are much closer to the truth. We do indeed have the power to conduct ourselves in morally admirable ways, specifically, the power to *resist* acting on the motives we do have. How could it be otherwise if we generally have the ability—which no virtue ethicist denies—to *improve* our character? However, I believe that such considerations undercut the significance of acting virtuously as Audi understands it, and tend to lead away from virtue-ethical accounts of right action altogether. The key to establishing this claim lies in the middle part of *AV*:

RW: We cannot at will determine for what reasons we act.[7]

In the next section I shall argue that *RW* is plausibly false: we can and not infrequently do determine at will the reasons for which we act. To this end I shall urge a sharp distinction between *acting from a virtuous motive* and *acting for a good reason*, and argue that any problematic feature of *acting virtuously* (as expressed in *AV*) stems from its connection to the former notion not the latter.

---

7 There is an ambiguity in *AV* and *RW*: is Audi's claim that we cannot at will determine *all* reasons for which we act, or that we cannot determine *any* such reasons? Perhaps the most charitable reading of the claim is that we cannot determine at will *some* of the reasons for which we act. As an anonymous reviewer puts it: "When we choose we select between a range of options. But we do not have (direct) control (in this moment) over the options that fall within that range . . . [since] . . . At the moment of choice some options will seem live and some won't." As I try to make clear in the text, I think even this charitable reading of Audi's claim is hard to square with our experience. For it seems that we do often have control over the options before us, in the sense that we can choose to act *on* any of those options or *for* any of those reasons. Of course, one must be aware of the relevant option/reason in the first place. The main point is that one is not, in general, unable to act on a reason associated with, or characteristically expressive of, a given character trait or virtue simply because one lacks the relevant trait or virtue.

Before getting to the argument, however, it is worth considering briefly the significance of a claim like *RW* to virtue ethics—specifically, to the notions of acting from virtue and acting virtuously. How do virtue ethicists conceive of the relationship between these two notions and *acting for a good reason*? As noted, my view is that they often do not distinguish *acting from a virtuous motive* from *acting for a good reason* as carefully as they should. In particular, they tend to conflate the *cognitive or intellectual* virtues associated with acting for a good reason, with the *conative or volitional* virtues associated with acting from a virtuous motive. This conflation is often reflected in the terminology they use.

Consider the well-known position of John McDowell (1979), according to whom virtue is a kind of knowledge. On his view a virtuous person has "*a reliable sensitivity* to a certain sort of requirement which situations *impose on behaviour*."[8] The first of these clauses suggests a broadly cognitive capacity (McDowell suggests the "sensitivity" is a kind of perceptual capacity), whereas the second suggests a broadly volitional capacity. Yet, these appear to be two quite different things, inviting an obvious objection: it is one thing to *know* what is right, another thing altogether to *do* it. Again, it is a truism that sometimes good people do the wrong thing. I would add: even a fully virtuous person *may* do the wrong thing—at least if she is a human being with free will and not a benevolent automaton. McDowell, however, explicitly denies this, claiming that "virtue issues in nothing but right conduct" (1979, 332). Although he skirts around the objection mentioned, he never really tries to answer it, and in a revealing footnote, concedes that his discussion is "meant to do no more than suggest that the identification of virtue with knowledge should not be dismissed out of hand, on the grounds that it poses a problem about incontinence" (McDowell 1979, 348, n. 10). I do not think it is unfair to say that, indeed, his discussion does no more than this.

Valerie Tiberius (2006) adopts a similar position to McDowell in trying to defend a reasons-based approach to virtue ethics. In particular, she responds to a well-known objection of Robert Johnson's (2003) by defending the following account of right action:

VR: An action A is right for S in circumstances C if it is the action in accordance with the reasons that would guide the action of a completely virtuous person in C.

As Tiberius recognizes, there is nothing distinctively virtue-ethical about VR. A Kantian and perhaps even a consequentialist could endorse it.[9] In trying to provide a distinctively *virtue-ethical* interpretation of VR, she

---

8 McDowell (1979, 331–32), my emphasis.
9 Tiberius (2006, 258) acknowledges the first possibility. See Driver (2015) for suggestions as to how a consequentialist might be able to endorse something like VR.

crucially appeals to McDowell's view that (in her words) "the reasons of the virtuous cannot necessarily be grasped by those without the virtues."[10] This interpretation suggests that acting rightly requires complete and/or comprehensive understanding of the relevant reasons, and that this is something only the virtuous possess.

In short, although Tiberius technically defines right action (merely) in terms of acting "in accordance with" the reasons of the virtuous, she appeals to the much stronger McDowellian standard—"grasping" the reasons of the virtuous—in order to give VR a distinctively virtue-ethical interpretation. The distinction in question is evidently similar to Audi's distinction between (merely) acting in conformity to virtue and acting from virtue.[11] And, although VR's reliance on the "in accordance with" standard leads Tiberius to consider objections not pertinent here, for our purposes we can say the following: *to the extent* that VR is interpreted in a distinctively virtue-ethical fashion, Tiberius, like McDowell, appears committed to a view which forges an implausibly tight connection between *knowing* what is right (being able to "grasp" the relevant reasons) and *doing* what is right (acting *on* or *for* those reasons, as opposed to merely acting "in conformity with" them).

Finally, and returning to Audi, it is worth considering the relationship between *acting from virtue* and *acting virtuously*. We have observed the difference between the two, but to this point I have said little about what they might have in common. Here is a suggestion broadly in line with Audi's discussion. An agent who acts virtuously, despite lacking the "firm and unchanging" dispositions definitive of one who acts from virtue, nevertheless acts from a desire-like state, a motive, which constitutes (in tandem with a means-end belief) a sufficient ground to act. This last point in particular, in my view, best *explains* why Audi thinks one cannot act virtuously at will. To be sure, Audi also thinks that one cannot act for a good reason at will, but this is precisely what I am going to deny. Again, I shall argue that distinguishing acting from a virtuous motive from acting for a good reason enables us to see that we *do* typically possess some ability to determine at will the reasons for which we act—even if we are unable to determine at will the motives for which we act.

## 3. Determining Reasons vs. Motives at Will

Let us return to *AV* and (in particular) *RW*: *we cannot determine at will the reasons for which we act*. In arguing against this claim I shall use Audi's rich

---

10 Tiberius (2006, 259). The modifier "necessarily" suggests that Tiberius understates McDowell's position: according to him, the reasons of the virtuous (simply) *cannot* be grasped by those without the virtues. An agent who *could* grasp the reasons of the virtuous would himself be virtuous; *no* non-virtuous agent can grasp such reasons.
11 Thanks to an anonymous reviewer for helping me to see this, and for saving me from a bad misreading of Tiberius' position.

discussion as a foil. Notably, he begins his argument by drawing a familiar distinction between motivational reasons (paradigmatically, desires) and normative reasons that is very similar to the one I wish to urge between acting *from a virtuous motive* and acting *for a good reason*. According to Audi, motivational reasons are psychological states that "generate actions and action tendencies," whereas normative reasons support an action, "in the sense that they count toward its rationality" (2009, 6).[12] In ordinary cases it would seem that we act for both types of reason; in particular, "myriad [normative] reasons for action are always with us" (2009, 6). In what follows, I shall retain Audi's more standard way of expressing the distinction. At the end of this section I shall say briefly why I think my way of putting the distinction is more useful in a virtue-ethical context.

Audi's main argument for *RW* consists in a consideration of six different types of case, in each of which an agent "*S already* wants to help a colleague, Sanja, and the question is what *S* can do *at will* in relation to grounds for the beneficent deed in question" (2009, 7). Audi argues persuasively that in such cases (those in which a relevant virtuous desire is already present) it seems unlikely that we have the power at will to act *solely* on that desire. For instance, suppose that in addition to wanting to help Sanja, *S* is also motivated by considerations of self-interest. It seems doubtful that *S* could at will make it the case that she acts to help Sanja solely out of beneficence, and not at all out of self-interest. Alternatively, suppose that *S* has an even better normative reason *not* to help Sanja (perhaps *S* has a special obligation to her child that precludes her helping Sanja). Again, it seems doubtful that *S* could "veto" the motivational force of her desire to help Sanja—even if, in the end, she chooses not to help her. More generally, it seems correct to say that we do not have the power "at will" to make *motivational* reasons, understood paradigmatically as desires, effectively "disappear," that is, to cease exerting any motivational force or pull on us.

However, it is not clear what if anything this implies about the control we have over our *normative* reasons, which are (after all) frequently in tension with our motivational reasons. Indeed, the type of case most relevant to our topic—whether we can determine at will the reasons for which we act—is that in which our motivational and normative reasons pull in *opposite* directions. What we really want to know is this: do we have any power to *resist* our motivational reasons in favor of our normative reasons? Unfortunately, Audi's discussion obscures this fundamental question, since in all six of his examples *S* already possesses a motivational reason, a desire, to help Sanja. Let us consider, then, the type of case Audi does not consider:

---

12 Cf. Smith (1994, 96), who suggests that whereas motivational reasons are psychological states (that play a role in explaining behavior), normative reasons are not.

*LM*: *S* has a normative reason to help Sanja but *lacks* any motivational reason to do so.

What can be said of this type of case? There appear to be three options. First, one could insist that if *S* lacks any motivational reason to help Sanja, then *S cannot* help her: it is nomologically impossible for an agent to do something that she lacks any desire to do. Second (and related), if it is claimed in response to this first point that surely it *is* possible for *S* to help Sanja, one could insist that if *S* does in the end help her, this just shows that our initial supposition was mistaken: *S did* in fact possess a motivational reason to help Sanja.[13] Finally, one could accept *LM* at face value—*S* lacks any motivational reason to help Sanja—but insist that she nevertheless has the power to act on one of her normative reasons to help her. On this view, if *S* does in the end help this does *not* show that *S* after all had an antecedent motivational reason. What it shows is that *S*, like most of us most of the time, has the power to determine at will at least some of the *normative* reasons for which she acts. More carefully (for those who insist that intentional action is always constituted by a desire and a means-end belief), it shows that the best *explanation* of why *S* acquired a hitherto absent motivational reason (e.g., a desire) to help Sanja may be her recognition of the normative reason to help—her *belief* that in this instance helping is the right thing to do.[14]

I think the third option best captures what we should say about *LM*. Sometimes, it seems, we act contrary to what we most *want* to do—typically, because we think it is the *right* thing to do. This way of putting things is, of course, deeply controversial, and I can't provide anything like a general defense of it here. Let me say a few things in its favor, however, and provide some evidence that it is congenial to Audi's considered view of virtuous action, if not to what he says in *AV*. Consider, first, some of the serious problems that confront the first two options listed above. If option 1 is correct, there are apparently many cases in which an agent is literally *not able* to act as morality or virtue requires, for instance, to act beneficently.[15] Although

---

13 Or, at least, it shows that *S* had some more general motivation from which the motivational reason to help Sanja could be derived.
14 Cf. Nagel (1970) on "motivated desires."
15 An anonymous reviewer asks: "Why many? One might think most well-socialized agents have motivational access to a reason to act as morality requires. Other motives might be readier to hand, but most agents will have access to a range of possible motives that would enable them to avoid blame." This is an excellent question, and the follow-up takes us right to the heart of some of the most interesting questions in metaethics about moral motivation. I cannot get into these questions here, but let me briefly state my position without trying to defend it. I think a distinctively virtue-ethical account of right action is committed to a broadly Humean picture of moral motivation, according to which agents act in accordance with their strongest motives, understood paradigmatically as desires. In line with what I argue in the text, it is far from clear that this picture can accommodate the idea that an agent may effectively *transcend* her present motivational set in order to do

one can certainly imagine that such cases exist, to suggest that they are common is a radically strong claim, deeply implausible on the face of it.

Next, consider option 2. Again, one who takes this option denies that S could have lacked a motivational reason to help Sanja and yet helped her: *if* she helped her, she must have had a motivational reason to do so. Taking option 2 thus apparently commits one to holding that the following is a *conceptual* or *definitional* truth:

HM: If an agent S performs some act A then S had a motivating reason to A.

While one is free to define "motivating reason" in this way, it is important to see that doing so *in cases where there is no independent evidence* that an agent has the relevant motive strips the concept of much of its explanatory power. In cases where an agent appears to act contrary to her strongest desires, it adds little or nothing to an explanation of her action to say that she (must have) had a desire to A. All it does is reflect a *definitional* assumption that if an agent performs some act A she has a desire to A. And this would seem to be quite different from explaining why she As.

Indeed, understanding motivating reasons in this way undermines much of the rationale for distinguishing motivating from normative reasons in the first place. Michael Smith (1994, 96), for instance, writes that "The distinctive feature of a motivating reason to φ is that, in virtue of having such a reason, an agent is in a state that is *explanatory* of her φ-ing," or, at least, explanatory of her being motivated to φ. Again, if there is antecedent *evidence* that the agent possessed a given motivational reason, then invoking such a reason is indeed explanatory of the agent's action. However, if there is no such evidence—if the agent's act is by all appearances *contrary* to everything we know about her motivating reasons—then it would seem to add nothing to the explanation to insist that she must have had a motivating reason all along. If this is right, then there are good reasons to reject HM, and to allow for the possibility that we may lack any motivational reason to perform an act A, and nevertheless perform A.

So option 3 best captures what we should say about the cases that are most salient to assessing *RW*, the question whether we can determine at will the reasons for which we act. Inherent in option 3, however, is a fairly sharp distinction between *motives*, understood as psychological states that are essentially "given," hence *beyond* our control at the time of action; and (normative) *reasons*, understood as *potential* psychological states that are "available," hence *within* our control to act upon at the time of action. In

---

what she thinks is right. If so, there will be cases in which agents are apparently unable to act rightly, due to the fact that what they most strongly desire is to do something else. Now, I am not sure how common these cases are, but I think they are common enough to support the "many cases" claim which prompted the reviewer's original query.

*LM*, *S* lacks any motive (or motivational reason) to help Sanja. That is a fact about her psychology, beyond her control at the time of action. Nevertheless, *S* possesses the *ability to recognize* (we are supposing) a normative reason to help Sanja at the time of action. Option 3 takes seriously the idea that possession of this reason is in an important sense under *S*'s control: she has in Audi's terms the ability to "harness" it—in short, to act *on* it.

The distinction between motivational and normative reasons is, as I have said, essentially the same as the distinction between acting *from a virtuous motive* and acting *for a good reason*. However, the latter way of putting the distinction has obvious advantages in a virtue-ethical context. The term "motivational reason" is not widely used in the virtue ethics literature, whereas "motive" and "virtue(s)" are ubiquitous. Moreover, we have seen that Audi and many others run together *acting from a good reason* and *acting from a virtuous motive*, and the plausibility of *AV* depends on doing so. Once we distinguish the two, however, we can see that Audi's problem of determining at will the *reasons* for which one acts is in reality a problem (only) of determining at will the *motives* for which one acts. And this is indeed a problem for any virtue-ethical account (notably including *acting from virtue* and *acting virtuously*) that evaluates action primarily with reference to an agent's motives or motivational reasons—more generally, with reference to her virtuous traits of character. The problem, again, is that because such states are not within one's control at the time of action, accounts such as acting from virtue and acting virtuously violate "ought implies can."

Nevertheless, it should be emphasized that what I have argued thus far captures much of what Audi (along, I suspect, with most virtue ethicists) ultimately wants to say about virtuous action. As noted, he wants to retain the idea that we have the power "in some sense" to conduct ourselves in morally admirable ways. He also agrees that we have a kind of "negative control" over our motivational tendencies, and that even if we cannot at will eliminate a motive, we often can at will resist acting on it. (Again, how could it be otherwise if we possess the ability to improve our character?) To hold on to these claims, however, I think we need to move away from virtue or motive-based assessments of action, from virtue ethics, entirely. The point is not that virtue ethics fails to build elements of will or volition explicitly into its account of rightness. The same, after all, is true of consequentialist moral theories. The problem, rather, is that the manner in which virtue ethics evaluates action—namely, in terms of relatively fixed traits of character that are beyond the agent's control at the time of action—leaves little or no room for the agent's ability effectively to *transcend* relevant aspects of her character, to act as she should.

## 4. Objection: Russell on "Ought Implies Can"

I now consider a possible objection to the view presented here, which derives from work by Daniel Russell (2009). Russell accepts the principle *ought implies can* but argues that it does not apply to virtue ethics.[16] This is because *ought* (a question of action *guidance*) does not imply *right* (a question of action *assessment*) and virtue ethics, as he sees it, is primarily interested in the latter question.[17] Russell's view, I believe, is nevertheless susceptible to the critique I have offered above. It ultimately rests on an implausible conception of right action that crucially includes relatively fixed elements of character beyond the control of agents at the time they act. I shall work toward this conclusion, however, by showing that his account is problematic on its own terms.

Chapter 2 of Russell's *Practical Intelligence and the Virtues* provides a sustained defense of the idea that virtue ethics can provide a plausible and distinctively virtue-ethical account of right action. His argument in this chapter forms a key part of the book's larger claim that "virtue ethics cannot survive without robust commitment to phronesis, pretty much as Aristotle conceived of it, as a crucial part of all the virtues" (2009, 3). Although this larger claim is not my target here, it merits a brief discussion insofar as it provides the context for that target claim, namely, that because "ought" does not imply "right," "ought implies can" does not pose a problem for virtue ethics, understood as an account of rightness.

For our purposes, the salient point about Russell's larger thesis is one that was made above in connection with Tiberius' reasons-based virtue ethics: there is nothing about phronesis (practical wisdom, or excellence in practical reasoning) that is distinctively virtue-ethical. Any minimally plausible account of right action—Kantian, consequentialist, Rossian, contractualist—will require the exercise of sound practical judgment.[18] If this is correct, then Russell's thesis appears vulnerable to the dilemma I have suggested above: virtue ethics is plausible roughly to the extent that it relies upon or incorporates elements—in this case, phronesis—that are not distinctively virtue-ethical. More specifically, the worry is that the implausibility of tying rightness to fixed virtuous *traits of character*, possessed in the fullest sense by few if any actual persons, is papered over by an appeal to *practical reason*—a flexible, adaptable ability the exercise of which is common to adult human beings across a wide normal range.

In any case, Russell sets up his discussion about right action in a way that appears to acknowledge the force of this dilemma, though he reformulates it

---

16 Conee (2006) and Hurka (2010) endorse the idea that a virtue-ethical account of right action violates "ought implies can." Slote (2001, 16–17) thinks a motive-based version of virtue ethics can meet this worry, "assuming only some reasonable form of free-will compatibilism." I briefly address Slote's solution in Das (2003).
17 Other virtue ethicists who distinguish between action guidance and action assessment (for broadly similar reasons to those of Russell) include van Zyl (2009) and Zagzebski (2010).
18 Russell is, of course, well aware of this, though I don't think he appreciates its significance, as the main text suggests.

in different terms. His reformulation crucially involves the concept of "serious practical concerns" reflecting the idea that:

> Differing ideas of what 'right action' is about rest on differing views about which [serious practical] concerns we think a theory of right action should cast light on, and how such a theory should do so. In this respect, theories that focus on external outcomes and theories that focus on internal states are all on an equal footing.
> (Russell 2009, 39)

In these terms, the question for virtue ethics becomes whether it can accommodate our serious practical concerns—in particular, our concerns about consequences—while still remaining distinctively virtue-ethical. Russell's affirmative answer to this question rests on a distinction between two ways of meeting our serious practical concerns, only one of which (the "act constraint") requires that these concerns be met by *each and every act*. A weaker constraint (the "account constraint") requires only that an account of right action "takes sufficiently into consideration all of our serious practical concerns" (Russell 2009, 44), without committing itself to the view that these concerns apply on an act-by-act basis. In short, Russell suggests that virtue ethics, understood as a general account of what makes actions right, can adequately accommodate our serious practical concerns without requiring that each and every act meets those practical concerns.

I believe that this view is implausible on its own terms. Granted that our serious practical concerns include both "external outcomes" and "internal states," it is very hard to see why we should settle for an account of right action that does not apply in principle to each and every act. We are, after all, trying to construct a normative account of right *action:* there is a natural and strong presumption that each individual act constitutes an *evaluandum*. I shall now show how this basic idea can be used to criticize Russell's argument that "ought implies can" does not pose a problem for virtue ethics. That argument crucially depends on the claim that "ought" does not imply "right," which in turn rests on distinguishing sharply between action guidance and action assessment. Let me explain.

Like a few other virtue ethicists (van Zyl 2009; Zagzebski 2010), Russell distinguishes questions of action guidance (what a person *ought to do*) from questions of action assessment (whether what a person does is *right*). Insofar as these are distinct questions, the fact that one ought to perform some act does not imply that the act is right. And insofar as virtue ethics is concerned with (theoretical) rightness rather than action guidance or "ought-ness," it follows that "ought implies can" does not impose any constraint on virtue ethics.

Now, it is of course possible to distinguish action guidance from action assessment. The question is why any ethicist who takes "serious practical concerns" *seriously* would want to do so. Why distinguish action assessment from action guidance so sharply? As far as I can see, Russell's use of the distinction is motivated entirely by a need to meet objections to virtue ethics which can be understood precisely as pointing to a *practical deficit* in the theory.[19] His response to Robert Johnson's (2003) widely discussed objection to virtue ethics provides a good example. Johnson's objection focuses on the problem of defining rightness in terms of what the ideally virtuous person would do, given that few if any of us are ideally virtuous persons. If virtue ethics is to be at all plausible, Johnson notes, it must make room for a genuine obligation to *improve* one's character. It must also address the apparent fact that an imperfectly virtuous person who tries to improve her character often does the *right* thing.

In response, Russell concedes that "remedial actions can be morally praiseworthy or excellent" (2009, 54). Nevertheless, such acts are not "*central* cases of excellent action," which he thinks are the only cases properly to be identified with right action (2009, 56). This invites the following question: what is the relationship between the praiseworthiness or excellence of *remedial* action and the excellence of *right* action? Russell does not address the question directly, but his discussion strongly suggests that there is some kind of linear relationship—that remedial action is in some sense "on the way" to right action. However, it is not clear why there should be *any* interesting relationship between remedial action and right action on the view of the latter that Russell defends. Indeed, this would seem to be a fairly direct consequence of *sharply* distinguishing action guidance from action assessment. A less sharp distinction would enable virtue-ethical rightness to serve at least as a rough guide to action, but relaxing the distinction appears to lead directly back to Johnson's objection.

If this line of thinking is correct, then any advantage gained by denying that "ought" implies "right" is purchased at a tremendous cost on Russell's own terms, for it renders virtue-ethical accounts of right action of dubious *practical* value in the vast majority of cases. After all, most (if not all) of us are imperfectly virtuous. We sometimes find ourselves in situations pondering a question that seems, prima facie, to have quite a bit to do with moral rightness: what, morally speaking, *ought we to do*? What can a virtue-ethical account of right action such as Russell's tell us? Very little, it seems—at least to the extent that it assesses rightness in terms of what an ideally virtuous person would do *and* sharply distinguishes rightness from "ought-ness." Again, imperfectly virtuous persons cannot acquire *at will* the relevant virtuous internal states in terms of which right action is defined

---

19 I don't deny that there may be other legitimate reasons to appeal to the distinction, which has been standard in ethical theorizing for a long time, as an anonymous reviewer has pointed out to me. My view is that many appeals to the distinction outside of virtue ethics are vulnerable to the same sort of objection I am raising against Russell's view, but I can't defend that claim here.

on Russell's view: those states are effectively beyond the control of agents at the time they act.

Indeed, this last and crucial point suggests that the problem with denying that "ought" implies "right" extends beyond the issue of action guidance, understood as a concern with an act's (external) consequences. For such a move is no less problematic when we consider the *internal* states of character or motive which, according to Russell, are also part of our serious practical concerns. Again, the internal states of greatest interest to virtue ethicists are not under our control at the time of action, in the sense that a person cannot change her motives (*qua* desires, not reasons) or broader character at will. It is, of course, a truism that changing one's character is a difficult, step-by-step process, requiring considerable time and effort. It consists, in short, in a series of *remedial* actions rather than right actions—at least up until the mythical point that one becomes fully virtuous. If so, then even with respect to changing one's motives or character, remedial action would appear to be of far greater practical significance than right action in Russell's sense. Indeed, it is not clear that an account of right action such as Russell's—one entirely divorced from action guidance—is of much practical significance at all.

Summarizing this section, and in line with what I have argued above, I believe the basic problem with Russell's account, like other virtue-ethical accounts, is that it defines rightness in terms of relatively fixed elements of character that are beyond the control of agents at the time they act. Not coincidentally, it accords a negligible role to the exercise of will or volition in its act-evaluations. Although Russell makes much of the distinction between action assessment and action guidance, this move comes at a significant cost given that he places practical concerns at the center of his account. As we have seen, drawing the distinction so sharply threatens to undermine his account on its own terms.

## 5. Conclusion

In earlier work (Das 2003, 2015), I have argued that virtue-ethical accounts of right action face a dilemma: roughly, they are plausible to the extent that they lose their distinctively virtue-ethical character. In this paper I have offered a diagnosis of why virtue ethics is in this predicament. The basic problem is that it accords far too much importance to relatively fixed traits of character that are *beyond the agent's control at the time of action*, and not nearly enough importance to the agent's ability effectively to *transcend* relevant aspects of her character at the time of action, to act as she should.

I have argued for this thesis partly through a critical consideration of Audi's claim that we cannot at will determine the reasons for which we act. I have distinguished *acting from a virtuous motive* from *acting for a good reason*, and argued that Audi's claim is plausible only for the former, not the latter. This leads to a reformulation of the dilemma for virtue ethics: it remains plausible roughly to the extent that it construes *acting for a good reason* in a way that is not distinctively virtue-ethical. On a distinctively virtue-ethical construal, the ability to act for good reasons is dependent on the possession of relatively fixed traits of character—virtues—which many ordinary agents simply lack at the time of action and cannot acquire at will. Yet, it is implausible that agents lack the ability to act for good reasons. The natural solution is that they have this ability, but lack the ability to act from good motives at will. The problem for virtue ethics is that in moving toward a more plausible construal of acting for a good reason—one that respects the truism that agents typically have the ability to act *out* of character—it moves away from any construal of that key notion that is distinctively virtue-ethical.[20]

# References

Annas, Julia. 2006. "Virtue Ethics." In *The Oxford Companion to Ethical Theory*, edited by David Copp, 515–36. Oxford: Oxford University Press.
Audi, Robert. 1995. "Acting from Virtue." *Mind* 104: 449–71.
———. 2009. "Moral Virtue and Reasons for Action." *Philosophical Issues* 19: 1–20.
Conee, Earl. 2006. "Dispositions toward Counterfactuals in Ethics." In *The Good, the Right, Life and Death: Essays in Honor of Fred Feldman*, edited by Kris McDaniel, Jason R. Raibley, Richard Feldman, and Michael J. Zimmerman, 173–88. New York: Ashgate Publishing.
Das, Ramon. 2003. "Virtue Ethics and Right Action." *Australasian Journal of Philosophy* 81: 324–39.
———. 2015. "Virtue Ethics and Right Action: A Critique." In *The Routledge Companion to Virtue Ethics*, edited by Lorraine Besser-Jones and Michael Slote, 331–44. New York: Routledge.
Davidson, Donald. 1963. "Actions, Reasons, and Causes." *Journal of Philosophy* 60: 685–700.
Driver, Julia. 2015. "The Consequentialist Critique of Virtue Ethics." In *The Routledge Companion to Virtue Ethics*, edited by Lorraine Besser-Jones and Michael Slote, 321–30. New York: Routledge.
Eshelman, Andrew. 2004. "Responsibility for Character." *Philosophical Topics* 32: 65–94.
Eylon, Yuval. 2009. "Virtue and Continence." *Ethical Theory and Moral Practice* 12: 137–51.
Hurka, Thomas. 2010. "Right Act, Virtuous Motive." *Metaphilosophy* 41: 58–72.

---

20 I would like to thank Robert Audi, Noell Birondo, Garrett Cullity, Simon Keller, Anton Killin, Don Locke, Justin Oakley, Vanessa Scholes, Justin Systma, members of the Working Papers Group at Victoria University of Wellington, and an audience at the New Zealand Association for Philosophy meeting at Massey University in December 2015, for comments and suggestions on previous versions of this paper. I am particularly grateful to the detailed and thoughtful criticisms of an anonymous reviewer, which have much improved the paper.

Hursthouse, Rosalind. 2006. "Are Virtues the Proper Starting Point for Morality?" In *Contemporary Debates in Moral Theory*, edited by James Drier, 99–112. Malden: Blackwell.

———. 2013. "Virtue Ethics." In *The Stanford Encyclopedia of Philosophy*, edited by Edward N. Zalta. Fall 2013 ed. http://plato.stanford.edu/archives/fall2013/entries/ethics-virtue/.

Johnson, Robert. 2003. "Virtue and Right." *Ethics* 113: 810–34.

Kawall, Jason. 2009. "In Defence of the Primacy of the Virtues." *Journal of Ethics and Social Philosophy* 3: 1–21.

McDowell, John. 1979. "Virtue and Reason." *The Monist* 62: 331–50.

Nagel, Thomas. 1970. *The Possibility of Altruism*. Princeton: Princeton University Press.

Roberts, Robert C. 1984. "Will Power and the Virtues." *Philosophical Review* 92: 227–47.

Russell, Daniel C. 2009. *Practical Intelligence and the Virtues*. Oxford: Oxford University Press.

Slote, Michael. 1990. "Ethics without Free Will." *Social Theory and Practice* 16: 369–83.

———. 2001. *Morals from Motives*. Oxford: Oxford University Press.

Smith, Michael. 1994. *The Moral Problem*. Malden: Blackwell.

Tiberius, Valerie. 2006. "How to Think about Virtue and Right." *Philosophical Papers* 35: 247–65.

van Zyl, Liezl. 2009. "Agent Based Virtue Ethics and the Problem of Action Guidance." *Journal of Moral Philosophy* 6: 50–69.

Zagzebski, Linda. 2010. "Exemplarist Virtue Theory." *Metaphilosophy* 41: 41–57.

# 6 Self-Knowledge and the Development of Virtue

*Emer O'Hagan*

## 1. Introduction

When we consider the nature of virtue, we often focus on the necessary and sufficient conditions of virtuous action and the constitution of the virtuous person, theorizing very little about the processes involved in the development of virtue. While it seems clear that virtue is to a large extent the result of conditions external to the individual, such as social, biological, and historical factors, it also seems clear that those who are interested in developing their own virtue have a variety of techniques available to them and varied opportunities for doing so. Some people put a great deal of effort into their own moral development and are admirably successful. To understand virtue more fully it will be useful to consider not only what the person already possessing virtue is like, but also the sorts of activities involved in its development. My focus here will be with the latter issue: the deliberate attempt to develop virtue or moral character, a project which is not universally adopted. To do this we will need to ask: to what extent, and how, can a person committed to developing virtue, exercise control over its acquisition?

A virtuous person acts for the right reasons and from a stable character. It is the stable connection to right reasons that makes the virtuous person's character truly admirable; she is so shaped in her reflective and motivational systems that well-motivated, right action for the right reason has become most choiceworthy for her. One objective in developing virtue will thus involve coming to stabilize her own responses to the question "What should be done?" by making appropriate reasons determinative of her actions. Given that we often have multiple reasons available to us for performing a particular act, the person interested in developing moral virtue will find attending to, and attempting to act on, the best reason for action a rich resource for developing virtue. Indeed it seems unlikely that one could develop virtue without such attempts. Consider that helping children come to see the connection between action and right reason is a commonplace feature of the most basic attempts to instill virtue in them. We see this, for example, when parents encourage a child to express gratitude for a gift received from a genuine sense of appreciation for the giver's kindness, rather than from a delight in a new toy—an ability which the child may find difficult to acquire without assistance.

In this paper I consider some issues related to the development of moral character, in particular, the practice of shaping one's reflective and motivational systems to promote action done from right reason. I set aside the issue of whether, and how, other techniques for moral development might focus on, or involve, strengthening the connection to right reasons; it seems likely that activities such as reading certain works of fiction, or engaging in volunteer work could contribute to moral development by means other than a strengthened connection to right reasons. Because a variety of non-rational variables influence character change, it seems plausible that moral development may sometimes result from activities that do not themselves aim at moral development, let alone moral development by way of a strengthened connection to right reasons. For example, a study comparing the "compassionate responses" of subjects who had participated in an eight week, secular meditation course, with subjects who received no training, found the meditators to be five times more likely to act to relieve another person's pain.[1] This too sounds like moral development, but it is not the sort of development I am focusing on in this paper. Nor am I here concerned with moral virtue that might have been arrived at naturally, by good fortune, or without moral effort.

My focus is thus on the intentional development of virtue, grounded in the development of self-knowledge, or a morally refined self-conception. In the following section I claim that because the person aiming to become virtuous must acquire a self-conception that is morally appropriate to virtue, the activity involved in its production should itself be considered a resource for moral development, and worthy of philosophical attention. I then look to Kant's ethics for an account which elucidates the reflexivity involved in moral reasoning generally, and the moral importance of self-knowledge. Turning to a discussion of potential methods for strengthening the agent's connections to right reasons, I take up Robert Audi's interesting notion of the harnessing and unharnessing of reasons, as well as his concerns about our resources for becoming virtuous. I argue that we can grant Audi's claim—that we lack direct control over harnessing good reasons at will—without this lack of direct control endangering our capacities to develop virtue, and I suggest that the focus on direct acts of will is ultimately, in this context, a red herring. I advance a view of moral development grounded in self-knowledge, a view that embraces our so-called indirect resources for developing virtue by creating a future self that is more sensitive and responsive to right reasons.

---

[1] The meditators were more likely than non-meditators to give up their seat to a confederate who evinced pain while walking with the aid of crutches into a crowded waiting room (Condon et al. 2013).

## 2. Virtue and Self-Conception

People interested in developing their moral character (becoming more benevolent, tolerant, or kind, for example) are interested in developing virtues. But the person who aims to develop moral excellence will not succeed by aiming directly at *being virtuous*, rather she must aim to develop capacities to act on particular right reasons, and so develop particular virtues in the process of becoming more virtuous. One would not become virtuously kind, for example, by aiming abstractly at kindness or even by directly aiming to do kind acts, for that would tend to make the ground of the kind action one's own moral well-being, and not the well-being of another. So if at a party I take the sting out of a critical remark directed at my friend by making light of my own inadequacies in order to support my friend (that is, for her sake), I will have done a virtuous act, whereas if I make the remark with the aim of becoming kind by doing such things, I will not have acted with the concern for the other that seems necessary for the virtue of kindness. Just as a person who aimed to become more knowledgeable would not succeed by aiming at knowledge in general, the aim of becoming more virtuous demands that virtue itself not be the goal, for virtues are conduits to the goal of being a good person. The person who aims to be virtuous so that he may be considered excellent, will strike us as self-righteous or smug. But the person who aims to be virtuous because she sees the virtuous life to be noble or good, will not. Such a person can attend to her moral constitution in a skillful manner. While caring about one's moral constitution in every specific case poses a problem for virtue, caring about one's moral constitution some of the time does not.[2] The morally ambitious person need not (possibly, cannot) be entirely unconcerned with the good of her own character.

Attempting to become virtuous will typically demand the agent's awareness (at least sometimes) of the self-evaluative attitudes concomitant with her actions, as virtue itself will be incompatible with some of them. To see this, imagine a casual acquaintance enthusiastically describing her aim of being in excellent physical condition. Now imagine a casual acquaintance enthusiastically describing her aim of being in excellent moral condition. In the second case, unlike the first, the explicitly self-conscious aim raises the prospect of a kind of corruption of the very end sought.[3] It seems that the act of casually self-identifying as someone aiming to achieve moral excellence itself indicates a quality inconsistent with its achievement. Conceived

---

[2] Glen Pettigrove and Michael Meyer (2009) take up some of the subtleties around this issue. In their interesting discussion, Pettigrove and Meyer argue for an account of moral ambition as a second-order virtue which itself facilitates the development of other virtues. The self-knowledge that I am discussing could, I believe, play a useful role in moral ambition.

[3] Such a remark made between close friends, spouses, or even client and therapist would not be similarly problematic. Thanks to an anonymous reviewer for pointing out that the context of the remark is relevant to an assessment of whether or not the moral aim is corrupted.

of as an excellence *to be possessed by me*, the moral achievement of virtue is miscast. One can achieve excellent physical condition and become quite vain about it in the process, but one cannot achieve excellent moral condition while becoming vain. Having certain virtues will preclude one's having certain attitudes about one's having those virtues. Thus, developing moral excellence involves a self-reflexive component, its achievement requires coming to see and assess oneself and the actions one authors, in a morally appropriate way.

This self-reflexivity is part of moral agency. When we act for reasons we simultaneously give expression to a mode of self-valuation. Christine Korsgaard describes the person's practical identity as the output of these deliberative operations. As she puts it: "The reflective structure of the mind is a source of 'self-consciousness' because it forces us to have a *conception* of ourselves" (Korsgaard 1996, 100). The loyal friend, for example, values loyalty itself but also values *herself* in relation to loyalty. To be a loyal friend is, in part, to have a sense of oneself that allows one to recognize opportunities for offering support to others, even giving their needs priority. In difficult situations even a loyal friend is likely to feel the strain of the demands of friendship. She might find herself feeling frustrated with and inclined to give up on her friend, and also find herself defying that very temptation—for that is not who she takes herself to be.

So intentionally developing moral virtue includes the development of a sense of oneself which is itself *morally appropriate to virtue*, a sense of oneself that other, non-moral virtues (for example, wittiness) do not. While this point is not original, it is significant in a discussion of the development of moral virtue. As a pursuit with a self-reflexive component, the development of virtue will involve the development of a sense of oneself suitable to the exercise of virtue. Being virtuous will not permit one to cast oneself as morally excellent, superior, or deserving of esteem, for example, when one is simply meeting the standards of morality. This is important not simply because our conception of the virtuous person includes humility or proscribes improper pride. It seems clear that even if a person does what is required, for the right reasons, but while doing so conceives of herself as morally superior to others, she is creating a sense of herself that will interfere with future moral action. Her sense of herself as superior might, for example, lead her to give her friend unwanted and unhelpful advice instead of the sympathetic hearing for which the friend was hoping. Skill in offering support to one's friends requires that one's ego be kept in check. As I am not here intending to advance a particular conception of virtue, I grant that different theoretical commitments may result in different appropriate self-conceptions.

My claim is not that the development of virtue requires the virtue of humility, although the process of coming to have a refined self-conception will ultimately involve qualities, beliefs, and attitudes related to virtues like humility. Instead I am targeting the knowledge or awareness of the sense of oneself that accompanies one's moral dealings, and drawing our attention to its potential role in moral development. This self-knowledge is an under-exploited resource in our philosophical reflections. By identifying one's own temperamental and behavioral tendencies, one is able to gain a measure of potential control over them. One's efforts to become kinder, for example, will be aided by greater knowledge of one's own characterological hindrances to kindness, as well as the sorts of circumstances that tend to inhibit or encourage kindness in oneself. This kind of self-knowledge is not knowledge of an unchanging essence or a metaphysical fact. Rather, it is knowledge of the impermanent, varying, and otherwise obscured beliefs and desires that shape one's agency. Our philosophical discussion of the nature and limits of our capacities for developing virtue, by strengthening our connections to right reasons, will be enriched by recognizing self-knowledge more explicitly. I hope to show this partly by discussing an example in the penultimate section of this paper, which illuminates how a person's self-knowledge can open and close different possible avenues for action. But first I want to motivate the claim that the development of self-knowledge has significance for the intentional development of virtue.

## 3. Kant on Self-Knowledge and Virtue

Kant clearly recognizes the essential role of self-conception in the development of moral character. This may come as a surprise to those who focus only on his earlier and preparatory works in moral philosophy, and ignore the later works such as the *Doctrine of Virtue*, for which the earlier ground was laid. In this later work Kant describes the duty of self-knowledge, a wide duty to the self, which demands of a person that she scrutinize her motives for action so that she can purify her heart:

> This command is "know (scrutinize, fathom) yourself," not in terms of your natural perfection (your fitness or unfitness for all sorts of discretionary or even commanded ends) but rather in terms of your moral perfection in relation to your duty. That is, know your heart—whether it is good or evil, whether the source of your actions is pure or impure.
> (Kant 1991, 191; Ak 6:441)

By tracking one's intentions, one gains knowledge of one's character and has an opportunity to improve the quality of one's willing. Kant's famous shopkeeper example in the *Groundwork* supplies a simple version of this: without first becoming aware that he is giving correct change because it is good for business, and not because the customer deserves it, he cannot become a virtuously honest shopkeeper. Kant recognizes that the development of moral character requires an on-going, dynamic development of self-knowledge, and about this he is surely correct.

Kant's account of self-knowledge is complicated both by his metaphysics and by his view of human nature. Famously, he holds that knowledge of the constitution of the soul (as having an independent noumenal existence) is impossible and beyond the limits of what is knowable; we cannot know whether we exist as substance or as accident (Kant 1965, 376; Ak B420). Moreover, knowledge of the phenomenal self is limited, according to Kant, because the empirical self is a dissembler even to itself, and seeks to create a positive self-presentation. But even while he expresses skepticism about our capacity for an accurate self-conception (he does not suppose the mind to be internally luminous) Kant identifies the duty of self-knowledge as the first among all of the duties to the self. He describes it as a kind of purification and regards it as "hellish" but necessary. Nonetheless, for the purposes of this paper, we need not consider the difficulties bedeviling Kant's metaphysics, nor his over-estimation of the role of duty in developing self-knowledge.[4]

What is relevant for the purposes of this paper is Kant's recognition that improving one's capacity for willing well has a reflexive component. Without coming to see the ways we are actually inclined to will, and to conceive of ourselves, we cannot improve these aspects of ourselves. For Kant, strengthening one's capacity for acting on the right reason involves committing to a complex procedure which is itself contextualized by the aim of becoming more effectively governed by good reasons. Earlier I argued that the aim of becoming more virtuous can be thwarted by being directly pursued. When Kant cautions us against puffing ourselves up, thinking of our actions as magnanimous or noble, when in fact they simply satisfy the requirements of duty, he is recognizing this possibility of moral corruption (Kant 1997b, 69–70; Ak 5:85).

Although my aim here is not to defend a Kantian account of virtue, it is nevertheless worth briefly outlining his own account partly to correct the misperception that Kant simply equates virtue with dutiful action, and partly to try to shift our concept of virtue by making a morally refined self-conception a prominent part of at least some forms of moral development. If it is not unreasonable to suppose, as Kant did, that the right operation of reason in us is partially obstructed by our nature, inclined by the "dear self" to make an exception of ourselves, then developing virtue cannot be construed simply as a process by which sentiments become appropriately aligned with reason.[5] For Kant, virtue is a strength of will: "the moral strength of a *human being's* will in fulfilling his *duty*, a moral *constraint* through his own lawgiving reason insofar as this constitutes itself an authority *executing* the law" (Kant 1991, 164; Ak 6:405).

---

4  I have argued elsewhere that Kant over-emphasizes the place of duty in his account of self-knowledge (O'Hagan 2012).

5  In the *Groundwork* Kant writes: "From love of humankind I am willing to admit that even most of our actions are in conformity with duty; but if we look more closely at the intentions and aspirations in them we everywhere come upon the dear self, which is always turning up; and it is on this that their purpose is based, not on the strict command of duty, which would often require self-denial" (Kant 1997a, 20; Ak 4:407).

Kant does not equate either virtue or the good will with the capacity to overcome temptation. In the *Groundwork of the Metaphysics of Morals* he relies on examples that include the dutiful motives winning out over non-moral motives in the course of a discussion aimed at showing that sentiment alone cannot be the ground of obligation.[6] Because his aim there is to identify what makes moral action *moral*, he chooses examples which cannot be confused with non-moral motives such as self-interest. His task is explicitly to articulate what moral action would be like if it existed, and famously he claims that it is possible that no dutiful action has ever been done, this we cannot know. In the Preface to the *Groundwork* Kant explains that because he is there doing pure (a priori) moral philosophy and not empirical moral philosophy—the kind of practical anthropology which includes a recognition of the particular kinds of rational beings we human beings happen to be—the concepts he is analyzing are not properly transferrable to a study of ourselves as empirical moral beings (Kant 1997a; Ak 4:387–9). This is why he describes morally good actions shaped by human moral sentiments such as sympathy as praiseworthy and to be encouraged but not morally worthy. Moral worth, as described in the *Groundwork*, is a technical term of pure philosophy and it applies to actions, not to agents. So although dutiful action is rightly prized by Kant, when discussing morality in relation to our empirical nature, he does not claim that sentiments have no role in the development of virtue. To the contrary, he holds that we have a duty to develop sympathy so as to be better able to fulfill our moral duties (Kant 1991, 204–5; Ak 6:456–7). He does not suppose that virtue involves a dour attitude, but rather claims that the virtuous person acts with a joyous frame of mind (Kant 1998, 48–9; Ak 6:23–4).

For Kant, to develop virtue is to develop a strength and while he does not equate virtue with moral character, it is clear that his ethics recognizes that moral development is not simply or primarily a matter of aligning the sentiments with reason, but also involves identifying and modifying aspects of the self which are not conducive to morality.[7] So the agent who is attempting to develop virtue will not be judging whether her actions are creditworthy; as already noted, Kant regards it as morally dangerous to lavish praise on ourselves when we are simply doing our duty. Kant's insight into the importance of self-knowledge for moral development has significance for our discussion of the relation between moral development and acting for the right reason because it shows that developing a connection to right reason will be mediated by the acquisition of self-knowledge. By contrast, Aristotle,

---

6 For example, the person who doesn't commit suicide because she is perfectly content, doesn't do a moral action, whereas the person who refrains from suicide while she wishes to end her life, because it would be wrong to commit suicide, does do a moral action (Kant 1997a, 10–12; Ak 4:397–8).
7 Allen Wood (2011) helpfully draws attention to how their different metaphysics and views of human nature influence Aristotle's and Kant's views of virtue.

who is thought to be sensitive to the psychology of virtue, seems to assume that we possess accurate self-descriptions and so advises us to correct our moral character by applying the appropriate opposing force as one would attempt to straighten a bent stick by applying opposing pressure (Aristotle 1985, 52; 1109b4–8).

Kant's duty of self-knowledge is more narrowly circumscribed than the morally refined self-conception I am here considering, but it does serve to establish the basic insight. Intentionally developing virtue naturally calls for developing self-knowledge, tracking one's self-conception and the reasons for which one is inclined to act. In developing this morally refined self-conception one accumulates knowledge about one's intentions, habitual tendencies to respond to circumstances in positive and regrettable ways (for example, having a capacity to accept constructive criticism, or a tendency to take on an unreasonable amount of work), as well as more robust character traits (for example, being short-tempered, controlling, or forgiving), and ultimately context-specific knowledge of how these factors relate to one's attempts to live up to one's values (for example, knowing that one's controlling nature interferes with one's aspiration to treat one's children respectfully). This sort of self-knowledge need not be infallible to be useful; indeed, its very fallibility is important for an agent to keep in mind. Given our tendencies to dissemble and to maintain a positive self-conception, it seems likely that when self-knowledge is achieved, it is hard won.

## 4. Harnessing and Unharnessing

Let us suppose that Kant's not-yet-virtuously-honest shopkeeper were both inclined to give his customers correct change for the moral reason and also inclined by the prudential reason, and let us suppose that he had some awareness of his overdetermined state. He would then have a chance to strengthen his connection to right reason. But how? Were it possible for an agent to strengthen his connection to right reasons—to cause himself to act for the right reason more frequently—he would need a capacity to connect with good or right reasons and a capacity to disconnect from bad reasons, or those not appropriate to virtuous action. Along these lines, Robert Audi has helpfully introduced the concepts of *harnessing* and *unharnessing* to describe some of what would need to take place were this sort of technique for moral development possible.

Because we often experience ourselves as having myriad reasons for action, sometimes reasons for doing different things and sometimes different reasons for doing the same thing, it seems possible that there is room to align oneself with a particular reason for action. As Audi notes, our tendencies to say things like "Do it because you should, not because it is convenient" or "Do it because you love me," indicate that we suppose ourselves to have the capacity to harness ourselves to right reasons, and unharness ourselves from wrong reasons, at will. Audi canvasses an interesting range of cases that involve attempts to secure right action for the right reason—some of which involve attempts to detach oneself from motivating reasons or emotions that oppose right reasons, and some which involve attempts to attach oneself to emotions and reasons that are conducive to virtue—and asks whether we can actually accomplish this. For example, do we have *veto-power*? Veto-power is relevant in cases where a person is motivationally inclined to act, but lacks a normative reason authorizing that action. She may be motivated by envy, which explains why she is inclined to act, but it doesn't *per se* give her a normative reason for acting. Or, perhaps she is caught in the gambler's fallacy, sure that the next coin toss will produce a head, given that the last dozen have been tails. Can a person in this state veto the motivational ground of action? Alternatively, to what extent can we enhance or reduce the psychological support for an action, augmenting or minimizing support for the ground of action? Audi plausibly suggests that by adopting additional reasons for a particular act, a degree of support is added, making it less likely that a contrary motivation will interfere and thereby increasing the agent's motivational strength. He describes this as *sustenance control of a ground*. This type of sustenance might also occur when a person adopts strategies to avoid forgetting to do something to which she is committed, such as making amends. It is not uncommon for people to speak about attempts to strengthen their resolve to successfully complete a difficult action.

We might add to Audi's list of techniques for attempting to secure right action for the right reason, practical reflection itself, as well as more commonplace strategies for increased sensitivity to moral reasons by way of enhanced empathy. Consider a not-yet-virtuously-honest shopkeeper who realizes that his practice of giving correct change is influenced both by prudence and by morality. Were he to reflect on the implications of the different reasons for giving correct change and realize that in different circumstances the guidance of prudence and morality would diverge and that prudence would recommend an immoral act, he might come to more clearly identify with the moral reason and feel somewhat alienated from the prudential reason. Such reflection shows that prudentially grounded honest action is importantly different than morally grounded honest action, the former allowing (*ceteris paribus*) for sensible knave cases that the latter does not. So the prudential reason which initially seemed justified and morally innocuous may, on reflection, seem unattractive to the morally serious person who aims at moral development. More commonplace strategies include asking questions that aim to put a person in another person's shoes. This may be interpersonal or intrapersonal and is pretty standard fare in the moral education of children. Asking your child "How would you feel if Ahmad did that to you?" is a way of causing the child to imagine how he'd feel and to provoke an appropriate moral attitude.

It seems both that we have these capacities and that their exercise can be morally commendable. Audi is, however, concerned with the nature and extent of our control with respect to them. His focus is on the harnessing and unharnessing of reasons and I will follow him in this. Audi describes harnessing as

> an ability, given that we have a reason to do something, either to *harness* it to the action, i.e., bring it about that the action is performed at least in part *for* that reason, or to *unharness* it, i.e. bring it about that the action is not performed even in part for that reason.
>
> (Audi 2009, 6)

Because developing virtue involves developing the capacity to act for the right kinds of reasons, so that over time a more stable moral character is created, a capacity to harness oneself to the right kind of reason, and to unharness oneself from the wrong kind of reason, strikes at the heart of something important in the development of virtue. While I will criticize some of the conclusions Audi draws from his analysis, I am largely in agreement with his account of the importance of these techniques, and the view that they are not accessible volitionally.

Harnessability and unharnessability seem essential for the development of virtue, but Audi argues that we have only limited direct negative control over the reasons for which we act, and believe. He argues that because acting virtuously requires that one act for the right kind of reason, and it is not possible to determine "at will" the reasons for which one acts, it is not possible to act virtuously at will. Audi holds that willful efforts can increase the proportion of acts virtuously done, and that certain kinds of reflection will enhance "the power of the kinds of reasons for which we should act and thus increases the likelihood that we will both do what they call for and do it on the basis of those reasons" (2009, 15), but concludes we "have only quite limited direct negative control over them" (2009, 17). Audi describes his conclusion as "disturbing," suggests that our capacity to act in morally admirable ways is largely indirect, and considers whether this fact undermines our autonomy on the grounds that it seems that we have less control over virtue than we might have hoped.

In order to evaluate the significance of the connection between harnessing and virtue, let us consider the following example: aware that I thoughtlessly broke my promise and thereby caused you hardship, I see that an apology is required. Given the nature of the power relation between us, it is also clear to me that making an apology would be prudent. Multiple motivations, and different reasons, for apologizing exist. If I further reflect that all persons deserve respect, admit that I did not give you your due, and so recognize that you deserve an apology, I can be moved to endorse the morally appropriate reason and to act virtuously. Audi doesn't deny that this may happen, but he does deny that this may happen via an act of will.

The capacity about which Audi expresses doubt is the capacity to bring oneself to act for a good reason, when one is inclined to do that act for a bad reason but also has a good reason available. He writes:

> If I can bring it about at will that either (1) I believe I should A for the good reason or (2) I want (strongly enough) to A for a good reason, I can thereby causing [sic] acting virtuously, i.e., A-for-r where r is a good reason to A and of a kind appropriate to some virtue. This would mean we could sometimes act virtuously, and perhaps contribute to becoming virtuous or to strengthening our virtuous character if we already have it, just by a kind of mental exertion: what some would call a volition.
>
> (Audi 2009, 14–15)

But this, he claims, is "doubtful."

Audi's expressed doubt can be interpreted in the following way: in the overdetermined situation, it is impossible to will to *A-for-r*, where *r* is the good reason, because the will simply lacks this reach. The will cannot *itself* produce beliefs or desires, and so acting for the right reason is not the sort of thing that willing can accomplish. Willing to be taller than I am, or willing to fly would be similarly ineffective. Considered this way, the argument amounts to the claim that in cases of overdetermination, one's will cannot itself elect to be governed by a particular reason. Audi's claim that direct control would require either willing a belief of the relevant sort, or a want of the appropriate strength, supports this reading. I can't simply directly will that I apologize out of respect for you, although I may want myself to do so or judge myself harshly for being moved by a bad reason.[8] The will by itself is impotent with respect to believing and wanting directly. So Audi has a point; we cannot (at least in standard cases) make our actions virtuous merely by willing to do so.

However, this claim neither establishes a significant or disturbing conclusion about the limits of our capacities to develop virtue, nor does it characterize the activity of harnessing and unharnessing in a sufficiently realistic manner that demonstrates its significance as a technique for moral development. First, the fact that something cannot be directly willed does not by itself entail that one is limited with respect to it. That I cannot will myself to believe that my cat is the Prime Minister does not limit me as a believer, nor restrict my capacity as a believer. That I cannot will myself to fly doesn't, in any ordinary sense of the term, constitute a limitation on my movement. It is true, of course, but simply not the sort of thing that creatures like us can do. If we could directly will ourselves to act for good reasons, and to believe for good reasons, and failed to do so under certain conditions then it would make sense to identify those conditions as limiting our practical and theoretical agency. Thus, the relevant question is can we effectively develop techniques that will cause us to take up good reasons for action in response to the rightness of the reasons? Clearly the answer is, with limits, yes. So

---

8 It should be noted that Audi doesn't deny that decision can be an action in some cases.

we can grant Audi's claim that we cannot will ourselves directly into acting for the right reason when overdetermined, without accepting his conclusion that this demonstrates any significant lack of control over the development of virtue. Whether or not this sort of willing is impossible, it seems not to the point.

Audi acknowledges the significance of the role of these so-called indirect strategies and does not disparage them. He describes the morally virtuous agent as one who can identify good reasons for action and who is appropriately moved to action by those reasons (2009, 17). My challenge to Audi's position is not a challenge to this claim. However, I have challenged the conclusion that our capacities for developing virtue are limited and indirect. It is misleading to use the language of *limited* and *indirect* to describe the capacities for moral development that we actually have, by reference to capacities that we lack. A route to an end may be described as indirect if it is less direct than another route, but not in comparison to a conceivable, but impossible route. Similarly, a set of strategies or practices may be limited in comparison with those that are more effective or ubiquitous, but not in comparison with a set of merely conceivable but non-actual strategies or practices. To describe our capacities for harnessing and unharnessing as indirect and limited for those reasons is to confound the matter. This is not a purely semantic issue. To concede this point is not merely to give up "limited" and "indirect" and replace them with unproblematic alternatives. What would they be?

It seems that what we do, sometimes, have direct but imperfect control over is a capacity to recognize the beliefs, desires, motives, and inclinations that shape our perceived experience prior to action. If our capacities for strengthening our connections to right reasons do not involve acts of will, but instead involve the refinement of natural cognitive, emotive, and reflective powers, then this refinement should frame our discussions of the development of moral character. It is, after all, the capacity that we actually have. Clearly, the moral significance of harnessing and unharnessing cannot be revealed without recourse to techniques involving cognitive processes and appeals to the suitability of emotional responses. So we should not conclude that the activity of attempting to develop virtue by strengthening one's connections to good reasons for action is indirect, but rather conclude that intentional moral development should not be characterized as an exertion of will. For example, when a friend exhorts you "Do it because it is right, not because it is convenient," she is not encouraging you to attempt an act of mental exertion that will harness the right reason or desire. She is likely encouraging you to remember the values to which you are committed, to attend to the motivations inclining you to convenience as well as to your duty, and to see that you are already committed to acting in accordance with your values. A capacity to directly will ourselves to act virtuously is not relevant because solutions to the overdetermination problem require a cognitive, reflective process, often involving emotion and self-awareness,

## Self-Knowledge and Development of Virtue

not an act of will. Overdetermination problems are opportunities for reflection and moral development.

"How would you like it if someone did that to you?" causes you to think, "I would not like it," and typically this brings one's attention back to the right reason. The recognition that these so-called indirect means are the means at our disposal for intentionally developing moral character is significant because it suggests that moral growth should not be conceptualized as a kind of willful self-determination, but as a kind of self-regulation. If, for example, people can reliably unharness themselves from bad reasons for action by thinking about how they will regret it after considering the suffering of a future self displeased with its past self, then it will be precisely the sort of strategy the morally ambitious person will adopt, for over time it will provide the connection to the right reason that is possible for creatures like us. It is a direct form of self-regulation, and a reliable route to action from the right reasons. Whereas, the picture of the self that wills its way to the right reason is a fiction, and should be abandoned. This supports the necessity of self-knowledge in some forms of moral development. Once we bring the dynamic, cognitive, and reflective attempt to gain self-knowledge into view as part of a comprehensive attempt to align oneself with right reasons for action, we acknowledge the activity's moral significance and advance a more plausible moral psychology.

## 5. Overdetermination, Self-Knowledge, and Moral Development

Let us revisit the case of the person who is attempting to develop virtue, finds herself owing an apology, and finds that her reasons for apologizing are overdetermined. This offers her an opportunity to reflect on her motives and beliefs. She will not will herself into virtuous action, but we can imagine her noticing the appeal of 'smoothing things over,' reflecting that if she doesn't, she is likely to face retribution. Suppose that she notices her own reasoning with some regret, recalling that she always appreciates it when she receives a heartfelt apology. She further reflects that she would like to be the kind of person who readily bestows heartfelt apologies when appropriate.[9] These considerations alone might move her to apologize for the right reason, but they might not.

Imagine that she makes her way to her colleague's office with the intention of apologizing as a sign of respect, to give him his due, before rushing home from work and preparing for the trip she is leaving on tomorrow. Her colleague barely looks up from his work to acknowledge her presence and his cold, superior attitude indicates to her that the retribution has already

---

[9] She might thereby unharness herself from the prudential reason and harness herself to the moral reason by way of her appreciation of the moral good that lies in heartfelt apologies.

begun. She feels deflated. She wonders, "Why do we have to play these games?" The situation is complex. Perhaps she will rally, recalling her aspiration to avoid office politics, or she may, partially in response to the icy reception, revert to the smoothing things over approach which may now feel less demanding, or even all that he deserves. If she feels very rushed it will be more difficult to act from the right reason, for that sort of harnessing requires a level of equanimity and responsiveness not typically available when one feels rushed.

Factors of which the agent is not necessarily aware can influence the agent's decisions. Recall that in the Princeton Good Samaritan study, where subjects en route to give a talk on a religious or non-religious theme encounter an apparently ailing stranger, the only variable that made a statistically significant difference to whether the subject stopped to help was how rushed the subject felt (Darley and Batson 1973). While 63 percent of the subjects who weren't in a hurry stopped to help, and 45 percent of the subjects who were in a moderate rush stopped to help, only 10 percent of those in a great hurry stopped to help. Or consider that it is very easy to feel self-righteous when slighted and to lose sight of the fact that the respect that is owed to others is owed even when they are ungracious. Without first recognizing that one is likely to lose sight of what is morally relevant by feeling slighted, unharnessing oneself from the bad reason won't be possible. This is just the sort of fact about oneself that the person aiming to develop virtue learns over time by attending carefully to her own inner states when she is acting. A person who is engaged in self-reflection, who attends to her current motivational states, and subsequently evaluates her moral action, will have more control over the conditions under which reasons are available to her, and thus more control over the reasons on which she acts.

To return to the example, whether or not she will act for the right reason will in part depend on whether she can at the time realize that she is feeling slighted, or rushed, or condemnatory of her colleague's behavior, and also on the ways in which these feelings motivate her to act by aligning themselves with different reasons. If she recognizes that they are in play she has a measure of control over them. Because she has, in the past, recognized the vice in playing office politics and determined to avoid it, she might avoid the bad reasons for action.[10] But she might not, and might later reflect that she was dragged back into the fray she had been determined to avoid. What she chooses on its own is not an indicator of virtue. Only in the context of this dynamic, reflective process can her choice be understood as acting for the right reason and from a stable character, or as a move toward virtue.

---

10 In which case it would seem that by recalling her disavowal of playing office politics, or perhaps her aspiration to be better than that, she might have unharnessed herself from the bad reasons for apologizing.

It might be objected that the position I am advancing relies on empirical claims that may be false.[11] I *am* suggesting that an awareness of one's inner states and the actions they promote (such as an awareness that feeling slighted can lead me to be less likely to give others their due) results in a possibility for control that is otherwise unavailable. This is an empirical claim and while I cannot fully defend it here, it seems consistent with findings in social psychology. Some of the work on implicit bias, for example, has found that a variety of factors influence the expression of automatic stereotypes, and concludes these stereotypes are more malleable (less automatic) than had been supposed. Techniques involving both the suppression of stereotypes and the promotion of counter-stereotypes were found to result in decreased stereotypic responses.[12] In one case, subjects were instructed by experimenters to adopt an "implementation intention" (an if-then plan to enhance goal attainment) that was aimed at diminishing stereotypical gender responses. The intention "Whenever I see Ina, I will ignore her gender" was found to be correlated with reduced automatic gender stereotype responses by contrast with subjects who were instructed only to make a fair and unbiased judgement in a subsequent measure concerning Ina (Gollwitzer and Schaal 1998). Effectively this seems like a long-term strategy for unharnessing. Other studies have reported that positive values, such as egalitarianism, can be reinforced in a manner that serves as a buffer against stereotyping. For example, Moskowitz and Li conclude that stereotype activation is not beyond individual control, and that a "goal shielding" process is effective in this (Moskowitz and Li 2011). They found that when an individual's expressed commitment to egalitarianism was primed or reinforced in individual subjects (interestingly, by having them reflect on an episode in which they failed to fully live up to their egalitarian values), it had the effect of shielding those subjects from the initiation of racial stereotyping. Effectively, this seems like a sustenance strategy of the type identified by Audi.

While there is much work to be done in this area, I take results of this sort to be supportive of the empirical claims to which I am committed. There is no reason to suppose that these techniques are only effective when initiated by an experimenter, and not the agent herself. The knowledge is transferable. When I read, for example, that people seated near translucent bowls filled with candy eat more candy than people seated near opaque bowls filled with candy, I can put that knowledge to use. I can reasonably suppose that I too am influenced by the visual impact of, and proximity to, the candy; and I can therefore adopt a plan to avoid sitting near translucent bowls of candy.

---

11 Robert Audi expressed skepticism about empirical claims of this sort in response to an earlier version of this paper presented at the Reasons and Virtues Conference at the Australian Catholic University, May 2015.
12 For a brief summary of some of the recent literature, see Saul (2012).

In doing so, I would be acknowledging a tendency of which I may never be conscious in the moment, and self-regulating with regard to it.

## 6. Conclusion

As stated earlier, the person who is attempting to become more virtuous doesn't aim to do virtuous acts in order to have acted virtuously, nor does she aim directly at being virtuous. So it should not surprise us that we can't will our way to virtue directly. Nevertheless, this does not imply that virtue is not up to us. By acknowledging the reflexive quality of moral judgement and introducing the need for self-knowledge in the development of virtue, we shift toward a conception of virtue grounded in self-regulation, away from a conception of virtue grounded in self-determination. This is important in two respects.

First, it marks a shift in thinking about virtue, one that is guided in reflection about how people deliberately come to be virtuous, rather than in a more abstract conception of what the virtuous person is like. Second, it promotes a more realistic moral psychology of selfhood—granting that the self and its propensities are not clearly and infallibly given to us in awareness, entirely unified and unobscured. Strengthening one's connections to the right reasons for action is important not just because it is good or virtue-enhancing to act for the right reason, but because the self is itself shaped by these determinations. On the account of moral development I am advancing, developing virtue, in effect, involves developing a set of skills. Although in Western philosophy we haven't much analyzed the techniques available to the person interested in developing virtue, this is not true of Eastern philosophy. In Buddhist philosophy, for example, a great deal of emphasis is placed on techniques for developing virtue, while the exact nature of virtue itself is not emphasized. It is edifying to approach the issue of the nature of virtue and its development from both ends, and given Buddhist philosophy's anti-essentialism about the self, it serves as a useful comparison.

In a famous Buddhist sutra, "Advice to Rahula at Ambalatthika," the Buddha instructs his son Rahula, now a monk, to be exceedingly reflective about and aware of his intentions in order to purify his actions.[13] He advises his son and disciple to reflect *prior* to action about whether or not the action is skillful or appropriate and will promote the qualities that lead to the end of suffering: and to reflect *while* doing the action about whether it is skillful or appropriate and so can lead to the promotion of the qualities that will lead to the end of suffering; and to reflect *after* the action about whether

---

13 In Buddhist philosophy actions are of three types: body, speech, and mind. In this sutra the Buddha claims that all three forms of action need to be purified in this manner (Nanamoli and Bodhi 1995, 523–26).

or not it actually promoted those qualities. In short he advises a maximal degree of vigilance over intention in order to perfect action. Self-perfection, and the moral development it requires, demands that the individual closely monitor what she is doing. It is not assumed that monitoring intentions is sufficient for willing well, but rather it is understood to be part of a program for developing virtue by coming to understand and modify the self.

It might be objected that my appeal to Buddhist philosophy in this context is problematic on the grounds that Buddhist philosophy's anti-essentialism about the self seems to be at odds with any account of self-knowledge.[14] If persons lack an essential self then self-knowledge seems impossible as, at best, persons could become aware only of illusory senses of themselves. However the knowledge of one's tendencies, particular motivations, intentions and beliefs that I have described is consistent with Buddhist philosophy's claim that a persistent sense of a self features in human action and that the person is not identical with that sense of self. Buddhism's no-self doctrine is not opposed to, but is part of, a practice of refining one's self-conception to produce less suffering by recognizing how one's experience is being shaped by one's attitudes, expectations, and desires.[15] One Buddhist scholar describes the account of no-self in the Pali Canon as ultimately practical: "the not-Self teaching is not a bald denial of Self, but a persistent undermining of any attempt to take anything as 'Self', and thus be attached to it. It is a contemplative strategy to induce, in the end, a letting go of everything" (Harvey 2009, 267). The meditative practices that are part of Buddhism serve to allow the meditator to become familiar with her own mind, and to understand the impermanence of the ideas and desires that inhabit it without identifying with them. The development of self-knowledge that I have described is entirely consistent with this.

It might further be objected that my account fails to advance a deep sense of self-knowledge.[16] For example, techniques employed to aid in fair judgement by ignoring gender when it is not a relevant fact, do not instantiate self-knowledge, but merely a commitment to ignoring gender. However, in response, it should be noted that my appeal to empirical evidence was intended to make plausible the claim that awareness of one's inner mental and emotional states results in a possibility for control over them that does not otherwise exist. The psychological evidence supports this. I am not claiming that a gender blocking technique is itself an instance of self-knowledge. But clearly, this technique used regularly by a person committed to making fairer, less sexist judgements would play a role in that

---

14 Thanks to an anonymous reviewer for asking that this issue be clarified.
15 I have taken up this point explicitly in O'Hagan (forthcoming), comparing different interpretations of the no-self doctrine. See also Flanagan (2015).
16 An anonymous reviewer has claimed this, suggesting that my discussion of the empirical evidence does not support self-knowledge.

person's acquisition of self-knowledge. She would doubtless uncover previously unknown beliefs, desires, and attitudes that have been shaping her judgements in possibly sexist ways and this will benefit the morally serious person. Whether or not this sort of self-knowledge is deep, it seems effective in moral development. I have not here argued that a robust metaphysical self is impossible. But anti-essentialists about the self, like Buddhists, and thinkers like Kant, who hold that we cannot know the self in its absolute manifestation, deny that deeper knowledge of the self is possible. Instead, they exhort us to keep a watchful eye on the sense of self accompanying our moral actions. From the practical standpoint, that is what is needed, and there is nothing deeper required for developing our moral character.

If the argument of this paper is correct we should make a philosophical investment in studies of the development of virtue from the first-person perspective; this aspect of the Western tradition is under-developed. The focus on the will has, perhaps, left us blind to significant features of the moral life, such as self-knowledge, that play a significant role in the development of virtue. We can harness ourselves to, and unharness ourselves from, reasons and emotions that enhance or degrade our moral qualities. The practical strategies for developing virtue are not direct acts of will and this does not imply a lack of control over virtue, but instead suggests that the development of virtue involves self-regulation as much as it involves self-determination. Indeed, developing virtue by strengthening action done from right reason is an activity aimed at creating a self which is sensitive and responsive to the right reasons.

## References

Aristotle. 1985. *Nicomachean Ethics*. Translated by Terence Irwin. Indianapolis: Hackett Publishing Company.

Audi, Robert. 2009. "Moral Virtue and Reasons for Action." *Philosophical Issues* 19 (1): 1–20.

Condon, Paul, Gaelle Desbordes, Willa B. Miller, and David DeSteno. 2013. "Meditation Increases Compassionate Responses to Suffering." *Psychological Science* 24 (10): 2125–27.

Darley, J. M. and C. D. Batson. 1973. " 'From Jerusalem to Jericho': A Study of Situational and Dispositional Variables in Helping Behavior." *Journal of Personality and Social Psychology* 27 (1): 100–108.

Flanagan, Owen. 2015. "It Takes a Metaphysics: Raising Virtuous Buddhists." In *Cultivating Virtue: Perspectives from Philosophy, Theology, and Psychology*, edited by Nancy Snow, 171–95. New York: Oxford University Press.

Gollwitzer, Peter and Bernd Schaal. 1998. "Metacognition in Action: The Importance of Implementation Intentions." *Personality and Social Psychology Review* 2 (2): 124–36.

Harvey, Peter. 2009. "Theravada Philosophy of Mind and the Person." In *Buddhist Philosophy: Essential Readings*, edited by William Edelglass and Jay Garfield, 265–74. New York: Oxford University Press.

Kant, Immanuel. 1965. *Critique of Pure Reason*. Translated by Norman Kemp Smith. New York: St. Martin's Press.
———. 1991. *The Metaphysics of Morals*. Translated by Mary Gregor. Cambridge: Cambridge University Press.
———. 1997a. *Groundwork of the Metaphysics of Morals*. Translated by Mary Gregor. Cambridge: Cambridge University Press.
———. 1997b. *Critique of Practical Reason*. Translated by Mary Gregor. Cambridge: Cambridge University Press.
———. 1998. *Religion within the Bounds of Mere Reason and Other Writings*. Translated by Allen Wood and George di Giovanni. Cambridge: Cambridge University Press.
Korsgaard, Christine. 1996. *The Sources of Normativity*. Cambridge: Cambridge University Press.
Moskowitz, Gordon and Peizhong Li. 2011. "Egalitarian Goals Trigger Stereotype Inhibition: A Proactive Form of Stereotype Control." *Journal of Experimental Social Psychology* 47 (1): 103–16.
Nanamoli, Bhikkhu and Bhikkhu Bodhi, trans. 1995. *Middle Length Discourses of the Buddha*. Somerville: Wisdom Publications.
O'Hagan, Emer. 2012. "Self-Knowledge and Moral Stupidity." *Ratio* 25 (3): 291–306.
———. Forthcoming. "Non-Self and Ethics: Kantian and Buddhist Themes." In *Ethics without Self, Dharma without Atman: Western and Buddhist Philosophical Traditions in Dialogue*, edited by Gordon Davis. Dordrecht: Springer.
Pettigrove, Glen and Michael Meyer. 2009. "Moral Ambition." *Australasian Journal of Philosophy* 87 (2): 285–99.
Saul, Jennifer. 2012. "Ranking Exercises in Philosophy and Implicit Bias." *Journal of Social Philosophy* 43 (3): 256–73.
Wood, Allen W. 2011. "Kant and Agent-Oriented Ethics." In *Perfecting Virtue*, edited by Lawrence Jost and Julian Wuerth, 58–91. Cambridge: Cambridge University Press.

# 7 Aretaic Role Modeling, Justificatory Reasons, and the Diversity of the Virtues

*Robert Audi*

The philosophical literature on virtue since Elizabeth Anscombe's "Modern Moral Philosophy" (1958) leaves no doubt that role modeling is important for the development of moral virtue. But particularly regarding intellectual virtue, role modeling, though widely explored in the literature on moral education, has not received adequate philosophical study. It will help us in understanding virtue overall if we begin by considering role modeling, proceed to explore its relation to reasons for action and belief, and, in that light, examine the nature and grounds of virtues of types that do not fall neatly into either the moral or the intellectual category. In exploring these interconnected topics, we can pursue another question needing more philosophical examination than it has had so far: whether reasons are conceptually, normatively, or psychologically more basic than virtues. If, as many considerations suggest, reasons are more basic in at least one of these ways, this does not entail that aretaic concepts are reducible or even that virtue ethics and virtue epistemology cannot illuminate normative questions in their domain; but it does indicate that both kinds of theory are best understood in the light of an account of virtue that clarifies the relation between virtues and the sorts of reasons essential for their realization.

## 1. The Role Modeling of Virtues

Role modeling, at least of the kind important for the development of moral virtue, requires action, but this is not merely any overt behavior of the sort characteristic of an agent exercising the virtue in question. To be sure, not all virtues can be conceived in terms of roles, even if there is a sense in which anyone acting virtuously is describable in terms of playing some role at the time. If you are kind and, from kindness, assist a lost child, you are acting in what may be broadly described as the role of a kind person—giving such help is the sort of thing a kind person does. If you are a teacher and criticize a student's paper, you are acting in the role of critic; and so forth. The relevant roles are not scripted and, within broad limits, are realizable in individualized ways. Still, where virtue is manifested in unexpected ways, but still role *modeled*, the relevant actions, even when exemplary, may, and ideally will, admit of imitation.

Role modeling of a moral virtue admits of great latitude, even eccentricity, but it must still meet a certain objective standard. To a properly sensitive observer, it must give the impression that the deeds partly constitutive of that virtue are motivated in a certain way, in a sense implying an explanation in terms of the agent's reasons for action. The conduct in question need not evoke a belief with exactly this content; but under appropriate conditions it should create a sense of action for an appropriate set of reasons. That sense, in turn, normally disposes the observer to form a belief to this effect. Consider a case in which we have only the behavioral bare bones of aretaic role modeling: binding someone's wound after a fall from a skateboard, done with absolutely no expression of sympathy or of caring about the victim. This is not role modeling for kindness or beneficence if done in that way. Duly sensitive observers who cannot perceive signs of caring or of some positive attitude may, to be sure, learn technique from it; but, if they were to regard the conduct as illustrative of kindness or beneficence, they might also come away thinking the proper expression of these virtues is simply instrumental.

By contrast, consider how one might role model considerateness and generosity. Imagine a summer Saturday when a family is having its house painted. They know the painter normally drives off at noon to lunch at a diner, but this time food is already arriving at a large table as the painter descends to go to lunch. Here both generosity and considerateness might be exhibited by inviting the painter to join the family for lunch and then, in a way the children can see, serving the painter first and themselves and the children less than usual. If this is done in the right spirit, the parents do not need to say anything to the children to communicate that on occasions for helping others in our domain, doing so is a good thing. Granted, saying to them (perhaps as the painter descends) that we should share with others might be desirable here, but endorsing action characteristic of a virtue is not role modeling the virtue and is likely less effective than the doing of the right kind of deed.

Role modeling, then, though not merely behavioral, does not require offering any commentary on what one is doing—valuable though that may be—but it would be at best abnormal for someone role modeling kindness not to be *disposed*, even if only afterwards, to attribute the relevant modeling deeds to some appropriate motive and to criticize certain failures either to perform such deeds in circumstances that call for them or to do so for a reason of the right kind. I take the latter to imply acting on appropriate motivation. Not all motivated action is for a reason appropriate to some virtue, as opposed to being simply purposively explainable, say aimed at making a profit; but all aretaically grounded action is performed for some reason appropriate to one or another virtue. All of this is illustrated, or anyway easy to imagine, in the painter case.

Aristotle's *Nicomachean Ethics* is sometimes interpreted in a way that neglects some of these points. One might think that when he says that virtue arises by habituation, he is taking overt behavior to be sufficient for the development of virtue in learners, such as children, and correspondingly, for role modeling aimed at moral education. But this understanding would not take account of much else that he says, particularly concerning what it is for an action to *express* virtue.[1] In many passages, he apparently has in mind the necessity of appropriate reasons as essential for action from virtue. If so, it would be strange indeed if he did not think that moral education, in role modeling and in other ways, should take account of the need for action from virtue to be motivated by appropriate reasons. This implies that moral education by role modeling should both communicate the appropriate underlying reason(s) and criticize doing the relevant deeds for reasons of the wrong kind.

I have described role modeling as partly constituted by overt behavior.[2] This implies that role modeling is not possible simply by stating the relevant standards of action—or even of action as based on appropriate motivation. But it does not follow that good role modeling over time, as for children or students, is possible without such expressions of standards. For certain virtues, it normally is not. Consider respectfulness. There is a generic notion of respect for persons that must inform this virtue, but the appropriate behavior toward others—especially elders or children—differs enough from one culture or subculture to another so that some descriptive explanation is likely needed to engender respectfulness, at least where there is not time and occasion for the full range of required behaviors to be demonstrated. Some subcultures tie respectfulness to protocol, and that is highly variable across cultures and with historical change. Granted, if respectfulness is a genuine moral virtue, it will have certain generic elements that transcend a particular culture, but even a plant that can grow in any soil must first be planted in a particular place.

With intellectual virtues, such as clarity, rigor in reasoning, and judgment, the same point appears to hold. With these, the same need for good role modeling to be combined with instruction seems evident. Indeed, intellectual virtues are closely bound up with conceptualization of a kind that normally requires instruction; this connection may be so intimate that role modeling them usually requires commentary and sometimes requires critique. There is, however, at least one important difference between role modeling intellectual virtues and role modeling moral ones. It concerns the extent to which intellectual virtue is manifested in the use of language. Parents who use language well can model clarity of expression, rigor in reasoning (at least oral reasoning), judgment (in matters in which their children can see them to be correct or incorrect), and other intellectual virtues, simply in teaching

---

1 See Book II, esp. 1105a. Consider, e.g., 20–30, in which he says, "actions are not enough" (for becoming just or even learning a craft) and explains why.
2 This is the normal case, but in principle someone could be given systematic hallucinatory experiences that suffice to teach the same patterns.

them to speak, which is of course largely a matter of simply speaking in their presence.

Much intellectual role modeling is morally neutral—not in the sense that it has no moral implications or moral value (that would be a kind of moral vacuity), but in the sense that it is not normatively determinate, say favoring a utilitarian view. As this point suggests, the kind of learning that is necessary for reaching high linguistic competence, even for certain kinds of conceptual competence, does not require manifesting moral virtue even if parents and teachers have it. Intellectual role modeling provides opportunities to manifest moral virtue, but whereas intellectual virtues manifest themselves in much ordinary communication either to or in the presence of children, moral virtues such as veracity, justice, and beneficence may not be so regularly manifested. Granted, there is a limit to how much *vice* in parents or guardians is compatible with bringing children to normal adulthood. But the mere absence of lying is not veracity; occasions to do justice, as opposed to avoiding gross violations of its standards, may be rare; and merely decent treatment of others need not represent beneficence.

## 2. Aretaic Uptake

Role modeling does not always yield the desirable results one might hope for. What kind of response to it indicates its success? Call this *aretaic uptake*, the kind of response to it that contributes to developing or reinforcing virtue in those who are meant to be (or should be) its beneficiaries. To understand both the nature of virtue and its development through responding to role modeling, it is important to bear in mind why habituation alone—conceived as a route (by a kind of repetition) to "automatically" doing a given kind of thing in a given kind of circumstance—does not guarantee the development of virtue. The kind of behavior that can become habitual simply does not suffice for virtuous action. That requires doing the thing(s) in question for the right kind of reason. We can of course distinguish between modeling act-types, as where we presuppose suitable motivation and are showing someone how to do a kind of deed, and the full-scale modeling I am calling aretaic, which entails acting virtuously—or at least doing something properly taken as such, as where the conduct is that of a highly skillful actor playing or illustrating a role in which some virtue is prominent.

Role modeling may succeed in the beneficiary's development of the virtue modeled even if its manifestations are not optimal. Consider courage in people with very limited power. Here we might expect the appropriate motivation to arise spontaneously where they see something they value to be under threat, but no automatic or even habitual behavior can be expected. When protective action is possible for them, they may see multiple options; this would complicate predicting action. But, more often than powerful people, they may also judge that the opposition is too strong to oppose and that resistance would be fruitless or foolhardy. Exemplifications of virtue in action need not, then, be either behavioral manifestations of habit or as frequent as one might expect in the absence of situational and personal variables.[3]

Another misunderstanding of virtue can come from the perfectionist strain in Aristotle, associated with his idea that happiness requires achieving the highest virtue. However one reads Aristotle, one should not take exemplifications of virtue to be invariably perfect instantiations of the virtue in question. A courteous response to an unwanted question may have a rough edge; a kindness may fail to benefit the person needing it. In a virtuous person, however, one expects the aretaically constitutive dispositions to be self-corrective, a point stressed by Julia Annas, among others.[4] Imperfection is one thing and surely common even in the conduct of virtuous agents; unresponsiveness to perceptible deficiency in one's conduct is another and is not compatible with virtuous character. As this suggests, however, virtues are possessed to varying degrees, and there is no precise quantitative measure of a threshold for possession, either in strength of the underlying motivational-cognitive elements or in frequency or strength of behavioral manifestations.

What I am calling aretaic uptake is important for judging the success of those role modeling virtue. Without it, role modeling may be observed, but not developmentally influential. Aretaic uptake may or may not take root and become "habitual," in the wide sense of being a settled characteristic of the person who has acquired the virtue. When it is rooted, the actions expressing the virtue in question must be performed for an appropriate reason. This is probably uncontroversial, but taken by itself the view does not make clear how the agent must understand the required reasons. They need not be conceived *as* reasons, though this may be common for sophisticated agents. Still, even a sophisticated virtuous agent may simply see certain deeds as, in the context, necessary or at least called for. This may require seeing some act or desirable goal as indicating a need, as fitting one's commitments, as benefiting another person, and in many other ways. But neither the notion of a reason nor any normative concept need figure in the agent's consciousness.[5]

The point that actions from virtue must be performed for an appropriate reason can mislead if we do not distinguish between action *from* a virtue and action that may, but need not manifest it. Take sensitivity to the feelings

---

3 I cannot here discuss the empirical issues that arise here, but I of course assume that many variables affect just how and in what way a virtue will be manifested. I also do not presuppose that trait-ascriptions, even virtue-ascriptions, are highly predictive. Virtues are conceptually, normatively, and philosophically important even if their predictive power is highly limited. For recent critical discussion of literature (e.g., by Mark Alfano, John Doris, Gilbert Harman, and Christian Miller) arguing that trait-ascriptions have little if any predictive or explanatory power, see Upton (2015).
4 See, e.g., Annas (2011), e.g., p. 14.
5 This is argued in detail in Audi (1995).

of others. This will manifest itself in a manner of treatment that may be exemplified by many actions that are non-intentional or at least not aimed at some goal that, in the context, figures in the sensitivity. One might furrow the brow on hearing something, draw closer to someone to allow a lower tone in communicating something personal, or simply avoid asking certain questions that are natural in the situation. Some of these actions or manners of action need not be intentional, even though none is *un*intentional. One important point here is that the manner of action—its adverbial dimension as opposed to its act-type—should not be overlooked in understanding virtue. The way in which we do things—even things not specifically required by any virtue—may indicate a virtue or at least constitute modes of behavior appropriate to it. Possession of the virtue of gentleness, for instance, may be what best explains the delicacy of someone's conduct toward a person the virtuous agent is evaluating—gently—in making a performance report.

For some virtues, including compassionateness, courage, and lovingness, not only is appropriate motivation required for acquisition and possession of a virtue; so is emotion.[6] To see the aretaic importance of emotion, consider empathy (as a trait) first. Normally, unless one has feelings significantly like those of others, or is at least disposed to have them in relevant eliciting circumstances, one cannot develop empathy. Similarly, if no affectionate feelings toward someone else occur, one cannot become genuinely affectionate in behavior at the time in question; and normally, if there is no fear to be overcome, one cannot develop courage. In any of these cases, if brain manipulation is capable of inducing virtue, it must produce not only the right behavioral patterns and its rootedness in appropriate reasons, but also emotional tendencies. If one thinks of virtues as *historical*, at least in the way remembering is, the idea of immediate producibility by brain manipulation will be ruled out a priori. No past, no virtue. I suggest, however, that duplication of a person is possible, at least by an omnipotent God, and that reflection will reveal no good reason to deny to my duplicate all my virtues that—unlike any that entail a past, such as appreciativeness that entails remembering people one has been helped by, which entails a past existence of the person—depend on my basic psychological constitution. This is arguable for all of the basic virtues.

Here courage differs from the others just mentioned in a way that merits comment: once courage is possessed, the courageous agent need not feel fear (even if there is a tendency to fear when danger looms) but can face danger without it—the crucial thing is a steadfast willingness to risk something one values for the sake of something else. If fear is normally required for

---

6 I refer to normal acquisition of virtue. On plausible assumptions about the relation between the mental and the physical and the determination of the former by the latter, certain brain manipulations could produce at least a large number of virtues. This would be an example of abnormal and doubtless not creditworthy acquisition of virtue.

development of courage—since mastering it is typically crucial for that—too much of it can make acquisition more difficult. A person too easily frightened may not be able to develop courage. There are, however, some emotions that may facilitate developing virtues of any kind. Such, for Linda Zagzebski, is (occurrent) admiration, provided it is directed toward the right elements in someone else's behavior and character (2013). One reason is that admiration usually implies desires to be like the person admired in respect of the element(s) for which the person is admired. Such desires can be long-standing and highly motivating.

## 3. The Place of Reasons in Understanding Virtue

Contemporary literature uses 'reason' and 'reasons' broadly. The category includes not just explanatory elements such as propositional attitudes but also their contents. For instance, a reason *for* consulting a dictionary of philosophy might be that it explains 'intentionalism', and one's believing this may be the (or a) reason *why* one does this. Non-intentional grounds, especially perceptual grounds, can play similar roles. Such grounds include the sense-impressions that occur when one sees the path one is walking on, memory impressions, mental images drawn from memory or imagination, and more. Elements from all these realms can be described in a way that displays them as explanatory reasons, say where the reason why one walks to the left is that one sees the forest path turn left, or as justifying reasons, for instance where one answers "What is your reason for believing the assailant was Moriarty?" with "I have a clear recollection of his face." Reasons are important in epistemology, where reasons for belief are the central case, and in all the major ethical traditions, where reasons for action are a central case. As above, I first consider reasons in relation to moral virtue.

I have assumed that actions from virtue must be performed for an appropriate reason. Similarly, and in more familiar language, actions not performed for an appropriate reason—even if they are both obligatory and have good effects—cannot be virtuous. An engineer could keep a promise to reinforce a building in fulfillment of a contract, but do so entirely for profit, and if the job is done well enough, it might have long-term good effects. For Kant and other leading deontologists, such as W. D. Ross, the parallel point holds, with 'moral worth' substituted for 'being virtuous': actions cannot have moral worth unless performed for at least one reason of the right kind.[7] It is consonant with their views (though not part of them) to emphasize, as I have, that we need only require a minimum of one reason of the right kind. I would add that at least one reason of the right kind must be motivationally sufficient. Take the engineer: if the job is done partly for profit but with a

---

7 These points are discussed by Kant in, e.g., Sect. I of the *Groundwork* and by Ross (1930), ch. 2, and elsewhere in that book.

motive of fidelity to the contract *sufficient* to yield its fulfillment without the aid of the profit motive, then the action can be virtuous—and a perfectionist about virtue likely would say this. I prefer to say that it is only *impurely* virtuous; but gold can be quite valuable even with impurities.

The matter is more complicated for utilitarians, but a similar point may be maintained (as indicated by J. S. Mill).[8] Given these points, one might think that in the virtue tradition, fully moral action is not possible without virtue. But this would surely go too far. Recall our discussion of how role models succeed in helping children to become virtuous. Mere imitation of the relevant act-types is not enough; but if the children do the right thing *for* an appropriate reason, this seems sufficient for the kind of conduct that, when spontaneous in an appropriate range of situations, bespeaks virtue. The point is that virtuous action can occur on the way to developing virtue and does not require already having it.

Once this point is appreciated, we can ask whether, normatively and conceptually, reasons are as basic as virtues or indeed, more basic. Suppose (1) that, for reasons indicated in sections 1 and 2, role modeling requires an understanding of an appropriate range of reasons (even if not in terms of the concept of a reason) for the behavior that is partly constitutive of the modeling. It is also plausible to assume (2) that if imitation of a role model's behavior for the right kind of reason is sufficient for performing a kind of virtuous action, that may be a step toward developing the virtue(s) in question, and (3) *having* a virtue is itself partly constituted by a proper reasons-responsiveness, a responsiveness to the kinds of reasons indicated in our discussion and referred to in (1). Given the plausibility of these points, should we not understand *fully* moral action—the kind that is both right and creditworthy for the agent—as a matter of doing the right thing for an appropriate reason, and in the right way?[9]

Suppose this understanding is correct. Proponents of virtue ethics may still plausibly claim that the act-types obligatory for an agent in a given situation are precisely those that would be intended by a perfectly virtuous agent who is aware of being in that situation. Nonetheless, given how virtuous action must be understood and role modeled, it is at best unclear how we can determine what virtuous agents would intend or do apart from a knowledge both of what should be done and of appropriate reasons for doing it. This point explains why reasons for action and hence, indirectly, right and wrong acts and good and bad acts are, in the normative order, conceptually more basic than virtues: roughly, such that the goodness of

---

8 See esp. note 3 in ch. 2 of *Utilitarianism*.
9 This needs qualification: the *way* an action is performed is aretaically important, and it would be a mistake to take descriptions of ways of doing things always to be simply actions in their own right, as I have argued in Audi (2016). On this adverbial dimension of action Davidson (1980) is instructive.

virtue in persons and of virtuousness actions must be understood on the basis of the nature and kinds of reasons to which aretaic development and virtuous actions are responses.

I am not suggesting that highly specific rules of action must be presupposed for the development of virtue, something one might take to be implied by Kant's emphasis on duty or from his apparently top-down conception of ethics. Indeed, we have seen how a broad spectrum of motivating reasons can be appropriate even to a single virtue, such as justice. The same spectrum is apparent in the range of types of aretaic modeling. To be sure, role models can exercise influence quite beyond eliciting virtuous action, say on the attitudes and emotions that are elicited in those their modeling influences. When they are admired or even simply identified with, moreover, their being the (or a) kind of person they are can be an aspiration and can generate its own psychologically autonomous reasons.

The case of consequentialism is difficult to deal with in connection with the issues we have been considering. But suppose we consider not a hedonistic version but a valuationally more pluralistic position such as we find in Sidgwick and Moore. (Hedonism is itself pluralistic given how many kinds of things yield pleasure and how many yield pain, but knowledge and virtue need yield neither, which is one reason their views are more pluralistic than hedonism.) Reasons for action may be considered conceptually autonomous even if the overall moral directive is to maximize intrinsic value. To illustrate, producing an equal distribution might be a basic reason for action of the kind important both for acting justly and for developing the virtue of justice. It need not be considered—on conceptual grounds alone—a reason for action only insofar as acting on it tends to maximize intrinsic value. If, however, a consequentialism is, like Mill's, top down and conceptual in its grounding of reasons in pleasure and pain, then virtuous action and virtue itself must be understood differently—as subordinate to the master reason for action: contributing as much as one can, given one's alternatives, to enhancing the balance of the intrinsically good to the intrinsically bad. This view does not provide a good basis for understanding either virtue or common-sense morality.[10]

## 4. Intellectual Virtue

It should not be assumed that intellectual virtues are precisely parallel to moral virtues, though it would be surprising if there were not some

---

[10] I have argued in detail for this in Audi (1989), reprinted in Audi (1997). I here assume that the kind of consequentialism in question is not "self-effacing," to use Parfit's term for a theory that directs agents not to think in terms of or be motivated by what, on the theory, is the source of their reasons. A consequentialist theory can be self-effacing in this sense and otherwise more sophisticated than Mill's. On this point see, e.g., Hooker (2000).

significant similarities as well as various differences. Certainly reasons figure in the exercise of intellectual virtues, especially reasons for believing some proposition relevant to the virtue. This is clear for such virtues as (intellectual) good judgment and, if to a lesser degree, intellectual rigor. Judgments should be responsive to reasons, and rigor should lead one to believe for good reasons or on good grounds and to reject, for some good reason or on some good ground, what needs support by a reason or ground and does not have it. Still, there is a contrast with moral virtue: even basic (intentional) actions are performed for some reason (if only to fulfill a whim), whereas it is common for beliefs and even judgments to be non-inferential and based on a ground that, like a visual experience, is non-propositional and (in my view) not properly considered a reason. A critic could rationally, even astutely, judge that the language of a poem is artificial on the basis of how it comes across holistically, not for a reason such as that there are too many French words present given that they merely fill out the rhyme scheme rather than enhance the poem's aesthetic value. This point does not imply that there is no reasonable basis or, in some sense, a reason, for the critic's judgment. Indeed, if the ground of a non-inferential judgment can be expressed in a proposition, it can *then* serve as an inferential reason for the judgment. Still, believing or judging on a ground does not entail being able to propositionalize that ground.

Intellectual virtue has an important connection to the venerable idea, traceable to Greek philosophy at least as far back as Plato (and no doubt to the historical Socrates), that truth is a kind of regulative ideal for the intellect much as goodness is a regulative ideal for the will. One way to take this is to say that intellectual virtues are features of character, or at least of intellect, that dispose one to discover a certain range of truths—"significant" truths, to put it broadly—and practical virtues, including the moral virtues as paradigms, are features of character that dispose one to honor, realize, and promote the good. I will return to the latter idea. Here I would stress that the idea of truth-regulatedness is a bit narrow if it is meant to capture the "telos" of all the intellectual virtues. But it should be added immediately that in speaking of truth and goodness as regulative ideas we include appropriate negative standards as well: falsehood is to be avoided in cognition, as is the bad in motivation and behavior. Truth and goodness are at best stymied ideals if they do not encompass avoidance of the false and the bad. Let me explain some applications of these points to intellectual virtue.

The first thing to be said here is that we can come closer to accommodating the intellectual virtues under this idea if we take it to include avoiding falsehood. Consider rigor. This virtue alone will help us see what is implied by truths, hence expand our store of them, but its main function is in reasoning and appraisal of content already before the mind rather than in discovery. Rigor is crucial, however, for avoiding contradictory beliefs and unjustified conclusions. Taken by themselves, in isolation from more "positive" traits, respectfulness of people's rights and certain nameless virtues such as avoidance of doing evil, no more promote or honor the good than rigor, by itself, promotes or honors truth. Such "positive" traits as gentleness on the practical side and creativity on the intellectual side need other traits, including respectfulness of rights and rigor in thought, for their full expression. Traits of character and intellect do not and should not operate in isolation from one another.

If, as I assume, intellectual independence and, especially, theoretical creativity are intellectual virtues, then a further limitation of the truth-regulatedness standard emerges. Neither of these virtues is mainly directed toward discovering truth, even if they often function better where truth is sought. Clarity is somewhat similar: it has value even apart from helping us seek truth and avoid error. Clarity of mind is rewarding in even its unsuccessful exercises if, as often happens, they have, in themselves, aesthetic value or intellectual interest. Clarity tends to assist theoretical creativity even where no conclusions are in the end drawn. To be sure, all the intellectual virtues bear on truth-seeking in some way, and some are necessary for its success. The point is that their "aims" and the standards for their proper exercise go quite beyond those governing the search for significant truth. Perhaps there are no pure and simple cases, but for, say, curiosity, there is a much closer approach to such purity.

## 5. The Diversity of Virtue

The truth-regulatedness standard may in part underlie a tendency prominent in some recent literature on intellectual virtue—to assimilate intellectual virtue to a kind of intellectual power. We should distinguish between an intellectual virtue and an intellectual power but also grant the importance of intellectual power *in* virtues, especially the intellectual ones. Certainly an intellectual power, such as the ability to do complex arithmetic problems accurately in one's head, can be a good trait. A more difficult case is that of creativity in fiction writing. This is both a power and good in a sense meriting praise. But whereas the arithmetic ability represents something like a handy calculating machine within the mind, creativity bears the stamp of individuality, and we understand it as showing both inventiveness and, typically, a kind of judgment of value or appropriateness and an exercise of will to achieve a worthwhile end.[11]

---

11 Representative works include Ernest Sosa (2007, 2011); and John Greco (2010). Critical discussion of the kind of externalist view developed in this tradition is found in Greco 2004. The critical appraisals include my "Intellectual Power and Epistemic Virtue," 3–16. For wide-ranging discussion of virtue epistemology in the context of virtue theory in both the practical and theoretical domains, see Battaly and Slote (2015). This paper also considers the virtue-responsibilism of James Montmarquet (1993, 255–56) and Linda Zagzebski (esp. 1996). The former takes an internalistic view of epistemic virtue, the latter, in part following Aristotle, an externalistic view.

It should be apparent from examples already considered that not all virtues are adequately classified as either intellectual or practical. A number of them might be called *cross-over virtues* ('mixed virtues' also describes them). Take judgment, sensitivity, and consistency, understood as either practical, say moral, or as intellectual, or as both. Given the way in which good judgment figures both in intellectual and in moral matters, it seems artificial to suppose there are two distinct virtues here under the same name—say intellectual sensitivity and moral sensitivity—rather than two aspects of a single virtue that involves discernment, comparison, weighting, and, often, selecting. Creativity and inventiveness also might be considered cross-over virtues. Indeed, what is sometimes called moral imagination is a kind of creativity directed (largely) to options that lie within the range of permissibility. These illustrate the requirement of reasons-guidedness without required limitation to particular reasons; reasons-essentiality without a determinate collection of essential reasons.

Prudence is an especially interesting case. In relation to action, it has been taken so broadly as to be considered equivalent of practical wisdom, but Aquinas called it "in essence an intellectual virtue," though in the same passage also describes it in practical terms as "right reasoning *about things to be done*."[12] In contemporary usage 'prudence' is often taken to be anchored in self-interest, and this may be thought to confine its scope to achieving goals of action; but even achieving just instrumental rationality in action requires intellectual competence. Consider also something not directly connected with self-interest. Might not a passage in an essay be imprudent on aesthetic grounds even where the author is aiming at entertaining the reader and not at aesthetic merit? It may be that prudence is in some way *goal-relative*, and that would leave open whether the relevant goal is broadly intellectual, rather than "practical."

In both the moral and the intellectual case, some virtues are open-ended in a way others are not. Veracity is directed toward symbolic acts, mainly speech acts, and its "outputs" are truthful (even if sometimes not true) representations. By contrast, creativity has no particular kind of output, even if we restrict it to a single medium, such as poetry. The input side, understood in relation to the virtue in question, is also important. Gratefulness has as inputs mainly a kind of good deed done toward oneself, whereas sensitivity is largely constituted by discernment of myriad kinds of deeds and other phenomena one experiences, whether intellectual or interpersonal. Judiciousness is open-ended on both the output and the input side. It governs

---

12 See Question LVIII, Art 3, in Oesterly (1966, 84). This passage is quite Aristotelian, but Aquinas should not be taken to follow Aristotle on every major point the former makes about virtue. For an indication of this point that applies to prudence, see Pinsent (2015).

action and speech, and it is crucial for interpretation of language one hears or reads and actions one witnesses.[13]

One thing these reflections show is that intellectual virtues commonly have characteristic expressions that are cognitive rather than actional and to which 'for the right kind of reason' does not always apply as it does with virtuous actions, which partly constitute the characteristic outputs of moral virtues. Nor is the contrast eliminated if we emphasize that manifestations of intellectual virtue are governed by grounds in the way manifestations of moral virtue are governed by reasons. Creativity may be manifested in elements produced rather spontaneously by the imagination, rather than in response to grounds. Clarity of mind may govern verbal expression in a similarly spontaneous way.

These contrasts should not be overstressed. Even what is not produced in response to reasons or grounds may be explained or rationalized, or both, by appeal to one or the other of these supporting elements. If a person exercising the virtue of creativity closes a poem with a couplet, there may be a reason the author could cite that would explain or justify using that couplet; it does not follow that the consideration(s) brought forward antecedently guided the choice or that, if they did, it was through rule-following or inference. Nor does it follow that what is cited is a mere rationalization; we can, by reflection, often cite elements that likely influenced us without implying that we intentionally or even consciously used those elements as guides in the activity in question. *Something* guided us, of course; but we should not assume that all the complexity to which our sensibility—and, at some level, our brain—responds is a guide in the way in which reasons or other kinds of grounds normally are. Clarity of expression can be appealed to in making the same point. Competent speakers of a language can follow a rule that they cannot readily formulate and may even have difficulty recognizing as governing their linguistic practice.

We have seen, then, two important and very general points about virtues: even if their exercise is not explicitly reason-guided, it may be guided by a sensitivity to grounds, and it is in any case reasons-appraisable. The modes of appraisal appropriate to it are determined by the character of the virtue in question. Such appraisability might be expected given that the concept of virtue (as distinct from that of a power) is normative. In a given person, virtues may or may not be normative in having targets that are normatively characterized. Virtues also may or may not be normative in having their characteristic exercises determined by responding to one or

---

13 A related view, compatible with mine, is proposed by Garrett Cullity in "Moral Virtues and Responsiveness to Reasons" (ch. 1 in this volume). He distinguishes reason-categoric, object-categoric, and response-categoric virtues, depending on the basis of classification under these three headings; and this taxonomy, though intended as applicable to moral virtues, apparently accommodates what I call cross-over virtues.

more normative reasons. Since virtues have beneficiaries or at least proper aims—either *beings* whose good is in some sense their target or *goods* they are seen as tending to realize—virtues and indeed their exercises are appraisable in terms of reasons that go with the good in question.

## 6. Objectivity, Internality, and Subjectivity

Given the normativity of the concept of a virtue—whether moral or intellectual—we should expect to encounter the question whether the concept is (in an epistemic sense) internal or external and, if internal, then subjective. The concept is internal, as I here use the term, provided the grounds for its instantiation are psychological elements in the person in question, normally elements accessible to introspection or reflection; external if these grounds are not, as with an excellence in inspiring others.[14]

A good way to pursue the question of internality versus externality is to ask, as epistemologists do with justifiedness for beliefs, whether virtues are *demon-proof*—i.e., may be possessed even in a world in which a Cartesian demon induces false beliefs about much of what one does and its effects, while giving inhabitants precisely the kinds of experiences they would have in our "normal" world. Take kindness. Can I be kind if my efforts to help those suffering cause them avoidable pain, but I don't see this because I am made to hallucinate their being relieved in just the way I intend? More concretely, suppose that after an accident I bind wounds gently and in the medically prescribed way, but the person gets infected at the sites. Or suppose my competent but ill-fated effort to repair someone's flat tire results in a crash after a few miles when the car is out of sight. My own reaction to these cases is to call them *star-crossed virtues* but virtues nevertheless. The agent should get credit for doing, for the right reasons, all one could reasonably expect.

This demon-proof character does not belong, however, to certain other virtues: if, without being interfered with, I get wrong answers to too many arithmetic problems or write too many unclear sentences, I do not have arithmetic virtue (if that isn't too narrow a trait to qualify as a virtue) or the intellectual virtue of clarity, even if I cannot be faulted for failing to prepare myself or to try to behave appropriately. It is one thing, however, to say that some virtues have external success conditions and another thing to say that

---

14 Cf. Thomas Hurka, for whom "an *internalist* view of virtue . . . holds that the value of a person's attitudes depends only on their appropriateness to his circumstances and not at all on what those circumstances are" (Hurka 2001, 117). Here "The moral virtues are those attitudes to goods and evils that are intrinsically good, and the moral vices are those attitudes that are morally bad" (20). My view differs in not giving attitudes the broad role needed for them to have the comprehensiveness and stability of virtues as I see them, and my conception of internality does not even presuppose that the person in question has any external circumstances; but on both Hurka's and my conceptions of the internality of virtue, non-relational, psychological elements play the central normative role.

the kinds of reasons for which aretaically relevant actions succeed need not be internally accessible. We have already seen ground for thinking that our reasons for virtuous action, say our sense of need to treat a wound we can properly treat, are internally accessible. External forces may prevent my knowing about an undiscovered allergy to the antiseptic I deem necessary, but they do not block my having a good reason in terms of the apparent curative value of the antiseptic and the obligating ground for my actions.

If, however, we affirm the internal accessibility of normative reasons, does that commit us to subjectivism? It may seem so, but the requirement that reasons be internally accessible does not imply that the standards for appraising their content are not objective and cross-culturally "valid." This is not to deny that some virtues, though not merely powers, do require a certain kind of objective success. Consider clarity, which is a virtue of expression in speaking and writing. This entails a power to communicate, but is not merely that, and its achievement requires a certain level of avoidance of vagueness and, especially, ambiguity. The point can also be seen in certain moral virtues. Take trustworthiness. Suppose the demon gives me excellent evidence of my doing what I must to keep my promises, but I have not kept them. I do not think I can then be said to be trustworthy, though I would deserve credit for trying and indeed for responding to the signs of need for my performances. Trustworthiness and other virtues that require achieving objectively correct results a significant proportion of the time entail powers but are not reducible to them.

We must, then, distinguish both between virtues and powers and also between virtues that are internal—in being possible even in a demon world—and those that entail a power in such a way that they must be conceived as partly external. Trustworthiness regarding promised deeds, for instance, like wisdom related to the content of judgment, requires an appropriate degree of external success. To be sure, even for virtues that are internal, the *criteria* for their possession are external in the sense that they are not derived from such internal variable states as desires or beliefs. On a desire-satisfaction view of the good, for instance, virtue would be understood in terms of actual satisfaction of the (non-instrumental) desires of the agent or those the agent interacts with or both. To be beneficent, for instance, would depend on what happens to be desired by the beneficiary.

Similarly, one could think that true virtue consists in an internalized tendency to follow one's conscience. It is indeed by and large true that virtuous agents strongly tend to follow their conscience in many kinds of actions. But conscience need have no external standards (beyond consistency, I assume). The kind of internality appropriate to certain virtues derives from the internality belonging to the notion of justification; for justified belief, in ways we have illustrated, is a necessary and major element both in the basis of agents' decisions regarding what to judge and to do and in their appraisal of their success.

Aretaic internality, then, is broadly epistemic and does not imply subjectivity or the relativity in normative matters that goes with it. Even excusability is internal without being subjective. If a beneficent surgeon makes a well justified but fatal decision to operate rather than rely on drugs, the action may yet be excusable, even justified in the aretaically crucial sense. We may pity the surgeon but can see that he acted as he should. The relevant kind of excusability and justification are objectively grounded, though justification is not truth-entailing, as is knowledge, which on that count is external.

The difference between subjectivity and internality can also be illustrated by the notion, prominent in Kant's *Groundwork*, of treating persons as ends.[15] One's evidence that an act is for the good of the other must be objective and, even if not conclusive, relevant to achieving some good for the other; but one may be excusable for failure when no better evidence could be expected to have guided action. The notion of end-regarding treatment is also mixed in the way trustworthiness is: we cannot achieve such treatment without both acting for the right kind of reason, roughly one of beneficence, and having a significantly high ratio of successes to failures (in contributing to the good of the others in question), just as we are not trustworthy in a given domain if we are motivated wholly by self-interest or there is no high objective probability of success in our performing the deeds entrusted to us.

If there is any commonly recognized virtue that manifests itself distinctively in treating persons as ends—end-regarding treatment—it is beneficence, but with a proviso. Beneficence as a virtue—rather than as just a stable behavior pattern—must be taken to imply a good measure of altruism, where this is roughly a trait constituted largely by suitably often doing things for others *for their sake*. Thus, a saint could be beneficent in doing, for the glory of God, good deeds for others; but this does not entail altruism, even if the behavioral implications of the two traits, given a plausible theology (or at least the saint's) never diverge. On my view, you cannot treat someone as an end unless you care about the good of the person for the *person's* sake and, in addition, this is at least a main reason why you do what you do. You need not, however, conceive the good of the other under that normative description. It is enough, for example, to be reducing the other's suffering for the other's sake. But suppose I am completely wrong about what will reduce your suffering and I put you through terrible pain in the misguided attempt to help you. If my evidence is good, I can certainly be *trying* to treat you as an end, but I do not succeed. The end-regarding beneficence in question, then, is normatively mixed, having both internal and external realization requirements.

---

15 That some such notion is important in Kant's *Groundwork* is not controversial, but the notion is difficult to capture. A detailed account that treats the notion largely independently of Kant (but without losing contact with his work) is provided by Part Two of Audi (2016).

Even in a demon world, one could have star-crossed beneficence with all the steadfastness and interpersonal expression one might hope for. To be sure, if the agent discovered the backfires in which the would-be beneficiary suffered as a result of the agent's false beliefs, there would have to be an appropriately corrective response. But a demon could also induce false beliefs about the success of would-be corrections. We might then continue to speak of star-crossed virtue, and even that is in one way admirable and has some inherent worth. Given removal of the cognitive blockage, it will yield the normal desirable results and thereby serve goodness.

For Aristotle and for many other philosophers, virtue is important as essential for the good life. For him, moreover, genuine flourishing—as actively leading a good life—requires a high level of virtue, indeed (on his unity of the virtues view) realizing all the virtues. There is dispute about the extent to which his view allows for degrees of excellence and, correspondingly, of flourishing. On my view, there are both degrees and levels of flourishing. Both bear on differences among kinds of good lives. There are at least three pertinent points implicit in our discussion.

First, even if a good life is not possible for someone with moral vices, it is possible, even if the *best* possible life is not, without having (as a perfectionist might require for a good life) *all* the virtues to the highest degree, and it may be possible for someone who, for some fields of virtue, such as courage, is neither virtuous nor vicious. A good life might not have the appropriate challenges that call for manifesting courage, and a person who is neither courageous nor cowardly could manage ordinary difficulties with conscientious efforts. Second, this pluralism about kinds and degrees of virtue in good lives applies perhaps more obviously to intellectual virtues. Insightfulness and rigor may enhance any life; but merely lacking them leaves room for many other virtues and much enjoyment. Third, none of these points implies that the good life is *conceptually* independent of virtue. It surely cannot be conceived wholly apart from the exercise of virtue as, to some extent, a constitutive element in any good life and as essential in any life truly admirable as one of excellence.[16]

## 7. Conclusion

Virtues and reasons are, in ways we have seen, interconnected. The former require a major role for the latter; but a virtue does not, and perhaps cannot, effectively play the role in guiding the thoughts and actions that express that virtue unless it is internally empowered by the cognitive and motivational

---

[16] For Zagzebski, "A *good life* (a desirable life, a life of well-being) is a life desired by admirable persons" (2013, 202). The parenthesized gloss leaves room for degrees, nor need a kind of life desired by all admirable persons be the only such kind or the kind most desired.

elements, above all desires and beliefs, by which it is at least largely constituted. Those elements, including, perhaps most importantly, a person's framework beliefs and deepest desires, empower thought and action and supply reasons—propositions in the case of beliefs and projected states of affairs in the case of the motivational elements—that go with the telos, the "aim," as it were, of the virtue.

Whether or not reasons are normatively fundamental or can be accounted for in terms of, say, reflecting values by being, roughly, valuing-promoting considerations (a matter left open here), it appears that reasons are conceptually, normatively, and psychologically more basic than virtues. The main conceptual point here is that we cannot explicate virtues apart from appeal to the kinds of reasons for which their genuine exercises must occur, but one need not—even if one can—explicate normative reasons by appeal to the virtues specially related to them. The main normative point here is that one cannot determine what we ought and ought not to do wholly by considering virtues in isolation from reasons for action. Determining moral obligation apparently requires determining what constitutes (moral) reasons for action and doing so in a way that need not proceed through an independent analysis of virtue. The main psychological point implicit in what we have seen is that, at least for moral virtues, we cannot understand what constitutes them as traits of character apart from positing longstanding and stable sets of wants and beliefs—psychological elements which can explain action and whose contents include reasons for action.

This third point does not hold, at least to the same degree, for intellectual virtues, particularly as applied to motivation as opposed to cognition. Our intellectual virtue depends far less on what we want than does our moral virtue, and arguably intellectual virtue is compatible with weak or even corrupted motivation of certain kinds. The overall view taken in this paper is connected both with epistemological points, such as those indicating how one can know that a person has a virtue, with ontological points connected with what psychological properties ground virtues, and with developmental points indicating how virtue is to be role modeled if it is to be well taught. None of this implies that virtues are of secondary importance in ethical or intellectual matters, nor even that, apart from having virtue, human beings can be relied on to act morally across time and with changing circumstances. Whether or not virtues are fundamental in one or another philosophically interesting way, they are theoretically important in philosophy and morally and intellectually essential in human existence.[17]

---

17 This paper is a much revised version of "Role Models, Reasons, and Virtues" presented at the Australian Catholic University's international conference on Reasons and Virtues in 2015. It has benefited from discussion at the conference and, especially, from a commentary by Garrett Cullity, and from previous work of mine (on which it draws), most notably Audi (forthcoming).

# References

Annas, Julia. 2011. *Intelligent Virtue*. Oxford: Oxford University Press.
Anscombe, G. E. M. 1958. "Modern Moral Philosophy." *Philosophy* 33 (124): 1–19.
Audi, Robert. 1989. "Internalism and Externalism in Moral Epistemology." *Logos* 10: 13–37.
———. 1995. "Acting from Virtue." *Mind* 104: 449–71.
———. 1997. *Moral Knowledge and Ethical Character*. New York and Oxford: Oxford University Press.
———. 2016. *Means, Ends, and Persons: The Meaning and Psychological Dimensions of Kant's Humanity Formula*. New York and Oxford: Oxford University Press.
———. Forthcoming. "Role Modeling and Reasons: Developmental and Normative Grounds of Moral Virtues." *Journal of Moral Philosophy*.
Battaly, Heather and Michael Slote. 2015. "Virtue Epistemology and Virtue Ethics." In *The Routledge Companion to Virtue Ethics*, edited by Lorraine Besser-Jones and Michael Slote, 253–69. New York: Routledge.
Davidson, Donald. 1980. "The Logical Form of Action Sentences." In his *Essays on Actions and Events*, 105–48. Oxford: Oxford University Press.
Greco, John, ed. 2004. *Ernest Sosa and His Critics*. Oxford: Blackwell.
———. 2010. *Achieving Knowledge*. Cambridge: Cambridge University Press.
Hooker, Brad. 2000. *Ideal Code, Real World*. Oxford: Oxford University Press.
Hurka, Thomas. 2001. *Virtue, Vice, and Value*. Oxford: Oxford University Press.
Montmarquet, James. 1993. *Epistemic Virtue and Doxastic Responsibility*. Lanham: Rowman and Littlefield.
Oesterly, John A., trans. 1966. *Treatise on the Virtues*. Notre Dame: University of Notre Dame Press.
Pinsent, Andrew. 2015. "Aquinas: Infused Virtues." In *The Routledge Companion to Virtue Ethics*, edited by Lorraine Besser-Jones and Michael Slote, 141–53. New York: Routledge.
Ross, W. D. 1930. *The Right and the Good*. Oxford: Oxford University Press.
Sosa, Ernest. 2007. *A Virtue Epistemology*. Oxford: Oxford University Press.
———. 2011. *Knowing Full Well*. Oxford: Oxford University Press.
Upton, Candace. 2015. "The Empirical Argument against Virtue Ethics." *Journal of Ethics* 20 (4): 354–71.
Zagzebski, Linda. 1996. *Virtues of the Mind*. Cambridge: Cambridge University Press.
———. 2013. "Moral Exemplars in Theory and Practice." *Theory and Research in Education* 11 (2): 193–206.

# Part III
# Specific Virtues for Finite Rational Agents

# 8 Practical Wisdom
## A Virtue for Resolving Conflicts among Practical Reasons

*Andrés Luco*

### 1. Introduction: The Plurality of Reasons

There are reasons that explain or motivate actions, and there are reasons that *justify* actions. The latter are known as *normative* reasons for action—or, normative practical reasons. Normative practical reasons are facts or considerations which contribute to the justification of an action. In Scanlon's phrase, a normative practical reason "counts in favor" of an action (Scanlon 1998, 17). A normative practical reason, or set of such reasons, may *favor* an action by supporting the judgment that the action *should/ought to be performed*. Conversely, a normative practical reason, or set of such reasons, may also *disfavor* an action by supporting the judgment that the action *should/ought not be performed*. The following is a discussion of normative practical reasons, which I will frequently abbreviate for convenience as "reasons."

Sometimes, normative practical reasons conflict. That is, there are some situations where there is a normative reason that favors doing some action, but there is also another normative reason that disfavors this action. There may be simultaneous reasons to go *and* not to go to a party that John will attend. If John is a mean person who I expect will insult me, this may be a reason I shouldn't go to the party. On the other hand, if everyone else at the party is kind and friendly towards me, this may be a reason I should go to the party.

Normative practical reasons are said to have varying degrees of *strength* or *weight*. Strength is a feature which enables us to resolve some conflicts among normative practical reasons. A reason (or set of reasons) in favor of doing some action may be stronger, or weaker, than a reason (or set of reasons) that would disfavor the same action. When all relevant reasons have been considered, an agent ought to do what he or she has the strongest normative reason(s) to do. Although John's unfriendliness may be a reason not to go to the party, I may have a *stronger* reason to go to the party based on the fact that I will be able to strengthen valuable bonds with many other party-goers who are friendly. In that case, assuming all relevant reasons have been considered, I should go to the party.

However, there are occasions where it appears difficult, if not impossible, to resolve conflicts among reasons by comparing the relative strengths of the reasons. It can be difficult, if not impossible, to determine whether I should donate an additional 1 percent of my income to fight world poverty, or instead spend that money on luxuries for my own enjoyment. Likewise, it can be difficult, if not impossible, to tell whether I should blow the whistle on corrupt activities going on in my workplace, or else remain silent and protect my job security.

There is a theory of practical rationality which purports to explain such seemingly irresolvable conflicts among reasons. This theory is known as *reasons pluralism*, and it comprises two central claims (cf. Copp 2009):

### Reasons Pluralism

(1) There is a plurality of different types of normative reasons; and
(2) the strengths of normative reasons of different types are *not rationally comparable*.[1]

From these claims, it follows that no normative reason of one type is stronger or weaker than any normative reason of another type. It is not even the case that a normative reason of one type is *equally* as strong as a normative reason of a different type.

Reasons pluralism is plausible, since it gives a compelling explanation for why it can be so hard to arrive at well-justified verdicts about what one ought to do when normative practical reasons conflict. Another not-so-obvious attraction of reasons pluralism is that it reveals an alternative way to adjudicate conflicts among normative practical reasons, apart from comparing the relative strengths of the reasons.

Given that reasons pluralism is a plausible theory of practical reason, it's worth addressing some of its potential difficulties. One potential problem with reasons pluralism is the worry that in *any* situation where different types of normative practical reasons conflict, there is no way to resolve such conflicts by arriving at a final, all-things-considered judgment about what the agent ought to do. Conflicts among different types of practical reasons seem quite commonplace, however, and it may be dubious to suggest that irresolvable conflicts among reasons are so widespread.

---

1 I shall follow Ruth Chang in drawing a distinction between *incomparability* and *incommensurability*. According to Chang, "two items are *incommensurable* just in case they cannot be put on the same scale of units of value, that is, there is no cardinal unit of measure that can represent the value of both items." By contrast, "two items are *incomparable* just in case they fail to stand in an evaluative comparative relation, such as being better than or worse than or equally good as the other" (Chang 2015, 205). Incommensurability does not entail incomparability, but incomparability does entail incommensurability (Chang 2015, 207; see also Chang 2016).

In this essay, I attempt to show that reasons pluralism does not imply that *all* conflicts among normative reasons of different types are irresolvable. On the contrary, I will argue that reasons pluralism is compatible with what I call the *Override Principle*. The Override Principle suggests that some normative practical reasons can *override* other conflicting reasons, even when the strengths of the reasons in question are not rationally comparable. Thus, apart from one reason being stronger (or weightier) than another reason, an additional way a normative practical reason may take priority over another one is by overriding it. Accordingly, the Override Principle illuminates another way to arrive at warranted verdicts about which of two or more conflicting reasons should guide our actions. It serves to dispel the worry that reasons pluralism overestimates the extent to which conflicts among reasons are irresolvable.

In the following, I'll present a rationale for the Override Principle. This rationale draws on Aristotle's conception of practical wisdom. I'll suggest that the virtue of practical wisdom, as Aristotle construed it, is needed to recognize different types of rationally incomparable reasons which correspond to different types of rationally incomparable goods. A practically wise agent would pattern her actions in such a way that she is as responsive as possible to all normative reasons she encounters. The Override Principle is one principle by which an agent with practical wisdom can make her actions fully responsive to all the normative practical reasons that apply to her. In section 2 below, I will identify some considerations in support of the reasons-pluralist claim that normative practical reasons of different types are not rationally comparable. My objective is not to provide a complete argument for reasons pluralism, but only to show that it is a plausible enough view to be worth defending against a particularly salient objection—namely, the objection that reasons pluralism wrongly implies that *all* conflicts among reasons of different types are irresolvable. In section 3, I introduce the Override Principle to show that even given reasons pluralism, it is possible to resolve some conflicts among reasons of different types. In section 4, I illustrate some applications of the Override Principle, and address a number of objections against it. Finally, in section 5, I discuss some refinements to the Override Principle that could be made from the perspective of either satisficing or maximizing/perfectionist theories of practical reason.

## 2. Conflicts between Rationally Incomparable Reasons

We've seen that normative practical reasons can sometimes conflict. In some of those cases of conflict, the strengths of the reasons in question may not be rationally comparable. Take, for instance, the conflict between a normative practical reason that I might have to spend an additional 1 percent of my income on luxuries I enjoy, versus another normative reason I might have to donate that extra 1 percent of my income to reduce death and suffering wrought by extreme poverty. If these reasons could be compared in terms of their strength, then the normative reason favoring a charitable donation would surely be, for the reasons I indicate below, stronger than the reason to buy luxuries.

Much of what follows will discuss our reasons to buy luxuries. I will adhere to the conventional definition of a "luxury." A *luxury* is something that adds to a person's comfort or enjoyment, but is not a necessity of life.[2] Life's necessities are goods necessary for a decent life. Food, medicine, and shelter are obvious examples of necessities. Goods needed for adequate social integration, such as conventionally acceptable clothing, may also be necessities of life.

Donating money that I would otherwise spend on luxuries could, in the long run, have life-saving effects on many people (cf. Singer 2010, 2015; MacAskill 2015). Even by spending only a small portion of my income on luxuries throughout my lifetime, I may be foregoing opportunities to prevent the deaths of scores of other human beings. Indeed, after reviewing the statistical evidence of the impact of several highly effective anti-poverty charities, Peter Singer concludes in *The Life You Can Save* that "the cost of saving a life through one of these charities is somewhere between $200 and $2,000 [USD]" (Singer 2010, 103). By comparison, being able to enjoy luxuries is hardly a matter of life or death. Luxuries are unlikely to have a positive impact on many people other than myself, and perhaps a few of my closest contacts. Furthermore, although I may well lose many significant life-enhancing goods if I went without any luxuries, these losses are meager when set against the poverty-induced loss of life and health in dozens of other people. The fact that I could alleviate the most devastating effects of poverty for many others by donating to effective charities seems to ground extremely strong reasons in favor of donating. On the other hand, my reason to instead spend the money on luxuries, and thereby enjoy the comforts and pleasures that luxuries bring, seems feeble by comparison.

And yet, the considerations above do not seem to establish conclusively that I ought to donate an extra 1 percent increment of my income to fight world poverty. Indeed, no matter how strong my reason to donate might be, it may still be the case that I should buy more luxuries instead, just by virtue of the beneficial impact luxuries have on *my own life*. In other words, the comforts and pleasures that luxuries bring *me* may ground normative reasons to buy more luxuries, and it may be the case that I ought to act on those reasons *in spite of* any greater benefits that I would fail to generate for others by not donating my money. For having some luxuries, as opposed to little or none, does seem essential to a *flourishing* life, even though luxuries are not essential to having a *decent* life. Indeed, it's hard to imagine a flourishing life that contained only scant few luxuries. For instance, a life

2 *Merriam-Webster Dictionary*, s.v. "luxury." Accessed August 3, 2016. http://www.merriam-webster.com/dictionary/luxury.

devoid of any deep engagements with music would seem to lack an important element of enrichment. Imagine a person who would appreciate music just as much as most people do, if she had encountered it, but who never had so much as an opportunity to play a musical instrument, never had the chance to attend a concert, never listened to a musical recording, nor even had occasion to listen to music that happened to catch her ear in the ambient environment. Such a person may be able to lead a *decent* life. But it is doubtful that she could have a *flourishing* life. So apparently we do need *some* luxuries to flourish. From this it evidently follows that we have strong normative reasons to acquire *some* luxuries. To be sure, there may be uncertainty and variation regarding the *amount* of luxury items an individual has strong reasons to obtain. It's a sensible conjecture, though, that the welfare of most people would be severely encumbered if they could not have some luxuries on a regular basis.

The point here is that strong normative reasons to donate an increment of my income conflict with strong normative reasons to spend that income on luxuries. And the task of discerning which reasons should ultimately guide our action cannot be based solely on a comparison of the relative strengths of the reasons in conflict. As I've argued, if a rational comparison could be made between the relative strengths of reasons to buy luxuries and reasons to donate to effective charities, then we should always opt to donate. But that seems not to be the case: even in the face of extraordinarily strong reasons to donate, it seems that *in some circumstances*, we should spend some money on luxuries for ourselves.

The contention made up to this point is that conflicting normative practical reasons sometimes cannot be rationally compared in terms of their relative strengths. Reasons pluralism offers a plausible explanation for this: namely, that there are different types of normative practical reasons which are grounded in different facts or considerations. And furthermore, the considerations that ground the different types of normative reasons are not rationally comparable. The conflict between my reasons to buy luxuries and my reasons to donate is an example. As I've suggested, the basis of my normative reasons to buy luxuries seems focused on *my own benefit*, as opposed to the benefit of others. There is reason for me to buy more luxuries, because having some luxuries makes *my* life go better than it otherwise would. And it seems this reason to purchase more luxuries is no less strong, if the purchase requires me to forego an opportunity to benefit many others in poverty. Thus, the reason to buy more luxuries is a member of a type of normative practical reasons grounded in a partial concern for one's own well-being. Following Kurt Baier, we can call these *self-anchored* reasons (Baier 1995).

At the same time, the basis of my normative reason to make a charitable donation has to do with the good of *others*, and *not* my own good. The potentially life-saving effects of a charitable donation ground very strong reasons to donate for the benefit of others. There are normative reasons to donate to charity instead of buying more luxuries, because I could produce greater benefits for others with the money I donate. And the strength of these reasons to donate would not seem to be diminished in any appreciable way, even if making the donation involves a foregone opportunity to acquire more luxuries for myself. A reason to buy a designer jacket does not undercut a reason to make a life-saving donation. Thus, we find that another type of normative reason for action is grounded in an impartial appreciation of the benefits or harms that an action brings to all affected persons. They are reasons that can only be recognized from "the point of view of the Universe," to echo Sidgwick's famous line (Sidgwick 1907, 382). We can call them *impartial reasons*, because they prescribe treating the good of one individual as having no greater or lesser intrinsic value than the good of another.

Impartial reasons are grounded in the point of view of the Universe. But this point of view excludes a partial concern for one's own well-being. A partial concern for one's own well-being is the ground of self-anchored reasons. Therefore, in light of the points made so far in this section, impartial reasons and self-anchored reasons are two different types of normative reasons, and their relative strengths are rationally incomparable.

Thus far I've outlined a few points to motivate reasons pluralism. Now we confront a problem raised by reasons pluralism. Suppose that reasons pluralism is true: i.e., there is a plurality of types of normative practical reasons, and the relative strengths of reasons of these different types are not rationally comparable. Does it follow that whenever someone faces a conflict between reasons of different types, there is no fact of the matter about what one ought to do, all things considered? This would be a troubling and dubious consequence. For it seems that there are numerous cases of such conflict. Furthermore, moral philosophers have devoted considerable energy to arguing that there is a correct way to resolve these conflicts. Consider once again the tension between doing what benefits yourself versus doing what benefits others. Or the dilemma between doing what is best for your loved ones versus what is best for society as a whole. Or, in general, any case in which doing what is morally right is burdensome for the actor. These situations are familiar, and they've commanded the attention of moral philosophers for thousands of years. Think of the debate between Socrates and Glaucon in Book 2 of Plato's *Republic*. If reasons pluralism is true, would we be forced to admit that difficult conflicts among reasons bear no resolution? Has so much of the tradition of moral philosophy been effort wasted?

In section 3 below, I'll argue that reasons pluralism can support the idea that when we face a conflict between reasons of rationally incomparable strengths, we can still arrive at well-founded judgments about what we ought to do. In some situations where normative reasons of different types conflict, normative reasons of one type may *override* normative reasons of another type. A normative reason of one type *overrides* a normative reason of another type when, all things considered, the agent ought to act in accordance with that reason and not the other. I will explain in the next section how in some instances, reasons of one type can override reasons of another type, in spite of the fact that they have rationally incomparable strengths.

## 3. The Override Principle

According to the proposal I shall defend, normative practical reasons of different types can override one another, in spite of the fact that the strengths of different types of reasons are rationally incomparable. The proposal, which I call the Override Principle, may be articulated as follows:

*The Override Principle*

Let $\{R_A\}$ be a set of normative practical reasons of type A. Let $\{R_B\}$ be another set of normative practical reasons of another type B. Suppose that $\{R_A\}$ favors doing φ, while $\{R_B\}$ favors doing ψ instead of φ.

Then:

$\{R_A\}$ overrides $\{R_B\}$ if

i. acting in accordance with $\{R_A\}$, rather than $\{R_B\}$, is necessary to promote some good that corresponds to $\{R_A\}$;

*and*

ii. not acting in accordance with $\{R_B\}$ does not involve the loss of any goods corresponding to $\{R_B\}$.

Note: Conditions (i) and (ii) are meant to be jointly sufficient conditions, but *not necessary* conditions, for $\{R_A\}$ to override $\{R_B\}$.

Again, one normative practical reason *overrides* another when—all things considered—it is the former reason that ought to guide the agent's action. In my usage, "overriding" reasons are reasons that provide sufficient justification for final, or all-things-considered, judgments about what one ought to do. Accordingly, if reason A overrides reason B, then it is conclusively the case that reason A, and not reason B, should guide the relevant agent's action.

I offer a virtue-ethical rationale for the Override Principle. The relevant virtue is practical wisdom, as Aristotle conceived it. In *Nicomachean Ethics* VI, Aristotle characterizes practical wisdom (*"phronêsis"*) as an intellectual virtue which enables its possessor to deliberate about his or her ends in such a way that achieving those ends will bring about a flourishing life (cf. *Nicomachean Ethics* 1140a25–9). As Daniel C. Russell interprets him, Aristotle understands practical wisdom to involve "a global understanding of the human good" (Russell 2012, 208). With this global understanding, a practically wise agent grasps "what is beneficial in all areas of human action," and then cultivates virtues needed to acquire human goods (Russell

2012, 215). Accordingly, on this Aristotelian view, every virtue requires practical wisdom (Russell 2012, 208–13).

Like Aristotle, I take practical wisdom to be a virtue that inclines its possessor to have a global appreciation of various goods, and to successfully pursue goods in a holistic way. For every good, there is a corresponding *pro tanto* normative practical reason that favors doing whatever would promote that good.[3] Therefore, practical wisdom is the virtue that involves a sensitivity to the normative practical reasons corresponding to human goods.

The Override Principle is a plausible criterion of rational action, I argue, because adherence to it is something that practical wisdom would demand. A practically wise agent would order her ends into a coherent system that allows for the attainment of many and varied goods. The Override Principle must be one ordering principle that the practically wise would follow, since it would prescribe that agents keep up a practice of pursuing a good whenever one finds oneself in a situation where the good could not be attained by doing anything else (condition (i)), and there would be no loss of any other good in the pursuit (condition (ii)).

I'll now discuss a relatively simple example to illustrate how the Override Principle can be applied. Suppose I could either act on a normative practical reason that favors pursuing a career in philosophy, which I find most fulfilling, or instead act on a normative reason to pursue a more profitable career in banking so that I could better support my family. Referring back to the Override Principle, let us say that the first reason substitutes for $R_A$ and the second reason substitutes for $R_B$. The reason to pursue a philosophy career ($R_A$) might correspond to the good that inheres in philosophical inquiry. It might also correspond to the good of taking on an autonomously chosen career path. On the other hand, the reason which favors pursuing a career in banking ($R_B$) might correspond to an affiliative good—i.e., the good that inheres in serving the welfare of my loved ones.

The reasons in question conflict with respect to which career I should go after. They are both strong reasons, because they both correspond to very important goods. However, it is difficult, if not impossible, to adjudicate which of these reasons should guide my actions. A reasons pluralist could take this difficulty to be evidence that the two reasons are of different types, and that the strengths of the two reasons are not rationally comparable. How, then, might the reasons pluralist suggest that I negotiate these conflicting reasons? Does reasons pluralism allow for a warranted all-things-considered verdict about what I ought to do, despite the incomparability of the reasons in conflict?

---

3 Here I need not commit myself to any thesis about whether goods are ontologically more fundamental than reasons, or *vice versa*. The claim that for every good there is a corresponding *pro tanto* reason to promote that good may be true if normative reasons are ontologically grounded in goods, and it may also be true if goods are ontologically grounded in normative reasons.

Here the Override Principle clears a way forward. A decision not to act in accordance with the reason to pursue a career in banking ($R_B$) would satisfy condition (ii) of the Override Principle. As long as I secure employment as a professional philosopher, this career choice wouldn't involve the loss of the affiliative good of serving the welfare of my family. It turns out that I'm fortunate enough to inhabit a society in which there are avenues for people to make a decent living as a philosopher. Professional philosophers have found ways to provide for their families while leading a life of philosophical contemplation.

Additionally, a decision to act in accordance with the reasons to pursue a career in philosophy ($R_A$) would satisfy condition (i) of the Override Principle. Pursuing a career in philosophy is *necessary* for attaining the goods that inhere in philosophical inquiry. Most philosophers will tell you that doing philosophy well requires a huge investment of one's intellectual energy. It also requires extended debate and dialogue among colleagues. The value inherent in philosophical activity could not be effectively attained, unless some people devoted most of their waking hours to it, and unless those who do that also have opportunities to share their work. In other words, the value in philosophical activity could not be realized unless there were a set of institutions, positions, and opportunities that make up the philosophical profession.

In light of the above, the Override Principle would suggest that my reason to pursue a career in philosophy overrides my reason to become an investment banker. Thus, when presented with conflicting reasons to choose one career versus the other, I ought to choose the philosophy career. (And thank goodness for that!) The main thought behind the Override Principle is that normative reasons to perform actions necessary to acquire certain goods (e.g., pursuing a philosophy career to acquire the goods inherent in doing philosophy) may override other reasons to perform other actions (e.g., pursuing a career in investment banking), provided that the goods associated with those other actions (e.g., caring for my family's welfare) can still be attained.

## 4. The Override Principle and the Demands of Morality

Considered in the abstract, the Override Principle may seem uninterestingly obvious. If you could do something necessary to promote some good without losing any other good, *of course* you should do it! But reflection on concrete cases will reveal that matters are not so obvious, and quite interesting. By exploring more complex examples, we can learn more about the potential applications and the limitations of Override Principle. In this section, I'll highlight the way in which the Override Principle offers a normative standard for balancing one's own self-interest against the good of others. I'll also explain how the Override Principle guides judgments about how to proceed when one could bring about great benefits to distant strangers, but at the cost of withholding relatively modest benefits to one's own family, community, or nation.

My examples will focus on potential conflicts between taking care of oneself or "one's own," and the high level of charitable giving prescribed by the effective altruism movement (see Carey 2015). I'll conclude that the Override Principle sometimes permits, or even requires, strong impartial engagement in alleviating the suffering of distant strangers.

Let's return to the dilemma between buying more luxuries and donating more to charity. It was already observed that people generally need *some* luxuries to lead a flourishing life. But how many luxuries are needed to flourish? And, is the amount of luxury items needed to flourish compatible with promoting other important goods, such as the survival, health, and flourishing of other people mired in extreme poverty? As leaders of the effective altruism movement have shown, many people can consume only a modest amount of luxuries while happily and energetically donating substantial proportions of their incomes to charity (see especially Singer 2015, chs. 3–6). Furthermore, recent research on the psychology of giving suggests that human beings typically draw great pleasure and happiness from helping others, whereas the psychological rewards that luxury items generate are surprisingly small by comparison (Singer 2015, ch. 9). All this goes to show that most affluent-world people could give a much larger part of their incomes to charity, while enjoying a supply of luxuries adequate to fulfill their needs for pleasure, comfort, fun, and self-cultivation. Therefore, for most people in affluent countries, a decision not to act in accordance with one's reasons to buy more luxuries, and instead donating more of one's income, would satisfy condition (ii) of the Override Principle.

On the other hand, the Override Principle may very well imply that there are overriding reasons to donate a large portion of one's income to fighting extreme poverty and other catastrophic forms of suffering. As Peter Singer has convincingly argued, global disparities in wealth are so great, and the deprivation suffered by the world's 1.4 billion extremely poor people so lethal, that a middle-income adult living in an affluent country has the power to save lives at only a minor cost to herself (Singer 2010, ch. 6). In *The Life You Can Save*, Singer surveys the activities of a number of effective charities that do life-saving work in less-developed countries (Singer 2010). For instance, Population Services International endeavors to stem the spread of HIV and malaria by selling condoms and bed nets at a nominal cost. Charity *evaluators* such as GiveWell and The Life You Can Save offer the vital service of estimating how much of an impact a donation to various charities can be expected to make in alleviating poverty and disease. These organizations also identify the most effective charities through rigorous evidence-backed assessments. Relying on GiveWell's analyses and others, Singer concludes that "we can reasonably believe that the cost of saving a life through one of these charities is somewhere between $200 and $2000 [in USD]" (Singer 2010, 103). Preventing loss of life is surely a good that we have reason to pursue. Moreover, this is a good that would not be attainable if people in affluent countries didn't donate much more money to effective charities than they currently do. Hence, a decision to act in accordance with one's reasons to save lives by donating to effective charities would satisfy condition (i) of the Override Principle. Ultimately, if we focus on the conflict between reasons to donate more and reasons to buy more luxuries, reasons to donate more satisfy both conditions of the Override Principle. The Override Principle would suggest that average-income inhabitants of wealthy lands can have overriding normative practical reasons to donate considerably more to life-saving charities.

However, the Override Principle would not require impartial benevolence in all situations where one's helpful action could benefit suffering strangers more than one could benefit oneself or one's own. Instead, the Principle may be construed as a specification of an idea that Garrett Cullity introduced in his book, *The Moral Demands of Affluence* (2004). Cullity identifies a set of *intrinsically life-enhancing goods* which include "friendship, achievements in the pursuit of worthwhile personal projects, and involvement in the life of one's community." An important feature of some intrinsically life-enhancing goods is that they are "goods the possession of which essentially involves attitudes of personal partiality" (2004, 129). This means that some life-enhancing goods cannot be possessed, unless the possessor has a special practical concern for his or her own personal relationship to those goods. You cannot participate in the life of your community, unless *you* personally take part in the customs and practices of *your* community. You cannot have a friendship, unless *you* take special care to play a positive role in the life of *your* friends. Hereafter, I'll refer to intrinsically life-enhancing goods whose possession requires attitudes of personal partiality as *partial goods*. Partial goods may be contrasted with *impartial goods*—goods that can exist without anyone having a special practical concern for their personal relationship to them. Life, happiness, and the reduction of suffering are paradigms of impartial goods. It can, for instance, be good that someone's suffering is alleviated, whether or not anyone has a special practical concern for that reduced suffering.

Cullity suggests that we may have normative practical reasons that justify the pursuit of partial goods, even when doing something else would bring about greater impartial goods. For instance, he proposes that members of affluent societies should make charitable donations up to the point that giving more would diminish their own access to partial goods (cf. Cullity 2004, ch. 8; Singer 2010, 147–48). A case can be made that having some luxuries is necessary to the attainment of certain partial goods. For example: to participate in the life of one's community, one might need to consume certain luxuries with others in order to perform convivial customs. People often cultivate friendships by accompanying each other to sports games, concerts, cinemas, museums, and pubs. In a community where people have a common practice of meeting their friends at the pub, you wouldn't be participating fully in the life of your community if you didn't occasionally go to the pub and buy a round of beers for your buddies. So, although drinking beer is a luxury, it can in some contexts be a necessary means of attaining a partial good like participating in communal life.

In line with Cullity's proposal, the Override Principle allows that reasons to pursue a partial good may override reasons to pursue great impartial goods, provided that both the conditions of the Principle hold. Suppose that you face a dilemma between buying beer for your buddies, as a necessary means of participating in the life of your community, and making a contribution to a life-saving charity project. If buying beer for your buddies really is necessary to attaining the partial good of participating in your community, then there are reasons that favor buying the beer. Moreover, these reasons would satisfy condition (i) of the Override Principle. The same reasons might satisfy condition (ii) of the Override Principle, provided that buying the beer instead of making the donation would not involve the loss of any goods associated with the donation. One way to satisfy condition (ii) would be to set an annual goal for how much you will donate to charity, and spend any amount beyond that goal on whatever you like (cf. Wise, in Carey 2015, 20). Your donations goal should be both reachable and sustainable over time. The donations should be such that they generate a maximal amount, *or* at least an adequate amount, of impartial goods that you can realistically contribute through your donations.[4]

Importantly, you should be wary of setting *too high* of a donations goal, as this might actually make you a less effective donor in the long run. Julia Wise—a leading effective altruist—recounts how she used to think of every single expenditure she made in terms of a tradeoff between her own desires and the needs of another person living in poverty somewhere else in the world. Wise usually imagined this person as a woman, and before she spent any money, she would ask herself "Did I value my new shoes more than her month's groceries? More than her children's vaccinations or school fees? Could I make that tradeoff? Sometimes I made it and felt awful afterwards." Wise now no longer makes decisions like this, simply because she could not bear to keep it up. She notes in the *Effective Altruism Handbook* that "I cannot spend the next 60 years counting dead children on every receipt. I would break" (Wise, in Carey 2015, 21). In her blog, *Giving Gladly*, Wise observed that, "Effective altruism is not about driving yourself to a breakdown. We don't need people making sacrifices that leave them drained and miserable. We need people who can walk cheerfully over the world, or at least do their damnedest" (Wise 2013). Currently, Wise and her husband spend 50 percent of their household income on charity, and spend the rest on whatever they want (Wise, in Carey 2015, 20).

It's remarkable that Wise has found a way to make tradeoffs between the partial goods that populate her life, and the impartial goods that she is in

---

4 The question of what *amounts* of the various types of goods we have normative reasons to pursue is touched upon in section 5 of this essay.

a position to create through her donations. If indeed this strategy of making an annual donations goal is a way of enabling Wise and her husband to keep up an optimally or adequately high level of charitable giving, without breaking down, then any non-donation purchases they made would not have involved a foregone opportunity to save lives and avert disease. Under these circumstances, a decision by someone like Wise to spend money on beer for her buddies, rather than donating it, would satisfy condition (ii) of the Override Principle. With conditions (i) and (ii) satisfied, as they are in the scenarios described, one may after all have overriding reasons to pursue a partial good instead of pursuing some highly significant impartial goods.

With all that said, one might worry the Override Principle is *too easy* to satisfy. The Principle would seem to imply that there are overriding reasons to pursue trivial goods when, *in a particular instance of choice*, there is no appreciable loss in the attainment of more important goods. This can be problematic when, *after a series of choices has been made*, the pursuit of the trivial goods reduces the attainment of the more important goods in the long run. For instance, suppose you spend an average of $30 per week buying beers for your friends and yourself while having a good old time at the local pub. At the same time, you maintain a goal of making regular charitable donations. Your expenditures on beers come out of the residual income you've set aside for pursuing other goods, like cultivating friendships. On first appearances, it may look as though your beer-buying habit does not undermine your effectiveness at being a charitable giver. After all, we're assuming that you are keeping up your donations goal. However, those beer expenses add up over time: at an average of $30 per week, you'll spend over $1500 per year buying beer at the pub. This amount is well within the range of a life-saving charitable donation. In other words, if you had saved that $1500 which you would have otherwise spent on beer, and donated it to an effective charity instead, the donation could have the impact of saving a life. Alternatively, a $1500 donation might have protected hundreds of people from contracting malaria, or have provided thousands of people with safe drinking water.[5] An objector may argue that the significance of consuming so much beer with your friends pales in comparison to preventing disease, dehydration, and death. Perhaps then, the Override Principle should be rejected *because* it dubiously implies that our reasons to buy weekly beers at the pub for our friends override our reasons to dramatically improve other people's lives. Reasons to pursue such comparatively trivial goods do not override reasons to secure those much more urgent goods.

If we examine things more carefully, however, the objection can be answered. The Override Principle is not so easily satisfied. All it takes to

---

[5] An excellent tool for assessing the likely consequences of a money donation to various charities is the Charity Impact Calculator maintained by The Life You Can Save: http://www.thelifeyoucansave.org/Impact-Calculator.

see this is that normative practical reasons do not only favor or disfavor individual tokens of actions, but also *patterns* of repeated actions that an agent undertakes. Let these patterns of repeated actions be called *practices*. Practices have cumulative effects over time, and oftentimes we can compare the cumulative effects of different practices. Indeed, in the light of these comparisons, we can apply the Override Principle to evaluate whether we have overriding reasons to follow one practice versus another. For example, if you had a practice of buying beers for friends that costs you $1500 per year, you could compare the impact of this practice to the impact of donating $1500 per year to an impactful charity. Now if you acted in accordance with your reasons to follow the beer-buying practice, it certainly *would* result in the loss of goods associated with donating more (viz. an extra $1500) to charity. So, condition (ii) of the Override Principle would not be satisfied. It's also doubtful that the specific practice of spending $1500 per year on beers for your buddies satisfies condition (i) of the Override Principle. Surely people can participate in communal life without drinking *that much* beer; surely people can find less expensive ways to bond with friends. When practices are incorporated into deliberations using the Override Principle, we see that the Override Principle does not imply that reasons to secure trivial goods override reasons to attain goods that are, intuitively, much more important.

One might argue that the Override Principle is inapplicable to most conflicts among normative practical reasons, since in most such conflicts either condition (i) or condition (ii) does not hold. While these cases of conflict among reasons certainly do exist, I will argue that they are not as prevalent as first appearances suggest. The Override Principle can offer practical guidance across a broad range of conflicts among reasons. For example, it often happens that someone faces a dilemma between two career options—career A and career B. And it might be true that pursuing each career is necessary to promote some type of good that could not be promoted by pursuing the other career. Consequently, if one acts in accordance with one's reasons to pursue career A, one loses the opportunity to promote goods associated with career B, and if one acts in accordance with one's reasons to pursue career B, one loses the opportunity to promote goods associated with career A. In a situation like this, it would seem that condition (ii) of the Override Principle is not met, regardless of which career is chosen. However, further analysis can reveal a way for the Override Principle to gain traction.

The choice of a career is doubtlessly an important one. The typical worker spends 80,000 hours on the job in his or her lifetime (MacAskill 2015, 12). Many people do a lot of good in the course of their careers. At the same time, whatever goods a person produces by working in their chosen career, other important goods might have been generated if one had chosen a different path. In *The Most Good You Can Do* (2015), Peter Singer describes several types of *"ethical careers."* Singer uses this term in reference to careers in which a person can wield enough resources and influence to save lives on a massive scale. One model of an ethical career is called "Earning to Give." This involves taking on a high-income career where one can earn a big salary, and thereby make larger donations to charities than one could by working in a lower-paying profession. Singer recounts the story of Matt Wage, who opted for a job on Wall Street instead of a promising career in academia. Soon after graduating university, Wage was donating a six-figure sum of money, and according to Singer, he "was on the way to saving a hundred lives . . . within the first year or two of his working life and every year thereafter" (2015, 3).

Earlier I suggested that one might have overriding reasons to take a career in philosophy, given that careers in the study and practice of philosophy are needed to facilitate the distinctive goods that philosophy has to offer. But an opportunity cost of most careers in academic philosophy is the chance to adopt one of Singer's ethical careers. Most obviously, academics earn well below the salary that people who Earn to Give make. In addition, some philosophers may have the skills to simultaneously follow another of Singer's ethical career paths: for instance, the "Advocate." Advocates are people who persuade or inspire others to make more altruistic donations (Singer 2015, 55). Singer is a philosopher who may count himself among the world's most influential advocates of effective altruism. But what of philosophers who specialize in other areas of philosophy that have little to do with practical ethics? What good does the logician, the philosopher of physics, or the meta-metaphysician do for the downtrodden peoples of the world? Although significant philosophical goods could not exist unless people embarked on careers in less socio-politically relevant branches of philosophy, it is equally true that significant goods could not be had unless more people went into ethical careers instead. Indeed, lives might have been saved, had the most renowned bimodal logician chosen an ethical career.

The question I've posed is: what practical guidance might the Override Principle give, when each of two incompatible career choices are necessary to the production of different goods? The answer, I suggest, calls for us to see that the goods that would flow from a particular individual's choice of career may be substituted by the goods created by others in the same career. It's very unlikely that every single academic philosopher (myself included) will make wholly unique contributions that no one else would make in their absence. And even if unique contributions are made, most of this work will not make a lasting, memorable impact on the field. Citation rates for philosophy articles and books are relatively low, and only a small handful of philosophers are fortunate enough to see their work become incorporated into the "canonical" literature of the discipline. In this sense, it is unlikely that an individual's choice to become a philosopher is necessary for the maintenance of goods that philosophy delivers. And in light of this, there seems to be an asymmetry in the dilemma between a philosophical career and an ethical career in Singer's sense.

While it is entirely possible that someone in an ethical career could fail to make much of a difference in terms of the good he or she does, it's less likely that this would be so. The work of people in many ethical careers cannot easily be substituted. A person in an ethical career is positioned to save and improve the lives of scores of people. Lives saved that would otherwise have been lost; suffering eased that would otherwise have continued—these are tangible, irreplaceable goods. Those who 'Earn to Give' supply cash flow to effective charities that would not be donated by someone else. Also, if someone decides not to go into an ethical career, it is unlikely that someone else is going to take on the same career and pick up the slack. Lamentably, few people aspire to ethical careers, since they can be difficult and unglamorous. Bureaucrats in anti-poverty and health institutions are not highly compensated, nor are they widely esteemed. Activists who lead charities and social change campaigns are often looked down upon as bleeding heart busybodies, or even troublemakers. Yet, Singer emphasizes these professions as precisely the areas in which people can do the most good—that is, the most *impartial* good. Further, Singer notes that people in some ethical careers do not have to be extraordinarily gifted to make a major difference. In *The Most Good You Can Do*, Singer tells the story of "Gorby," a health economist at the World Bank, who led projects that saved the World Bank $2 billion by finding more cost-effective ways to prevent unwanted pregnancies in developing countries. Gorby has pointed out that there is less competition for positions in development institutions like the World Bank, and that "one does not have to be exceptionally talented or work seventy-hour weeks in order to reach a level at which one can make a real difference" (Singer 2015, 55–56).

In sum, an ethical career can be an efficient good-making career: it can enable one to do a great deal of impartial good while placing only moderate stresses on one's time, energy, and aptitudes. This certainly isn't true of *all* ethical careers. Nevertheless, the fact that *some* such ethical careers exist has implications for the way we should deliberate about our career paths in light of the Override Principle. In the face of a dilemma between an ethical career and, say, a career in academic philosophy, the Override Principle challenges us to consider what goods we would forego creating by virtue of our choice of one career over another. The goods one wouldn't create by choosing an ethical career over a philosophy career are likely to be replaceable—i.e., others are likely to take up the slack. Meanwhile, the goods one wouldn't create by choosing a philosophy career over an ethical career are likely to be significant and non-replaceable. (And the same is undoubtedly true of other careers that don't qualify as one of Singer's ethical careers.) These considerations suggest that some goods could not exist, unless one acted in accordance with one's normative reasons to choose an ethical career. And so, reasoning by the Override Principle, there may be overriding reasons to choose an ethical career over a philosophy career.

On the other hand, there may be circumstances in which the Override Principle entails overriding reasons for some individuals to choose a philosophy career over an ethical career. And these reasons don't just apply to philosophers of exceptional genius whose work has shaped the tradition. For apart from the goods that philosophy itself can bestow, the act of going for a career that one finds most stimulating or worthwhile may generate *partial* goods. These partial goods may include the realization of *your* values and interests resulting from the choice of the career that *you* are most passionate about. They could also include the promotion of *your* sense of *self*-respect that flows from success in a career of your choice. These partial goods correspond to normative reasons that favor choosing a career as a philosopher. And those reasons may indeed be overriding, in the specific case that an aspiring philosopher reasonably anticipates that she couldn't produce any non-replaceable goods through an alternative career.

Nevertheless, the values and interests a person has at a particular time will not always establish overriding reasons to choose one career rather than another. William MacAskill, another prominent effective altruist, contends that choosing an ethical career can *transform* one's passions, interests, and values *after* one commits to it (MacAskill 2015, 150–51). MacAskill argues on the basis of an extensive psychology literature that your values and interests may be served just as well, and possibly even better, *after* choosing an ethical career than they would be served by choosing a career that you're initially more interested in or passionate about. Indeed, the lesson MacAskill draws from the "job characteristics theory" literature in psychology is that "the most consistent predictor of job satisfaction is engaging work" (MacAskill 2015, 151). Engaging work need not be work that a person was most passionate about from the start. Instead, engaging work is described as work that involves a degree of worker-independence, a sense of contributing to a complete end product, the performance of a variety of skills and activities, receiving constructive feedback, and making a positive contribution to the well-being of others ((MacAskill 2015, 151). If engagingness rather than initial passion reliably leads to job satisfaction, then for at least some individuals there would be no partial good foregone by choosing an ethical career instead of a different career that one had been more passionate about before making the career choice. In that type of case, then, partial goods would not confer overriding reasons to pursue a non-ethical career instead of an ethical career.

In some ways, the Override Principle upholds commonsense judgments about what normative reasons for action we have. Under the Principle, we may in some circumstances have overriding reasons to consume luxuries and choose the career which inspires us the most. But in other conditions, the Override Principle identifies overriding reasons to bring about considerable impartial goods while foregoing certain personal pleasures, comforts, and interests. This is an appropriate conclusion, I've argued, since practical wisdom demands an appreciation of varied kinds of rationally incomparable goods. By adhering to the Override Principle one can efficiently attain a large endowment of rationally incomparable goods. For instance: when the Override Principle directs a person to select an ethical career instead of another non-ethical career that they are more interested in at the time of selection, he or she can be expected to bring about great impartial goods through that career, while *also* developing a deep interest in the work over time. Thus, the person attains more goods than she would have attained, had she merely chosen the non-ethical career that she was most interested in at the outset.

## 5. Qualification, Refinements, and Conclusion

For all its attractions, it still has to be conceded that the Override Principle cannot rule out the possibility of genuinely unresolvable conflicts among normative practical reasons. There may be cases where acting on a given normative practical reason is necessary for the pursuit of some type of good, but taking that action eliminates the possibility of pursuing some other, incomparable type of good. In cases like this, where tradeoffs among rationally incomparable goods are inevitable, condition (ii) of the Override Principle is not fulfilled. For instance, a truly multi-talented student who wishes to embark on a career in philosophy may well be able to offer a non-replaceable contribution to philosophy scholarship, but would also be able to save scores of lives by choosing an ethical career. Suppose that the goods afforded by philosophical scholarship and the goods involved in saving lives are not rationally comparable. Given this reasonable assumption, the Override Principle would not provide guidance in the case of the multi-talented student.

However, continued inquiry may reveal that genuinely irresolvable conflicts among reasons are few and far between. To see this, we can consider how two potential refinements of the Override Principle may help to resolve conflicts among rationally incomparable reasons. First, there may be some warrant for refining the Override Principle into a satisficing principle. To *satisfice* is to seek a satisfactory or adequate result, instead of the best or maximal result.[6] A satisficing version of the Override Principle would state that normative reasons $\{R_A\}$ override reasons $\{R_B\}$ if (i) acting in accordance with $\{R_A\}$ is necessary to promote an *adequate level* of goods that correspond to $\{R_A\}$; and (ii) not acting in accordance with $\{R_B\}$ does not involve the loss of an *adequate level* of goods corresponding to $\{R_B\}$. Going by this satisficing version of the Override Principle, the multi-talented student described above may have overriding reasons to pursue a philosophy career, provided that she can make adequate non-replaceable contributions to philosophy

---

[6] For a defense of satisficing in rational choice, see Slote (1989).

scholarship *without* failing to secure an adequate level of impartial goods for the world's less fortunate. Perhaps the amount she donates from her salary, and/or the volunteer work she does in her spare time, enables her to secure that adequate level. Even if the multi-talented young student could, strictly speaking, generate more impartial goods in an ethical career, she could still satisfy condition (ii) of the satisficing Override Principle, just by virtue of meeting the threshold for an adequate provision of impartial goods.

Satisficing accounts of practical reason have their difficulties.[7] In particular, some theorists insist that a practically wise agent would aim to acquire the most goods possible. In other words, we should strive for a *maximal* endowment of goods; we shouldn't settle for whatever is merely adequate. These points invite an alternative refinement of the Override Principle: namely, a *maximizing* version. The maximizing formula of the Override Principle states that normative reasons $\{R_A\}$ override reasons $\{R_B\}$ if (i) acting in accordance with $\{R_A\}$ is necessary to promote the *maximal level of* goods that correspond to $\{R_A\}$; and (ii) not acting in accordance with $\{R_B\}$ does not involve the loss of the *maximal level* of goods corresponding to $\{R_B\}$. If the maximizing version of the Override Principle were the correct one, the problem of irresolvable conflicts among reasons would be very acute. Still, even the maximizing Override Principle may be practically relevant. Some conflicts among reasons may occur only because of background conditions that are entirely contingent. Given the background conditions, such conflicts may not be resolvable. But if the background is changed, the conflicts may become resolvable. The multi-talented student may face a tragic situation where she cannot make maximal contributions to philosophy while also pursuing a maximally impactful ethical career. Recognizing this, she may yet see a way to cut off one horn of the dilemma. Most saliently, the student might enter a philosophy career, but also champion social reforms—such as Thomas Pogges's proposed Global Resource Dividend—that would eventually put an end to extreme poverty (Pogge 2001). As a professional philosopher, she may not be able to reduce quite as much suffering as she would through an ethical career. But at least her reform efforts would work toward freeing future generations of conscientious people from the currently irresolvable dilemma between a philosophy career and ethical careers in poverty eradication. Changing the background conditions that create conflicts among reasons may be all that has to be done for a maximizing version of the Override Principle to gain relevance as a guide to action. Now if, as in the case of the multi-talented student, the agent cannot change the background conditions generating conflicts among reasons in time for her to maximize various types of goods *directly*, through *her own* action, she may still have normative reasons to bring about the conditions that would

---

7 For a thorough critique of satisficing in the framework of consequentialist ethics, see Bradley (2006).

enable *others* to maximize plural goods through *their* action at a later time. In normative ethics, non-egoist forms of maximizing consequentialism and maximizing perfectionism offer theoretical foundations for the claim that we do indeed have reasons to maximize the good, or the perfection, of all persons at all times.[8]

In the end, the plurality of reasons is so radical that it would be naive to think all conflicts among reasons can be resolved. But it should not be assumed that the Override Principle specifies the *only* conditions under which reasons of one type may override reasons of another type. For this reason, conditions (i) and (ii) of the Override Principle are jointly sufficient *but not necessary* conditions for reasons $\{R_A\}$ to override reasons $\{R_B\}$. To be sure, it is the burden of the reasons pluralist to pinpoint more ways that reasons of different types can override and be overridden. Nevertheless, the Override Principle should be recognized as one among many arrows in the practically wise agent's quiver. Although the plurality of reasons does introduce complexity into our rational decision-making, practical wisdom can serve to put the unruly house of reason in order.

# References

Aristotle. 1995. *Aristotle: Selections*. Edited by Terence Irwin and Gail Fine. Indianapolis: Hackett Publishing.
Baier, Kurt. 1995. *The Rational and the Moral Order: The Social Roots of Reason and Morality*. Chicago: Open Court.
Bradley, Ben. 2006. "Against Satisficing Consequentialism." *Utilitas* 18 (2): 97–108.
Carey, Ryan, ed. 2015. *The Effective Altruism Handbook*. Oxford: Centre for Effective Altruism.
Chang, Ruth. 2015. "Value Incomparability and Incommensurability." In *The Oxford Handbook of Value Theory*, edited by Iwao Hirose and Jonas Olson, 205–24. Oxford: Oxford University Press.
———. 2016. "Comparativism: The Grounds of Rational Choice." In *Weighing Reasons*, edited by Errol Lord and Barry Maguire, 213–40. Oxford: Oxford University Press.
Copp, David. 2009. "Toward a Pluralist and Teleological Theory of Normativity." *Philosophical Issues* 19: 21–37.
Cullity, Garrett. 2004. *The Moral Demands of Affluence*. Oxford: Oxford University Press.
Hurka, Thomas. 1993. *Perfectionism*. Oxford: Oxford University Press.
MacAskill, William. 2015. *Doing Good Better: How Effective Altruism Can Help You Make a Difference*. New York: Penguin Random House.
Pogge, Thomas. 2001. "Eradicating Systemic Poverty: Brief for a Global Resource Dividend." *Journal of Human Development* 2 (1): 59–77.

---

8 Thomas Hurka (1993) argues for non-egoistic maximizing perfectionism.

Russell, Daniel C. 2012. "Phronesis and the Virtues (*NE* vi 12–13)." In *The Cambridge Companion to Aristotle's Nicomachean Ethics*, edited by Ronald Polansky, 203–20. Cambridge: Cambridge University Press.
Scanlon, T. M. 1998. *What We Owe to Each Other*. Cambridge: Belknap Press.
Sidgwick, Henry. 1907. *The Methods of Ethics*, 7th ed. London: Macmillan.
Singer, Peter. 2010. *The Life You Can Save: Acting Now to End World Poverty*. New York: Random House.
———. 2015. *The Most Good You Can Do: How Effective Altruism Is Changing Ideas About Living Ethically*. New Haven: Yale University Press.
Slote, Michael. 1989. *Beyond Optimizing: A Study of Rational Choice*. Cambridge: Harvard University Press.
Wise, Julia. 2013. "Cheerfully." *Giving Gladly: Altruism and the Good Life*, June 8. http://www.givinggladly.com/2013/06/cheerfully.html.

# 9 The Virtue of Modesty and the Egalitarian Ethos

## S. Stewart Braun

## 1. Introduction

Assuming that modesty is a virtue, then it is certainly a virtue that has generated an immodest amount of discussion and debate. At issue are questions about what constitutes modesty, why it is admirable, and whether an agent can be modest and also cognizant of the full value of her accomplishments. These questions are answered in different ways. For instance, in Julia Driver's (1989, 2001) well-known account, modesty involves an "underestimation" or ignorance regarding the value of one's accomplishments or self-worth, and modesty is valuable because of its positive social consequences. Against Driver, other theorists have contended that true modesty requires knowledge or awareness of the value of one's accomplishments. However, for modest agents the value of their accomplishments are put into their proper limited perspective as Ben-Ze'ev (1993), Brennan (2007), Flanagan (1990), Nuyen (1998), and Schueler (1997) have all separately argued; or played down and de-emphasized as Bommarito (2013), McMullin (2010), Raterman (2006), and Woodcock (2008) have contended. In contrast to Driver's approach, all of these 'awareness accounts' of modesty, as I call them, reflect a traditional approach in which the virtuous agent is aware of the relevant situational and normative factors, and acts appropriately given those factors.

Despite the different approaches to modesty, there is more unity than commonly supposed. In particular, all the accounts seem to explain modesty as a virtue that reflects a broad commitment to something like equal social standing and respect. Therefore, instead of developing yet another entirely separate account, I contend that an interpretation of modesty can be developed that explains what modesty is, how it functions, and why it is valuable in a way that accommodates the insights of the other accounts. According to my analysis, a modest agent is disposed to act in a manner that attempts to avoid establishing or endorsing distinctions in social standing or social respect regarding herself. This 'Egalitarian Account', as I call it, shows that modesty is admirable because it reflects a broad commitment to social equality.[1] It also explains why modest individuals may underestimate, play-down their achievements, believe that those achievements are of limited value when fit into a larger perspective, or not care what other people think about those achievements, since all of these dispositions are consistent with efforts to maintain equal social relationships and standing.

The upshot of this claim is threefold. First, a more unified account of modesty is provided. Modesty manifests itself in people's character and dispositions in different ways. Therefore, a successful account of modesty will need to explain that diversity. The Egalitarian Account meets this requirement because it explains the diversity of dispositional behavior with reference to the value of equal social respect and standing. So, in explaining what constitutes modesty, the account also explains why modest agents act in the diverse ways highlighted by the competing theories. Second, the Egalitarian Account also simultaneously demonstrates why modesty is valuable. If a modest agent is in some manner committed to social equality, then the agent's purportedly modest behavior follows naturally from that commitment. In other words, the behavior expresses that commitment. The Egalitarian Account, therefore, knits the value of modesty more closely to the dispositional behavior. In so doing, it helps to avoid the problem of false modesty (see below). Third and finally, the Egalitarian Account also provides a unique approach to the issue of knowledge that splits the difference between Driver's ignorance account and the various awareness accounts. As I argue, the modest agent knows that she is successful or accomplished; however, because she is disposed to act in a manner that safeguards social equality, she does not engage in behavior, like ranking behavior, that would provide her with full knowledge of the value of her accomplishments.

## 2. The Competing Accounts of Modesty

It is easiest to enter into the debate by looking at the issue of false modesty and Driver's response to it. Traditionally, the virtues are understood as requiring a virtuous agent to act in accordance with practical wisdom. This means that the agent must understand the virtue and act from it knowingly and in the correct circumstances. But this requirement creates a problem in the case of modesty since if a person claims that she is modest—that is to say, she correctly understands what modesty entails and recognizes herself as being

---

1 Even though modesty reflects the value of equal social respect or standing, that fact does not entail that modesty is valuable only for the states of affairs it brings about, as it is in Driver's account. A commitment to social equality is more than a commitment to the formal notion of equal rights. It involves a deeper commitment to structure personal and civic relationships in particular ways. It, therefore, reflects *on the type of person the agent is* and how that agent views others. Therefore, this account of modesty is seemingly consistent with a wide-range of virtue-ethical theories.

modest—she seems to undermine her own claim to modesty. A modest person cannot claim to be modest because such a claim amounts to highlighting one's virtuousness, which is, of course, to exhibit immodesty. Analogously, it seems that a successful and accomplished person cannot recognize the full value of her achievements since if she were to do so she would not be internally modest. She would recognize the superiority of her accomplishments, along with the extent to which she was praiseworthy or esteemed for those accomplishments. Therefore, it might be argued that true modesty requires a certain degree of ignorance regarding the extent of one's success.

This analysis led Driver to argue that if modesty is a virtue, then it is a virtue of ignorance. According to Driver (2001, 18–19), the modest person is "one who underestimates his self-worth to some limited degree" and who thinks of themselves as "less deserving, less worthy than she actually is." Therefore, in contrast to the traditional Aristotelian-inspired account of virtue ethics, Driver contends that the virtuous agent does not need to act from practical wisdom: modesty is a virtue of ignorance. On Driver's understanding, modesty is a virtue because the disposition to underestimate the value of one's accomplishments reduces the likelihood of producing an "envious response" in others that may disrupt relationships (2001, 27). In more general terms, modest behavior is conducive to a positive state of affairs. Given the emphasis on ignorance, Driver's account stands as the preeminent representative of what I call the 'ignorance account.'

Many commentators have found Driver's account implausible because it runs against the idea that a virtuous agent is one that acts from practical wisdom and should be as free from defect as possible. More specifically, these critics have charged that turning modesty into a virtue of ignorance does not properly explain what constitutes modesty. First, it has been argued that underestimation cannot guarantee modesty since a person may be disposed to underestimate her abilities or accomplishments, but still not be modest. For example, a person may actually be the best writer in the world but brag incessantly that he is the third best (Schueler 1997). Second, in some cases, a disposition to underestimate the value of a skill or accomplishment may seem to fall far short of virtue. For instance, if a scientist underestimates her technical ability, she may fail to address an important global problem that she could play a fundamental role in solving (Bommarito 2013). In this case, the underestimation seems unvirtuous since it leads to a failure of action. Underestimation may also be interpreted as a lack of self-esteem (Flanagan 1990). Moreover, it may lead to servility because, from ignorance of self-worth, a person may be disposed to defer to the authority of others, which the individual should not do given her numerous accomplishments and high level of ability (Statman 1992). So, many commentators conclude that modesty cannot involve ignorance.

Overall, these criticisms may be too quick, especially since Driver does not seem to preclude self-knowledge of the entire value of one's skills and accomplishments. For example, she says that a modest agent "does not spend a lot of time ranking . . . and thus remains ignorant to the full extent of self-worth" (2001, 27). So, according to Driver, the agent simply lacks some specific information that would allow him to accurately assess his accomplishments and status in society. Nevertheless, not only is that statement vague, since we do not know the contexts where ranking is acceptable and where it is not, but Driver actually claims that what we value in modesty is the actual ignorance of the individual, not the reticence to engage in systematic ranking (27). If that is the case, then it seems to turn modesty into a propensity for error or to render the virtue dependent on luck. An agent is modest, then, if he happens to be disposed to make errors when evaluating his accomplishments or if he is simply lucky enough to lack access to all the relevant information regarding the degree to which his accomplishments are valued by others. The trouble is that there is then nothing particularly admirable about the individual in those types of cases. Driver might claim that it is the reduction in envy produced by the purported modesty that causes admiration (26, 39), but that seems insufficient, since a great many things may reduce envy that we do not admire, including things like clumsiness or ugliness. In order for an account of modesty to be successful, it should explain why we think of modesty as a virtue by identifying something admirable about the character trait. Driver's account fails in that respect.

Given the problems with Driver's account, many theorists have attempted to demonstrate that modesty can coexist with the self-knowledge of one's abilities and accomplishments. These alternative accounts accept a more traditional view of the virtues as requiring knowledge and practical wisdom. According to this interpretation, a modest person will be aware of her successes and perhaps the esteem in which she is held; however, she will act to minimize attention and praise. Given the awareness that the modest agent possesses, I call these alternative approaches, 'awareness accounts.'

Awareness accounts may themselves be loosely subdivided into two categories: 'perspectival accounts' and 'de-emphasis accounts.' Perspectival accounts broadly argue that a modest agent is one that keeps things in perspective. The manner in which an agent is required to keep things in perspective vary by account, but typically it involves comparing oneself to a suitable high standard or recognizing that one's accomplishments matter little in the scheme of things. For example, Ben-Ze'ev (1993) argues that a modest person is one that, despite her success, adopts the attitude that everyone is of equal *moral* worth. Therefore, she acts modestly because she realizes that her success does not separate her from others or render her more *morally* valuable. Nuyen (1998) challenges Ben-Ze'ev's account on the grounds that it requires an evaluative attitude about human moral worth that some agents simply may not have developed. Nonetheless, he argues in a similar vein that a modest person keeps her achievements in perspective because she recognizes how contingent factors have contributed to her success.

Flanagan (1990) and Schueler (1997, 1999), both early critics of Driver, have also developed perspectival accounts. Flanagan (1990) contends that a modest agent possesses an accurate understanding of her accomplishments and does not overestimate their value. Schueler (1999) argues that a modest person does not care whether others are impressed with her accomplishments because she is her own person and only concerned with satisfying herself. In both of these accounts, the modest agent's perspective is accurate and constrained. She does not think of her accomplishments as more important than they are, nor is she interested in advertising or boasting about her success. More recently, Brennan (2007) has refined this type of approach and contended that a modest agent is one that assesses her achievements against an ideal she sets for herself, while at the same time assessing the achievement of others against the average. The agent's modesty results from the fact that her accomplishments fall short of meeting her own ideal standards. So her perspective serves to limit self-aggrandizement.

Perspectival accounts do seem to get something right about modesty. Certainly, modest agents do not get carried away with their own accomplishments. They interpret them correctly and in a constrained manner. Nevertheless, there is a central problem afflicting the account. The issue is that in order to keep things in perspective, one's frame of reference must be indexed to a particular standard. However, that standard may do little to ensure modesty. This phenomenon is most easily observed in Brennan's account in which it is argued that a modest person recognizes her failure to achieve at an ideal level. The problem is that although an agent may recognize her failures to achieve at an ideal level, she may still believe that she is superior as a result of what she has accomplished. For example, a highly decorated runner may have elevated standards that she fails to meet, but she may still be better than 90 percent of her peers. So, the fact that she has fallen short of her ideal does not entail that she will be modest about her accomplishments when compared to the large majority of other people. Now, Brennan may reply by insisting that the modest agent will not judge others harshly because she will not evaluate them against her own high standards. However, the fact that the agent does not judge others harshly does not entail that the agent is modest. All it demonstrates is that she does not criticize people who have failed to reach her ideal. So this formulation shows that the agent is not callous, but it does not exclude her from bragging about what she has accomplished or ranking herself far ahead of others (even as she simultaneously acknowledges how much more she needs to accomplish to satisfy herself).

Ben-Ze'ev's and Nuyen's accounts are saddled with similar issues. Even if the runner accepts the fundamental moral worth of others, that commitment does not prevent her from acknowledging that she is a superior runner since she is in the top 10 percent. The standard of moral worth is too broad to limit self-aggrandizement regarding specific qualities. Nuyen's account is perhaps more promising. However, it fails as well because even if the runner recognized the contribution of contingent factors, she may still think that the majority of that success is the result of her individual will and effort.

For example, the runner may claim that she was blessed with good running form, but simultaneously assert that "form is nothing without all the hard work and dedication for which I am famous." So even if her perspective serves to limit the most egregious forms of self-congratulatory behavior and praise, it seemingly does little to exclude more commonplace vanity.

Flanagan and Schueler also face difficulties along these lines. Even if the runner correctly judges that she is better than 90 percent of her peers and is concerned only with her own performance, she may still not be modest. For instance, and in contrast to Flanagan's approach, if the runner regularly refers to the fact that she is in the 90th percentile and constantly brings up her running prowess, it would be justifiable to wonder whether she was modest, even if she could back up her claims with the appropriate proof to demonstrate that she was not overestimating. In regards to Schueler's account, we might wonder about the runner's modesty if she was too inwardly focused and not appropriately responsive to the accomplishments of others. A single-minded focus on one's own performance can seem vain and self-centered, not modest.

So even though perspectival accounts pick out aspects of character and behavior that seem to be linked to modesty, they don't adequately portray what constitutes modesty. Persons may attempt to keep things in perspective and ensure that they are not overemphasizing the value of their accomplishments, but that does not ensure modesty, especially when the worth of the accomplishments strongly exceeds the average. Overall, then, in perspectival accounts the behavior of an agent can become disconnected from the trait of modesty since there is no clear appeal to an underlying value that clearly links the two.

De-emphasis accounts offer an alternative approach to explaining how an agent may be modest while at the same time remaining aware of the full value of his accomplishments. According to de-emphasis accounts, a modest agent acts to play down the importance of his accomplishments or direct attention away from those accomplishments. For example, Raterman (2006) contends that a modest person is reluctant to evaluate himself as praiseworthy because the person recognizes how such praise can negatively impact others, is aware of the role of luck in his success, and recognizes his own failings. In McMullin's more recent version, modesty is described as being a virtue of character that is strongly "other regarding" (2010, 786). A modest person is one who accepts that he will be defined by social rankings, but refuses to view himself as entirely reducible to that ranking since he believes that accomplishments do not determine value. Therefore, he acts to de-emphasize his accomplishments because he is concerned to insulate others from feelings of insecurity or envy. Woodcock (2008) takes a similar approach, arguing that a modest agent does not allow the value of his accomplishments to be overestimated because he is disposed to avoid harming others by causing jealousy or envy. According to Woodcock, modesty plays an important social role by discouraging "unhealthy competitive ranking" (2008, 3). Bommarito (2013) contends that modesty involves the recognition of positive contingent factors, which leads the modest agent to focus attention away from himself and toward others.

De-emphasis accounts are certainly plausible, and they capture the intuitive idea that a modest agent downplays the value of his success. However, de-emphasis accounts prove problematic because, in general, they fail to adequately explain why an agent acts virtuously when he downplays his success. The reason given for why an agent downplays his success is under-developed in the case of Bommarito and mistaken in the cases of Raterman, Woodcock, and McMullin.

In Bommarito's account we are told that modesty is a virtue because it is a "manifestation of morally good desires or values" (2013, 100–131; 115). While that may be true, it is necessary to identify what is valuable or admirable about modesty. If it is admirable to downplay one's accomplishments, why is that so? We need some account of the virtuous nature of modesty. Bommarito's account is, unfortunately, too skeletal to provide a clear answer.

Woodcock and McMullin may be interpreted as answering that last question by pointing out that modesty may prevent others from feeling envious. Although it is true that an emotion like envy can be destructive and is a vice, there are two problems with understanding the value of modesty in terms of its ability to reduce envy. First, it is not clear that modesty is an effective antidote to envy. Envy, understood as hostility toward another person's good position or accomplishments, represents faults or weaknesses in an individual's constitution. As Perrine and Timpe (2014) define envy, it is a vice that arises from a feeling of inferiority and the perception that the envious agent's accomplishments are not as valuable as those of the envied. But although Perrine and Timpe think envy arises through comparison, envy is almost certainly not the result of a lack of modesty on the part of another agent.[2] Quite simply, people do not feel envious of an individual with few accomplishments, even if he brags about what (little) he has achieved. Envy, therefore, has more to do with the success or accomplishments of another and not simply their behavior. Additionally, envy is irrational. Assuming the accomplishments of another person were obtained fairly and on merit, there are no justified grounds for spite or resentment. And since it is irrational, it then becomes extremely difficult to prevent, even with genuinely modest behavior. An envious person may feel resentment at another's success regardless of the agent's modesty since it is the success that is generating the envy. Consequently, there is no reason to think that a modest agent is

---

2 Perrine and Timpe contend that humility corrects or prevents envy. I have my doubts about whether this is correct. First, to the extent that I am correct that it is the agent's success that generates envy, then humility seems incapable of correcting for envy. Second, I am not sure that humility, as distinguished from modesty, should count as a virtue. For more on this second point, see sect. 3.

primarily motivated to reduce envy since modesty is likely to prove ineffective in many cases. Moreover, to the extent that the modest agent closely embodies the ideal of the virtuous person, she will realize that modesty cannot often limit envy. Since a virtuous agent is endowed with practical reason and presumably understands human emotionality quite well, the agent will recognize the true nature of envy and recognize that if her accomplishments are known, modesty will do little to prevent envy in a person prone to an envious reaction.

Of course, this last claim should not be taken as asserting that modesty can *never* reduce envy. Certainly in cases where the potential envious person is unaware of the modest agent's accomplishments, restraint in discussing those accomplishments can reduce the likelihood of envy because the accomplishments will not become fully known. Nevertheless, that motivation to reduce envy seems limited or highly contextual. It is not robust enough to motivate a general disposition or deep commitment to modesty, one in which the agent is modest regardless of the situation or context; or, in other words, when modest behavior will not necessarily lead to any beneficial outcome.

This last point brings me to the second problem, namely, that the motivation to avoid generating envy does not prevent the occurrence of false modesty. If an agent acts modestly in order to prevent envy, then that individual may not be acting from sincere modesty but rather to avoid the unpleasant effects of envy. In that case, the agent may think of himself as superior or excellent and worthy of praise, but act in an outwardly modest manner because he is mindful of the negative and disruptive effects of envy, not because he has internalized a modest disposition. Consequently, the purported modesty would not be grounded in the proper feelings or normative commitment. Of course, false modesty is a potential problem under almost any account since it is nearly impossible to evaluate the agent's internal motivation. Nevertheless, a successful account of modesty should explain what is admirable about modesty in a manner that links the motive as consistently and strongly as possible to the dispositional behavior, so that the possibility for false modesty is limited.

Given these issues, it can be concluded that the de-emphasis accounts are also inadequate. Although modest agents do downplay their success, it does not appear that their reason for doing so is adequately explained either in terms of unanalyzed moral goodness or in the desire to avoid envy. In order to properly account for modesty, we require a deeper sense of what makes it an admirable part of a person's character or constitution.

To summarize, all of the accounts of modesty face difficulties. Although Driver's ignorance account can avoid false modesty, underestimating the value of one's accomplishments or abilities does not guarantee modesty since an agent may miscalculate the value of her accomplishments or abilities while still being immodest. Underestimation may also lead to a less than virtuous failure to act. The two subcategories of awareness accounts fare no better. Perspectival accounts founder because an internal perspective or standard (elevated or not) may do little to check the agent's attitude that she is better and more praiseworthy than her peers. Therefore, a gap is left between what constitutes modesty and the agent's behavior. Relatedly, de-emphasis accounts fail because they do not adequately explain what makes modesty valuable or admirable.

In light of these problems, it is possible to identify the requirements that a successful account of modesty should be able to meet. First, it should be able to explain modesty in a way that allows the agent to remain substantially aware of the value of her skills and abilities. This requirement will prevent modesty from being the result of a lucky misapprehension, which strips it of a large part of its value. It will also ensure that the agent is capable of using her skills appropriately. Second, it should provide a description of modesty that properly accounts for the agent's modest attitude and behavioral dispositions with reference to an underlying value. When that requirement is met, the value of modesty—what makes modesty admirable—is explained and the behavior of the modest agent is accounted for. Third and finally, a successful account will also need to connect with practical action. An agent may downplay her success in order to create the *appearance* of modesty, so a defensible account will need to demonstrate how a modest agent can act from the virtue without having the virtue directly in mind. This criterion, together with the second criterion, will enable the account to largely avoid the problem of false modesty.

## 3. Modesty and the Egalitarian Ethos

Although all of the different accounts of modesty face problems, there is no need to be overly critical since it is certainly true that modest agents are disposed to act in the ways described and may also be motivated by some of the concerns the theories highlight. Nevertheless, the general problem facing the accounts is that they prove incapable of explaining why modesty is virtuous because they have difficulty linking the purportedly modest behavior consistently with the reasons people have to be modest. There is always space enough to drive a wedge between what constitutes modesty and the reasons people have for being modest. In order to properly explain modesty, then, it is necessary to develop an account that more closely connects the dispositional behavior of a modest agent with what is admirable about modesty.

The Egalitarian Account accomplishes that goal because it identifies equal social status and respect as the underlying value that explains or motivates the different behavioral dispositions of modest agents. Therefore, according to my analysis, modesty should be understood as follows: *A modest agent is an agent that is disposed to act in a manner consistent with attempts to avoid establishing or endorsing distinctions in social or civic standing, ranking, or respect, which are applicable to herself, both at an institutional level and at a local community level*. I call this the Egalitarian Account of modesty because of its obvious connection to the egalitarian ideal of social equality.

This commitment to equal social respect and standing seems implicit in all the major accounts. For instance, an agent who in line with Driver's ignorance account underestimates his accomplishments despite strong success, may be disposed to do so out of a commitment to ensure that his success does not mark him out as superior to his fellow community members. As noted earlier, Driver argues that a modest agent does not engage in a great deal of social ranking. So, to a large degree, her account is amenable with the Egalitarian Account; although she clearly would not endorse the motivational claim. (More on that issue below.) Perspectival accounts also seem to incorporate this commitment. An agent, like Brennan's modest agent, who does not judge others by her own ideal standards but rather by an average standard, is adopting a more egalitarian standpoint since evaluating others with reference to the average reflects a commitment to a more inclusive standard. De-emphasizing one's accomplishments is also consistent with equal social standing. When an individual downplays his achievements he is making it difficult for those achievements to be used to rank him or assign him an unequal status. Overall, then, a commitment to the value of equal social respect and standing seem to undergird modesty.

However, more needs to be said to fill in the account. In particular, it is necessary to better explain the concepts of equal social standing, ranking, or respect, and to also clarify what the Egalitarian Account intends to capture by distinguishing between institutional and local levels of application. In stating that a modest person is not disposed to engage in behavior that establishes or endorses distinctions in social status, ranking, or respect, the account intends to demonstrate that a modest individual engages with others as equals and does not think of herself as superior, deserving of privilege, entitled to deference, or general adulation. However, it should not be interpreted as asserting that individuals are equal in terms of their abilities and accomplishments. A modest agent is willing to admit that she has accomplished much of value and that she possesses valuable skills. Nevertheless, she understands that these accomplishments and skills do not entitle her to a distinct social standing, position, or ranking in comparison with others who may be less successful. She recognizes and intends to remain an equal member of her society as well as her smaller local community. All the same rules and regulations apply equally to her as they do to others, she does not expect deference in relationships, and she is responsive both to the needs and accomplishments of others. She views herself as an equal citizen, organization member, or professional practitioner and she acts accordingly. So, the point is that although a modest agent's accomplishments and skills may be highly valued, the agent is disposed to act in a manner that prevents those accomplishments from impacting the agent's social standing or respect in relation to others.

This point may be further elucidated by appealing to Stephen Darwall's well-known distinction between "appraisal" and "recognition" respect (2006, ch. 6). According to Darwall, appraisal respect involves the judgment or assessment of an individual's behavior, and it is something people can earn or merit as a result of their conduct. In contrast, recognition respect is a type of moral respect persons are entitled to qua person and regardless of their conduct. Although Darwall uses the distinction to analyze the concept of moral recognition, it may be stretched to help make sense of the idea that two individuals can differ in their accomplishments, yet still hold the same social status. So, as a result of her accomplishments, a modest agent will warrant higher appraisal respect, but she also recognizes that her recognition respect should remain the same as any other person, and she acts to ensure that that occurs.

But although Darwall's terminology is useful in terms of its ability to separate the respect a person earns as a result of her accomplishments from her general social or community standing, two important points must be kept in mind. First, as Darwall uses appraisal and recognition respect, they reflect general ideas about moral standing and human dignity, not social equality. So it needs to be remembered that in the case of modesty, the focus is at the level of civil society, not at the level of human value and moral equality. The type of moral value and equality that Darwall is referencing is already assumed in the modesty case. Second, the distinction assumes a strict division between an agent's appraisal standing and his recognition standing that is, unfortunately, not often adhered to in a practical social setting. According to Darwall's account, regardless of how an individual is appraised that individual will retain the same recognition standing as any other individual. Now, conceptually speaking, this division is defensible and useful. However, in applying it at a social level and in the case of modesty, it should be recognized that a person's appraisal standing can come to influence his social standing. Ideally, an agent's appraisal standing and recognition standing should be kept separate, but we know that persons with valuable accomplishments often use those accomplishments to curry special treatment, gain unique benefits, and demand deference on important social/community matters. The distinction between appraisal and recognition respect is of vital importance though, because it enables the fundamental point to be made that the appraisal of an individual's accomplishments and talents can and should be kept separate from his social standing. This point is vital to understanding modesty since a modest individual is one that seeks to prevent his accomplishments and talents from being used to establish a difference in his social standing, ranking, or respect. The modest agent is aware of how achievements can be used to separate, categorize, and rank individuals, so he acts in a manner that makes the judgments more difficult or, at least, he does not act in a way that encourages those judgments.

However, it may be objected that this account of modesty is too strong and will exclude any person who engages in competitive activities and/or whose accomplishments are highly lauded or ranked from being modest since the modest person is supposed to eschew rankings and social distinctions.[3] For example, it might be argued that my account prevents someone like Rafael Nadal from being modest. Nadal was ranked as the number one tennis player in the world, he has won 14 Majors, and is guaranteed to be inducted into the Tennis Hall of Fame. Therefore, it might be argued that Nadal's success has led to rankings and judgments about his standing that prevent him from being classified as modest. There are three replies to this concern.

First, it is necessary to keep in mind the difference between appraisal and recognition respect (as I am employing them). Of course, Nadal can and should be *appraised* extremely highly as a tennis player. But that does not entail that Nadal, if he is modest, will brag about all the times he won the French Open, expect a general sense of social deference from his peers and the general public,[4] or insist he is entitled to special privilege on the ATP Tour. A modest individual can accept the legitimate rewards of success without coming to think of himself as a 'breed apart' and of a different standing than other community members.

Second, the phrase social or civic standing is to be understood as referring to one's status as an equal member of the community (regardless of the size of that community), not one's *reputation* or *eminence* within the community. In any community some persons will be more successful, famous, and wealthy than others. However, a modest individual does not use those differences to establish distinctions in social standing between himself and others. To draw the contrast as bluntly as possible, being ranked the number one tennis player in the world (and accepting that ranking) is vastly different than accepting a Knighthood, or at least using it to obtain social deference.[5] The latter establishes, or may be used to establish, a special civic or social distinction that serves to separate the person from the 'common folk' and institutionalizes a hierarchical social standing, while the former simply acknowledges one's accomplishments and skills in a particular arena. Nadal may accept that he has been ranked as the number one tennis player in the world without constantly highlighting that fact and acting as if it secures for him special privilege over and above other community members.

Third and finally, we should expect modesty to be difficult to attain, especially for those with vast amounts of success. The adulation and attention

---

3 I thank an anonymous referee for highlighting this issue.
4 Of course, deference on something like the proper execution of a top-spin forehand is different, since in that case there is an appeal to a knowledge base that Nadal clearly possesses. A 'general' sense of deference refers to deference of social/civic matters and personal relationships that Nadal's world-class forehand does not entitle him to receive.
5 It is possible to imagine cases where rejecting a Knighthood would lead to more attention than quietly accepting it. What a modest agent should choose to do will depend on the circumstances. Regardless, a modest agent would not use the Knighthood in ways designed to garner special treatment or adulation, if he accepted it.

that come with extreme success can skew perspectives, rendering it difficult to act virtuously. But it is precisely that difficulty that makes the modesty of extremely successful and accomplished people so admirable.

The Egalitarian Account therefore captures the idea that modest agents are disposed to downplay or underestimate their success because they are concerned to avoid establishing or endorsing distinctions that may serve to undermine equal social standing and respect. But it is important to emphasize that the equal social standing and respect picked out by the Egalitarian Account is not the same as simple moral equality. Although social equality is typically taken to imply moral equality, social equality is a more robust concept that opposes distinctions that may serve to ground or legitimize unequal or deferential social relationships or community structures that are not affected by moral equality. Severe economic inequality is often cited as a paradigmatic example of a distinction that grounds social inequality, but not moral inequality. Of course, it is not the only thing, and depending on what society values, other distinctions in ability and accomplishment may do the same. Regardless, the problem with simple moral equality is that it is not sufficient to prevent an agent from boasting about specific accomplishments or leveraging them for social gain. For instance, an immodest person could hold that she and another individual are moral equals, or that they are part of the same moral community, or that they have the same natural rights, or that they are equal in the eyes of God—all ways of articulating moral equality—while at the same time highlighting her success and/or claiming that it qualifies her for special privilege and deference on community matters. A benefit of the Egalitarian Account of modesty is that it prevents that type of behavior since it is grounded on a robust notion of social equality that limits self-aggrandizement on specific accomplishments because the modest agent seeks to prevent her appraisal respect from affecting her social or civic standing.

The Egalitarian Account also accommodates the fact that people are embedded in a range of communities and social structures that range from large institutional structures, such as states, to local community structures, such as clubs and neighborhoods. Modesty entails a commitment to equal standing and respect within all of these communities. So if Nadal is modest, then he interacts with other tennis players and the general public as an equal and he does not use his accomplishments to impress, intimidate, or gain general adulation and deference. Overall, the disposition to modesty can consistently be linked with the idea of equal social standing or respect, and it is operable across a variety of contexts.

But it may be objected that the Egalitarian Account offers an implausible formulation of modesty because it links modesty too directly to a political/social account of equality. Why think that a modest person is motivated by something like equal social respect and standing? After all, it seems possible that a person could either be modest and not endorse anything like equal social standing, or, alternatively, not be modest but endorse equal social standing. It might further be argued that if the account were accepted, modesty would be possible only in communities that valued social equality. But many societies have failed to endorse social equality and surely some modest people have lived in those societies. So, how can the Egalitarian Account deal with these issues? Responses are offered in reverse order.

First, a modest person need not be consciously aware that his modesty arises from a commitment to something like equal social respect or standing. The commitment may be implicit in his character and motivations without ever rising to conscious acknowledgment. This may be especially likely to occur in societies that do not endorse social equality and where there may exist no external encouragement in that direction. Relatedly, that a society does not endorse equal social standing does not entail that an agent cannot be committed to those ideals either implicitly or explicitly and act modestly as a result. In that type of inegalitarian society, it might simply be the case that the agent's modesty would not be considered virtuous.

Modesty has not always been considered a virtue; it is certainly not on Aristotle's list. In fact, there is a degree to which modesty conflicts with Aristotle's magnanimous person, who Aristotle seems to exalt as an epitome of virtue in the *Nicomachean Ethics*. According to Aristotle, the "magnanimous person" is concerned with honor and "thinks he is worthy of great things, and is worthy of them . . ." (1124b). He also attempts to prove his superiority over others that have a good reputation since superiority over them is "impressive" (1124b). So although the magnanimous person may not boast, he is certainly not modest since he is concerned with proving his superiority and winning honor for himself. But if anything, the fact that magnanimity, not modesty, is a virtue for Aristotle should lend support to the Egalitarian Account. Aristotle infamously did not endorse equality, arguing instead that some persons (barbarians, non-Greeks) were unsuited for inclusion within a polis and incapable of virtue (*Politics*, Bk. 5). So it is reasonable to assert that Aristotle lacked the moral framework that would allow him to fit modesty into his account of the virtues.

Although this is no place to trace the genealogy of modesty, it is plausible to assert that modesty has come to the fore only recently in the modern era when concerns about social equality began to present themselves as fundamental moral issues. Of course, in medieval Christendom humility was considered a virtue; and some have interpreted modesty and humility to be synonymous.[6] However, there is much to distinguish humility from modesty, since humility is more consistently associated with deference and servility. A humble person is one that seeks to serve others; accordingly, he subsumes his desires to those of others. The phrase 'to humble oneself' captures this aspect of humility, as when a Christian humbles himself before another individual or before God. Humility therefore involves a lowering of

---

6 For example, see Sinha (2012).

oneself—an acknowledgment that the demands of others take precedence or that one is in some respect less worthy than another. In contrast, modesty involves no diminution in one's status. The modest person recognizes his own value and the general worth of his accomplishments, but he does not seek to use his accomplishments to elevate his social standing above others. Although he may seek to accomplish much, those accomplishments are internally motivated.[7] So, perhaps most fundamentally, a person that is modest possesses something to be modest about. The modest agent has significant accomplishments, but does not attempt to mark himself out as deserving of esteem, privilege, or deference by highlighting those accomplishments. By contrast, a humble person may lack any significant accomplishments or skills. One is humble simply if one is willing to accommodate or serve others. Modesty requires no such deference; in fact, it would trend against the sense of equality on which modesty is based.

Therefore, given Aristotle's failure to include modesty as a virtue and assuming that the contrast between modesty and humility is correctly drawn, it is reasonable to conclude that the recognition of modesty as a virtue is linked historically with the acknowledgment of egalitarian social values. Because of the modern commitment to social equality, we are now better positioned to see that modesty is a virtue.[8] But this does not imply or entail that modesty is only a virtue within an egalitarian type of society. Nothing precludes an individual from acting modestly in a society that does not accept egalitarian ideals, so long as the individual holds a commitment, at least implicitly, to equal social standing. Of course, as I have said, within an inegalitarian society the modest individual may not be considered virtuous. But that is a shortcoming of the society and not the individual.

This brings me to the second response. Although according to my account of modesty the egalitarian values undergirding the virtue need not be explicitly endorsed nor recognized in society, it still may be asked why a commitment to equal social standing in the broader, institutional sense is required? Typically, we think of modesty in terms of localized personal interactions. It is a matter of character, not a political/social concept. Why believe that an individual cannot be modest if he endorses an inegalitarian type of society?

Although this is an important question, it is misguided because the separation it posits leads to a disconnection in motivation or character, leaving the account vulnerable to the problem of false modesty. If an individual acts modestly among his peers, but then endorses a deeply inegalitarian society—for instance, he endorses an aristocratic form of government—he evinces a commitment to hierarchy that runs against modesty. If the aristocrat

---

[7] See Schueler (1999), who is in agreement with this assertion.
[8] This claim should not be interpreted as endorsement of any sort of deep relativism about the virtues since all it asserts is that we now possess better insight into the demands of morality and the virtues.

believes that he is entitled to institutionalized social privilege, then he believes that he is superior in some fundamental manner to other members of the community or society. This attitude is problematic since it seems to entail vanity and egotism. For an agent like the aristocrat to believe that he stands above others and that in some fundamental respect other people are inferior to him, is for the aristocrat to express a judgment of his superior worth vis-á-vis other people. In this case, the social distinction that the aristocrat accepts functions as an implicit acknowledgment of his superior value in much the same way that an immodest tennis player would highlight or employ his world ranking in order to establish a social pecking order on tour. So even if the aristocrat did not brag, his commitment to inegalitarian social structures demonstrates a strong degree of immodesty. In the end, then, a broader commitment to equal social standing and respect is necessary to guard against false modesty as well as to ensure that the agent acts from the proper grounds.

Of course, none of this is meant to deny that the aristocrat may be incontinent or that he may be more modest than another individual that is *both* a braggart and a proponent of aristocracy. It is certainly possible that he may be struggling to understand and act on the demands of equal social respect and standing. Perhaps he sees the logic of the demand more closely with reference to his peers, but is unable to internalize it in a manner that would allow him to act virtuously with reference to 'common' people. Nothing in the account denies that possibility. Nevertheless, it cannot be said that the aristocrat fully possesses the virtue of modesty because his broader commitments and dispositions demonstrate otherwise. The aristocrat uses the social distinctions as a way to highlight his value. So, the larger point is that to possess the virtue of modesty one needs to be disposed to act for the right reasons that undergird the virtue in all contexts.[9]

But how does the theory deal with the third and opposite problem, namely, one in which an individual is clearly committed to equal social standing and respect, but is disposed to immodesty? Take for example an individual who works for an NGO committed to equality that constantly talks about his work claiming that he does an excellent job, has helped thousands, and that the NGO has consistently awarded him for his effort. Is he modest? The short answer is 'no.' Even though the individual may be committed to social equality, his self-promotion prevents him from being classified as modest because, at least at the local community level, he engages in actions that might serve to distinguish him from others and highlight his skill and dedication. In essence, the individual is stating that he is a better citizen and that he is uniquely deserving of praise for his work. So the individual has betrayed his larger egalitarian commitments. As in the earlier example, modesty requires consistency in character and commitment. Of course, this

---

9 See Garrett Cullity's "Moral Virtues and Responsiveness for Reasons," ch. 1, this volume.

fact makes the virtue difficult to possess, but difficulty in attaining virtue should be expected since they represent excellences of human character.

In summary, then, the Egalitarian Account asserts that a modest agent is one who is disposed to avoid behavior that would serve to endorse or establish distinctions in social standing, ranking, or recognition respect (as I have used that concept). Moreover, the commitment to equal social standing and respect that undergirds this disposition requires consistency. The agent must respect people equally both in the larger institutional context and the more intimate local context.

## 4. Egalitarian Synthesis

The Egalitarian Account not only accommodates the insights of the alternative theories, but also improves upon those theories by avoiding the pitfalls that ensnared them. As I demonstrate below, the account therefore meets the requirements for a successful theory, as detailed at the close of sect. 2.

In Driver's ignorance account, an agent is modest when she is disposed to underestimate the worth of her accomplishments. The Egalitarian Account is also consistent with a degree of underestimation. If an agent seeks to avoid establishing distinctions in social status or standing, then she is obviously disposed to avoid the type of ranking exercise that would allow those distinctions to be clearly drawn. She may also be unaware of the rankings made by others given her disposition not to endorse distinctions in status and her reticence to engage in behavior that emphasizes those differences. However, that does not preclude her from possessing knowledge that she is successful; she just may be somewhat unaware of the magnitude of that success. What matters though, is that, despite her knowledge, she does not seek to use her accomplishments simply to distinguish herself and/or acquire esteem. Moreover, in the Egalitarian Account it is not the ignorance that is valued, but rather the disposition to avoid establishing or endorsing distinctions in social status or respect. In other words, it is the modest agent's commitment to social equality that is admirable. Consequently, the Egalitarian Account avoids rendering the agent defective in some respect.

In perspectival accounts, the modest agent views her accomplishments from a larger vantage point that serves to demonstrate the limited importance of those accomplishments. The Egalitarian Account is certainly consistent with that understanding of modesty since a modest agent refuses to highlight the value of her achievement in order to prevent them from being used to establish social distinctions or rankings. But the Egalitarian Account also improves upon the perspectival approach. As noted earlier, the general problem with the perspectival approach is that the vantage point or standard the purportedly modest agent uses to place her accomplishments into perspective might do little to limit immodesty. Take Ben-Ze'ev's (1993) otherwise promising account as an example: according to Ben-Ze'ev, the modest agent realizes the moral value of all persons and recognizes that an individual's successes do not affect moral standing. Although Ben-Ze'ev is partially correct, his account does not go far enough because it allows immodesty when it does not affect moral equality. In fact, Ben-Ze'ev acknowledges this point, claiming that a virtue of his account is that it allows for "local, professional immodesty" (1993, 238). But why should we accept immodesty at a local or professional level? We are often most aware of immodesty in our workplace and local communities. This type of immodesty can be as disruptive to respectful social relationships as broader, more encompassing forms of immodesty. Moreover, it may allow potentially pernicious social inequities to develop that can detrimentally affect people's standing and respect in the local context, even if they still possess the same formal set of moral rights. The Egalitarian Account rectifies this oversight because it relies on a more robust account of social equality that serves to limit local or professional immodesty, thus connecting the value of modesty with modest behavior in all contexts.

The Egalitarian Account is also consistent with de-emphasis theories. According to de-emphasis approaches, a modest agent plays down or shifts attention away from her accomplishments. The Egalitarian Account is clearly consistent with that type of behavior. One way to demonstrate a commitment to social equality is to downplay one's success so that clear social distinctions cannot be made. But the Egalitarian Account also avoids some of the problems that haunted the de-emphasis approach. As noted, a general problem for the de-emphasis account was that it failed to explain why playing down one's success was admirable. For instance, Woodcock and McMullin argued that that behavior would reduce envy. Perhaps that is true in some limited contexts, but if envy is problematic and should be avoided, then the agent has a reason to downplay his success regardless of whether he is truly modest or not. In other words, if the agent wishes to avoid social conflict, then his motivation for downplaying his success does not result from a true internalized sense of modesty, but rather from the desire or thought that social conflict is bad. But obviously many types of dispositional behaviors are consistent with that view. The Egalitarian Account avoids this problem because modesty is not explained in terms of a disposition not to cause envy or avoid conflict, but rather as an internalized character trait that leads to the disposition to act in a manner that is consistent with equal social respect and standing. The modest person views himself as equal to others and acts in a manner that respects that equality. Since modesty involves a refusal to highlight or separate oneself from others, the behavior amounts to an attempt to remain equal with other people. Thus, the Egalitarian Account knits the dispositional behavior and moral motivation more closely together.

Given the improvements described, it is clear that the Egalitarian Account meets the three requirements for a successful account of modesty detailed at the end of sect. 2. First, the account allows the modest agent to remain aware of his own success. Although the modest agent is disposed not to establish or endorse social distinctions or rankings, he can know that he is successful. Even with that knowledge, all he needs to do to remain modest is to refrain from using it in a manner that would establish meaningful distinctions in social standing or respect. Of course, as I have argued above, the agent's refusal to establish distinctions in social standing and rank may lead him to underestimate the full worth of his accomplishments since he will lack the points of comparison necessary to make firm judgments. Nevertheless, in the Egalitarian Account the agent's modesty does not depend on luck or circumstance as it could in Driver's account. The agent is modest because he is committed to social equality and equal respect. Even if he underestimates his accomplishments, that underestimation can be said to result from the egalitarian perspective he has adopted; it is not simply the result of a lucky misapprehension. Moreover, given that he is not fully ignorant of his skill and abilities, he still should possess enough information to use them appropriately.

Second, the Egalitarian Account avoids the problem regarding the disconnect between an agent's actions or behavior and what make modesty admirable, which plagued the perspectival and de-emphasis accounts. It is successful in avoiding that issue because it directly connects the modest agent's dispositions with a description of what constitutes the virtue of modesty. If an agent is appropriately disposed to avoid establishing or endorsing distinctions in social standing and respect, then she is modest. The account, therefore, explains what modesty is and why it is admirable in one step by appealing to (something like) the value of social equality. This prevents a gap from opening up between the agent's motivation and the description of the virtue. In the Egalitarian Account, the agent is modest because she accepts the value of social equality and her behavior expresses that commitment.

Third, the Egalitarian Account explains how an agent can act modestly without having the virtue in mind. Recall that this was important to avoid problems with false modesty. If an agent acted modestly because he had the virtue in mind, then there would be some danger that the agent was exhibiting false modesty since he may be acting modestly only to appear modest. Under the Egalitarian Account, an agent acts modestly out of a commitment to social equality. Hence, there is less danger that the agent is acting modestly only in order to seem modest. Even if the agent is aware of his commitment to social equality, it does not mean that he is aware of his modesty. He acts modestly not to seem or appear modest, but rather in order to respect social equality. His modesty arises naturally and largely unconsciously. Therefore, he is acting virtuously, even though the virtue is not directly held in mind.[10] The agent is committed to social equality, but not aware of his modesty.

---

10 Some support for this claim can be drawn from Bernard Williams' observation that "a courageous person does not typically choose acts as being courageous, and it is a notorious truth that a modest person does not act under the title of modesty" (1985, 10). See also Robert Audi (1995).

## 5. Conclusion

The general upshot of the Egalitarian Account is, then, that it provides a unified interpretation of modesty that properly explains the behavioral dispositions of modest agents while simultaneously accounting for the value of modesty.

According to the Egalitarian Account, because a modest agent is disposed to avoid engaging in ranking behavior regarding the value of her accomplishments, it can help to pull the ignorance and awareness accounts back together. An element of ignorance remains because the agent may be unaware of how her accomplishments specifically rank or how deeply they are valued. However, there is a certain degree of awareness as well. The agent is aware that she is successful or accomplished. She may also be aware that she is committed to social equality (although it is not necessary that she be consciously aware of egalitarian theory or even have explicitly egalitarian thoughts on specific occasions). She is modest, then, because she accepts the value of social equality and acts from it.

The Egalitarian Account also provides a description of modesty that explains what is admirable about modesty. The modest agent is disposed to avoid establishing or endorsing distinctions in social status, ranking, or respect, and this disposition is admirable because it reflects a commitment to social equality. Modesty is valuable, then, not (only) because it reduces envy as Driver, Woodcock, and McMullin argue, but because it reflects the morally valuable commitment to equal social respect and standing. Although modesty might accomplish the goals identified by the other theories, the accomplishment of those goals is not what makes it valuable. It is valuable because of the moral and social commitment it highlights and what that commitment reveals about the character of the individual.

A final and overriding benefit of the Egalitarian Account is that it helps to unify the divergent approaches to modesty. In so doing, the account helps to secure modesty's status as a virtue. If I am correct that modesty exhibits an underlying unity of theme regarding the idea of social equality, then it may be easier to justify the claim that modesty locates an admirable human moral trait. It may further be argued that even though all of the competing approaches highlight different aspects of modesty, they are all still pointing towards a larger understanding of modesty as a moral virtue that derives its importance from the value of social equality. So the emphasis on smooth, non-envious, and cooperative social interaction that all of the accounts stress in one way or another, amounts to an implicit endorsement of equal social respect and standing.[11]

---

11 An early version of this paper was presented at the Reasons and Virtues Conference (Melbourne 2015). I wish to thank the audience for their helpful comments. Special thanks are owed to Robert Audi, Steve Matthews, and Noell Birondo as well as an anonymous referee for their guidance.

## References

Aristotle. 1988. *Politics*. Edited by Stephen Everson. New York: Cambridge University Press.
———. 1999. *Nicomachean Ethics*. Translated by Terence Irwin. Indianapolis: Hackett.
Audi, Robert. 1995. "Acting from Virtue." *Mind* 104: 449–71.
Ben-Ze'ev, Aaron. 1993. "The Virtue of Modesty." *American Philosophical Quarterly* 30: 238–46.
Bommarito, Nicolas. 2013. "Modesty as a Virtue of Attention." *Philosophical Review* 122: 93–117.
Brennan, Jason. 2007. "Modesty without Illusion." *Philosophy and Phenomenological Research* 75: 111–28.
Darwall, Stephen. 2006. *The Second Person Standpoint*. Cambridge: Harvard University Press.
Driver, Julia. 1989. "The Virtues of Ignorance." *Journal of Philosophy* 86: 373–78.
———. 2001. *Uneasy Virtue*. New York: Cambridge University Press.
Flanagan, Owen. 1990. "Virtue and Ignorance." *Journal of Philosophy* 87: 420–28.
McMullin, Irene. 2010. "A Modest Proposal: Accounting for the Virtuousness of Modesty." *Philosophical Quarterly* 60: 783–807.
Nuyen, A. T. 1998. "Just Modesty." *American Philosophical Quarterly* 35: 101–9.
Perrine, Timothy and Kevin Timpe. 2014. "Envy and Its Discontents." In *Virtues and Their Vices*, edited by Kevin Timpe and Craig A. Boyd, 225–42. New York: Oxford University Press.
Raterman, Ty. 2006. "On Modesty: Being Good and Knowing It without Flaunting It." *American Philosophical Quarterly* 43: 221–34.
Schueler, G. F. 1997. "Why Modesty is a Virtue." *Ethics* 107: 467–85.
———. 1999. "Why IS Modesty a Virtue?" *Ethics* 109: 835–41.
Sinha, G. Alex. 2012. "Modernizing the Virtue of Humility." *Australasian Journal of Philosophy* 90: 259–74.
Statman, Daniel. 1992. "Modesty, Pride and Realistic Self-Assessment." *Philosophical Quarterly* 42: 420–38.
Williams, Bernard. 1985. *Ethics and the Limits of Philosophy*. Cambridge: Harvard University Press.
Woodcock, Scott. 2008. "The Social Dimensions of Modesty." *Canadian Journal of Philosophy* 38: 1–30.

# 10 Virtue and Prejudice
## Giving and Taking Reasons
*Noell Birondo*

> We might ask, for example: how could Socrates talk philosophy and set the discussion in order without a body? But if he could not, and if the interlocutors believe that the ability to participate in the give and take of dialectic is essential, as part of being human, to the Socrates they know . . . then we must concede that there is some incoherence in the wish that *Socrates* go off from his body to the happy life of the blessed.
> 
> Martha Nussbaum (1995, 93)

## 1. Introduction

The most long-standing criticism of virtue ethics, at least in its traditional, eudaimonistic variety, centers on its apparently foundational appeal to nature in order to provide a source of normativity: its attempt to validate, by appealing to the nature of human beings, that certain traits of character amount to exemplary, excellent, or virtuous traits of character. But many defenders of virtue ethics have insisted that a naturalistic validation of the virtues might proceed in two quite different ways. One side of the distinction is sometimes cast in this Neurathian image: that when we extol certain traits of character as virtues of character, and when we give our reasons for doing so, we are like sailors rebuilding our ship on the open sea. Any particular conception of *eudaimonia*—the vessel by which one might navigate the ethical waters—remains always open to revision, an acknowledgment of its fallibility. That approach contrasts with a more ambitious validation of the ethical virtues, one that proceeds from naturalistic materials that lie, already in dry dock, external to the ship. A traditional candidate here is Aristotle's alleged appeal to an "absolute" conception of nature, replete with its metaphysical biology.[1] With this distinction in hand, virtue ethicists can claim that the long-standing criticism applies only to very ambitious 'external' appeals to nature.

---

1 The allusions here are to Bernard Williams (1985, ch. 3) and Alasdair MacIntyre (1984, ch. 12). For other influential advocates of this general reading of Aristotle, see the works cited in Nussbaum (1995, n. 2).

A less ambitious validation of the ethical virtues—one that appeals, self-consciously, to a conception of human nature that is, of course, open to dispute—can still seem well worth our philosophical attention. Indeed, the Neurathian image looks like an invocation of mere modesty: in this context it amounts to the familiar liberal idea that 'our' conception of the best way to live, something that is of course the product of culture, might be in various ways mistaken. Ethically sound practice involves, according to this modest outlook, not only the giving of reasons for our ethical conceptions, but also the taking of such reasons from those whose conceptions differ from our own. This idea of the "giving and taking of reasons" is something that I mean in a completely mundane sense—it is the mundane sense employed by Martha Nussbaum when she appeals, without explication, to the "give and take" of philosophical dialectic, in the quotation with which this paper begins. Such give and take implies neither—absurdly—accepting all of the reasons which one is offered no matter how irrational or outlandish, nor—stubbornly—merely claiming that one will consider the reasons which one has been offered. The claim that "I'll consider it" is often meant to indicate that genuine discussion has come to an end. Such a claim is often meant, indeed, as a shut down. Hence, the phrase "taking reasons" is more helpful in this context than the phrase "considering reasons," since "taking reasons" is helpfully ambiguous between someone's genuinely and open-mindedly taking into consideration the reasons that have been offered by others, and actually taking (or accepting or embracing) those very reasons as her own.[2] My claim in this paper is that a failure to appreciate both the giving and the taking of reasons in sustaining an ethical outlook—a failure to appreciate the kind of understanding and transformation that can be effected by a rational exchange of practical considerations between different ethical communities—can distort one's understanding of what an 'internal' validation of the virtues would ultimately amount to. To insist only on giving reasons, without also taking (maybe even considering) the reasons provided by others, displays a sadly illiberal form of prejudice.

In order to illustrate the distortion just mentioned, I will consider its appearance in one recent discussion of virtue ethics; but I hope that the considerations advanced in what follows make it clear that such a distortion is hardly confined to the discussion I single out for attention. The distortion I have in mind makes a prominent appearance in Jesse Prinz's recent criticisms of virtue ethics (2009) from the perspective of what he calls the "Normativity Challenge." An examination of Prinz's views regarding this challenge will help illuminate the importance of both giving and taking reasons in sustaining an ethical outlook; but the discussion of Prinz's views

---

2 Of course, one can specify which of these two things one means in a specific case; the point is that the phrase can helpfully do double duty in this way.

(§§2–3) will also help bring into focus what I have thus far referred to only opaquely as the long-standing criticism to virtue ethics.

## 2. Prinz on Well-Being and its Relation to *Eudaimonia*

The challenge that Prinz sets for virtue ethics can itself be brought into focus by first specifying more precisely the difference between an 'external' and 'internal' validation of the virtues. An external validation of the virtues of character is an attempt to demonstrate that possession of the virtues of character is necessary in order to secure some good, or to avoid some harm, where the good in question, or the harm, is recognizable as such independently of the particular evaluative outlook provided by possession of the virtues themselves. The validation will thus rely on resources that are 'external' to the particular evaluative outlook to be validated. By contrast, an internal validation of the ethical virtues would be one according to which the good unattainable without the virtues, or the harm unavoidable without them, is only recognizable as such from within the evaluative outlook provided by possession of the ethical virtues themselves, although this evaluative outlook might also be shared by people who (like most of us) never manage to proceed further than Aristotelian continence.[3]

The aim of Prinz's "Normativity Challenge," as I understand it,[4] is to press the following thought: that neither an external validation nor an internal validation of the ethical virtues is at all likely to succeed. This can be demonstrated, he thinks, by appealing to empirical studies from cultural psychology that emphasize the differing conceptions of 'well-being' across cultures. If neither type of validation can succeed, then the alleged "normativity of the virtues" will remain unexplained. According to Prinz this "Normativity Challenge" constitutes a more serious challenge to virtue ethics than the much-touted "Situationist Challenge." This is a challenge that Prinz thinks can be adequately answered, on behalf of virtue ethicists, by

---

3 For this account of the distinction, and for discussion, see Birondo (2015a, 2015b). On the non-matching overlap between the continent person's outlook and the virtuous person's outlook in specific cases, see McDowell 1979, especially §3.
4 An interpretation of Prinz's argument here is somewhat hampered by the fact that, in the section of his paper devoted to explicating the "Normativity Challenge" (sometimes also the "Normative Challenge"), various views are attributed to Aristotle, and to contemporary "Aristotelian virtue ethicists," without there being any citations to Aristotle, or to any contemporary Aristotelian virtue ethicists. A possible exception is Prinz's reference to Martha Nussbaum, in support of the claim that, in Prinz's words, "some cultures may find exposure to the natural environment more important than others" (Prinz 2009, sect. 4, "Normativity: Another Empirical Challenge to Virtue Ethics"). Hence, Prinz's new empirical challenge to virtue ethics relies on what he apparently considers to be the a priori options for it.

appealing to the same types of studies from cultural psychology.[5] In this paper my concern will be with what Prinz says about the "Normativity Challenge" to virtue ethics.

Before turning to that, some preliminaries are in order. Specifically, something needs to be said about Prinz's understanding of the appeal, within Aristotelian versions of virtue ethics, to the notion of *eudaimonia* or "flourishing." For it immediately becomes unclear which proponents of virtue ethics Prinz has in mind in his discussion. The question that Prinz puts to virtue ethics is this (2009, 132): "What is the source of this obligation," he asks, the one that says that we "*should* cultivate the virtues?" Having asked this question, Prinz goes on to characterize, on the subsequent page, what he apparently takes to be some genuinely Aristotelian answers to it.[6] He insists that, whereas theists might see the normativity of the virtues in terms of divine command, Aristotelians "tend to go another route." More specifically, they argue "that morality derives from natural teleology." By appealing to such natural teleology, the proponents of an Aristotelian virtue ethics maintain that, "The normativity of the virtues derives from the fact that they are the end to which our nature directs us, and thus constitute human flourishing."

However, flourishing is not at all constituted, on an Aristotelian view, by any state or disposition of character, not even virtue. Aristotle's own view, which has hardly been rejected by prominent defenders of virtue ethics,[7] maintains that *eudaimonia* is, over a complete life, rational activity in accordance with virtue (*NE* 1098a16–18). Thus, on Aristotle's view, the flourishing life is a life constituted by a certain type of activity, not by a state or disposition of a person's psychology. No state or disposition of a person's psychology, not even virtue, could possibly constitute flourishing as Aristotle understands it. This is because the possession of that state or disposition, whatever it is, remains consistent with a completely inactive life, a life that involves no virtuous activity (*NE* 1098b30–1099a5; cf. 1102b5–8). Hence, whatever traits of character the ethical virtues turn out to be, activity in accordance with those traits, over a complete life, just is what flourishing, according to Aristotle, ultimately is.

A life of virtuous activity is also, of course, a life of affect: it is a life of both doing and feeling, a life that good people find enjoyable. Perhaps it is on the basis of such Aristotelian thoughts that Prinz says that flourishing is "widely presumed to involve certain affective states." He then claims

---

5 However, even this much is unclear: Mark Alfano (2013, 51–52) has issued some worries about whether Prinz's appeal to such studies, on behalf of virtue ethicists, actually does answer the situationist challenge.

6 The quotations from Prinz in this section of my paper will accordingly be from that page of Prinz's paper: (2009, 133).

7 See, for instance, Annas (1993), Hursthouse (1999), McDowell (1980), and Nussbaum (1995). Any complexities introduced by the indispensability of 'external goods' can safely be put to one side here; the crucial point is the one about activity.

(1) that flourishing is "related to" well-being and (2) that well-being is "an affective construct," a "subjective state." Prinz goes on to clarify that for Aristotelians the virtues are good "not simply because they make us feel good, but because they make us feel good in a way that is indicative or constitutive of having fulfilled our natural ends as a species." The view that Prinz has in mind maintains that, "Well-being confers normative status not because of its hedonic qualities, but because of its teleological status." Thus, according to the 'Aristotelian' versions of virtue ethics that Prinz has in mind, Aristotelian flourishing (*eudaimonia*) drops out of the picture altogether, except insofar as it "relates to" subjective conceptions of well-being. One might therefore characterize the target of Prinz's arguments here as "Aristotelianism without *eudaimonia*."[8] What is the new empirical challenge that Prinz takes to be problematic for virtue ethics so understood?

## 3. The Long-Standing Criticism of Virtue Ethics

The "Normativity Challenge" seems to press the idea that neither an external validation nor an internal validation of the ethical virtues is at all likely to succeed. Consider what Prinz says about each of these approaches for validating certain traits of character as genuine virtues of character.

An internal, 'Neurathian' validation of the virtues would be, as I said above, an attempt to demonstrate that there is some good, say, that is unattainable without possession of the ethical virtues, where the good in question is recognizable as such only from within the evaluative outlook provided by possession of the ethical virtues themselves. However, as Prinz points out in considering this type of proposal, showing that a certain tendency is *natural* obviously falls well short of showing that it is *good*, since whole cultures might have natural tendencies toward violence and warfare. Perhaps we can draw a distinction, though, between natural tendencies that are "noble" and those that are not. But Prinz insists that, "It is hard to do this without circularity." This is because one "cannot define noble natural tendencies as those that accord with virtue, and then

---

[8] Sebastian Purcell (2014) has argued, in response to this "Normativity Challenge," that Prinz's understanding of Aristotelian *eudaimonia* relies on presuppositions "that are not supported by a careful reading of the *Nicomachean Ethics*." My own response cannot quite muster Purcell's admirable charity. But although this interpretation of an "Aristotelian virtue ethics" does not strike me as especially accurate, the example does provide a recent version (2009) of the criticism that I described, in the first sentence of this chapter, as the "long-standing criticism of virtue ethics." This long-standing criticism—when directed at an 'external' interpretation of an Aristotelian virtue ethics—presumably persists because it can be difficult to see any alternative to that interpretation (cf. McDowell 1995a, 150, 1995b, passim); appreciating such an alternative is what this chapter is about. (Those last two sentences respond to a comment by an anonymous reviewer for this volume.)

argue that virtues derive normativity from their status as natural" (2009, 133–34). That is Prinz's argument against an internal validation of the ethical virtues. I will return to it briefly below in §5, after considering the alternative, external approach.

An external validation of the ethical virtues is an attempt to demonstrate that there is some good, say, that is recognizable as such independently of the evaluative outlook provided by the ethical virtues and that is clearly unattainable without possession of those virtues. In order to articulate such a validation, virtue ethicists might want, Prinz says, "to beef up their notion of well-being" (2009, 134). The strategy would be this: "If a substantive account of well-being can be offered that makes no reference to virtue, then we can define the virtues as the natural behaviors that promote well-being without any circularity" (2009, 134). Here one might compare Prinz's formulation of a substantive account of well-being to Thomas Hurka's formulation (unacknowledged in Prinz's paper) of the same idea. As Hurka puts this idea: "A *substantive* conception equates flourishing with some determinate state F of people or their lives, where both the nature and the goodness of F are defined independently of the virtues" (Hurka 2001, 235; quoted in Annas 2008).[9]

Prinz, however, thinks that there is an obvious problem with this substantive strategy. This is the fact that "there are well-documented cultural differences in which factors matter" for well-being (2009, 134). After noting some of the empirical studies documenting these cultural differences (studies which I have no reason to question for my purposes here), Prinz sums up this line of thinking as follows:

> This variation has serious implications for virtue ethics. Virtue ethicists have traditionally assumed that there is a universal set of virtues; indeed many virtue ethicists try to list them. And, they assume that these virtues are universal precisely because they are all part of a universal human nature. But that supposition is untenable. What leads to fulfillment in life is neither universal nor entirely natural. Culture can shape our conception of the good life.
>
> (2009, 134)

In this passage, the word "fulfillment" presumably refers to well-being, achieved according to a specific conception of it. Hence, Prinz's thought can be put like this: subjective conceptions of well-being, resulting as they do from the influence of culture, are neither universal nor entirely natural. Thus, the prospects for "deriving" a universal list of the virtues from an

---

9 In defense of virtue ethics, Julia Annas responds by insisting that, "Where success is defined independently of the virtues, it will always be hopeless to try to show that the virtues are a good way of achieving *that*" (2008, 214).

account of well-being, construed in these terms, seem especially dim. An external validation of a set of universal virtues—a validation that takes a subjective conception of well-being to be the good that is unattainable without the virtues—is not, as Prinz sees it, very likely to succeed. He nevertheless considers what he takes to be the available options, at this point, for defenders of an Aristotelian version of virtue ethics.

The options constitute, he says, an unattractive dilemma. On the first horn of the dilemma, virtue ethicists might defend the idea that—in spite of the wide cultural variation in subjective conceptions of well-being—there is, nevertheless, a *universal* set of ethical virtues that promotes "all forms of well-being" (2009, 136). This is what we might call the *off-brand* conception of virtue. Prinz rightly passes over this idea without comment.

On the second horn of the dilemma, virtue ethicists might maintain that some conceptions of well-being are, after all, better than others. But Prinz says that "such an argument would inevitably hinge on one of two mistakes" (2009, 136). The first mistake is this: in assessing alternative conceptions of well-being "from within" (or better: from) our own evaluative outlook, we would "inevitably," Prinz says, "impose our own conception of well-being on others, when determining which is best" (2009, 136). This would amount to an objectionable form of cultural chauvinism. (I will return to this point below in §4.) The second mistake would be to go further external: to argue from an allegedly neutral, cultural-free standpoint, that some conceptions of well-being emerge as more natural, and therefore as 'better,' than others. Prinz's passionate rejection of any such appeal is worth quoting at length, since it encapsulates the 'long-standing' criticism of virtue ethics that I referenced at the outset. Prinz points out that this external strategy "assumes a conception of the human species that is profoundly false." He elaborates:

> We are a cultural species, and it is part of our nature that our values should be forged in the context of human interactions. To the extent that those interactions engender different conceptions of well-being, as the empirical literature shows, we cannot pretend that there is some pre-social, purely natural conception. That is the myth of the noble savage. Indeed, if we could find such a pre-cultural conception, it would have scant normative force, for conceptions of well-being that did not emerge through cultural processes would hardly be applicable or conducive to thriving once we find ourselves situated in a cultural context. Faith in a universal form of well-being teeters between cultural chauvinism and a form of naturalism rivaling Spencer's in its naiveté and vulgarity.
> (2009, 136)

The main thing to say, however, about the position targeted by this long-standing criticism is that many quite prominent defenders of a eudaimonistic version of virtue ethics have explicitly rejected it.[10] Certainly as an interpretation of Aristotle, the view has been fairly well repudiated. Julia Annas, for instance, writing more than twenty years prior to Prinz's paper, insists quite generally that:

> The Greeks did not support their various claims about happiness and virtue by an appeal to teleology, nor to a fixed and determinate pattern of human nature which would impose on the recalcitrant agent a rigid and specific set of aims and mode of life. The appeal was rather to what we would call the best available moral psychology—something much more general, and disputable.
>
> (1988, 165)

Regarding Aristotle in particular, Annas writes that, "Aristotle does not have a 'universal teleology,' and the teleology he has is not a theory about human lives" (1988, 156).[11]

Hence, the long-standing criticism of virtue ethics, as Prinz seems not to realize, is well off the mark. The appeal to an allegedly neutral, teleological conception of nature—as many contemporary virtue ethicists have long recognized—ought to be abandoned. Nevertheless, if a certain culture stands equipped with a subjective conception of well-being, one that its members consider to be better than the alternative conceptions, won't this attitude of superiority "inevitably" lead, as Prinz says, to imposing their conception of well-being on others? Won't insisting on the superiority of 'our' conception of well-being amount to a form of cultural chauvinism? The answers to these questions will help illustrate the distortion that I hope to bring out: the culprit is failing to appreciate the importance of both giving and taking reasons in sustaining an ethical outlook. In order to illustrate the phenomenon I have in mind, in the next section I consider, at some length, a case that Prinz deploys from cultural psychology. It involves two contrasting conceptions of well-being from two different cultural communities. What can we learn from such a case?

---

10 See, for instance, Annas (2008), Hursthouse (1999), McDowell (1995a, 1995b), and Russell (2009). MacIntyre is a special case here, since he rejects the natural-teleological position targeted by the long-standing criticism (1984), but also again (1999) feels its attractions. But even on MacIntyre's later view, as Christopher Toner has recently stressed, some Neurathian considerations are at work (Toner 2008, sects. 5–6).

11 Some of the material from this article, Annas (1988), was later incorporated, in an expanded form, in an even more prominent venue: Annas (1993, Part II, "Justification and the Appeal to Nature."). See 136, n. 4. Other prominent interpretations of Aristotle's ethics that would show the long-standing criticism to be quite off target include McDowell (1980, 1995b) and, in exquisite detail, Nussbaum (1995).

## 4. Agrarian Toleration and Imperialism

Suppose that the well-being of a certain agrarian community depends upon various forms of cooperation in the sharing of agricultural resources (cf. Prinz 2009, 129). The members of this community therefore tend to value cooperativeness in the sharing of such resources. Moreover, they insist that their own cooperative conception of well-being is better than the one embraced by the herders in the hills. The herders work in isolation and are, as a result, more prone to violence, for instance in defense of their flocks. Do the agrarians display a form of cultural chauvinism, insofar as they consider their own cooperative conception of well-being to be better than the violent alternative? Are they bound "inevitably" to impose their conception of well-being on others? There are many things to say in response to these questions, the answers to which, as we saw above, Prinz takes to be obviously affirmative. Here I will mention three points that suggest otherwise.

First, if the agrarians can prosper without interference from the herders, then the agrarians may not be, and perhaps should not be, especially concerned about the herders' tendencies toward violence. If a life that is overly prone to violence contributes to the different type of well-being enjoyed by the herders—given that the hills are so dangerous—then so much the better for the herders, and for their flocks. The agrarians need not be, and perhaps should not be, in any way involved. They need not even understand the way of life in the hills in order to adopt this attitude of toleration.[12] In any case, even if they did understand it, what reasons could the agrarians give (left as the herders are to fend for themselves) to embody the 'agrarian' virtues—e.g., the virtue of trust? The agrarians could of course insist that the virtue of trust contributes, as they themselves see it, to the well-being of agrarians. But they cannot plausibly insist that such a trait contributes to the well-being of herders: if the hills are especially dangerous, then such a claim is simply false. (Recall that we have already dismissed the implausible 'off-brand' conception of virtue.) Hence, the question of imposing a specific conception of well-being on others need not arise. Nor need the agrarian attitude of tolerance amount to a form of cultural chauvinism. The attitude that I have described can be maintained in full awareness that the herders look down in condescension on the agrarian way of life. This all remains perfectly consistent with the agrarians' insistence that their own conception of well-being is much better than the alternative conception, the one that incorporates habitual violence.

Of course, the situation becomes rather different—this is the second point—if the herders descend from the hills. It may be that the herders

---

12 These claims are not meant to deny that there can of course be cases in which humanitarian intervention is justified.

threaten, not the agrarian way of life, but at least the lives of certain agrarians. In this case there may be no alternative to threatening sanctions against the herders: if the case becomes desperate, this will become the threat of violence, or, at the limit, simply violence. But in this case the imposition of a peaceful co-existence, by means of threatened external sanctions, looks like a justifiable imposition. (I will come back to "looks" in the next paragraph.) The situation becomes different again, of course, if the herders threaten, or even seem to threaten, the agrarian way of life. In that case the well-being of the agrarians becomes, or seems to become, compromised. The question that arises then—whether defending one's way of life justifies the threat of sanction, and even violence, in the face of a real or perceived threat from some new cultural element—is obviously a question that is too large to address adequately here. But what I do want to insist upon should be predictable. In a society comprising members from both the agrarian and the herder communities—i.e., in a multicultural society—only a regrettably illiberal form of prejudice can seem to justify giving reasons for one's own conception of well-being while refusing to take into consideration the reasons provided by others for their differing conceptions. Charles Taylor remarks in a similar context on what he takes to be a "general truth" about life in a society that is both multicultural and democratic; this general truth is that "contemporary democracies, as they progressively diversify, will have to undergo redefinitions of their historical identities, which may be far-reaching and painful" (Taylor 2011, 317). What this observation highlights is that, although the agrarians may initially consider their own conception of well-being to be better than that of the herders—and although there may be nothing objectionable about that—the agrarians still cannot justifiably close their minds to the reasons offered by the herders for their different conception of well-being, violence-prone though it may be. Presumably there are reasons (which, for all we know, may be excellent reasons) for their traditional security concerns; and so presumably there are also reasons for their tendencies toward violence. Perhaps it will be the agrarians who come to realize—after taking (or accepting or embracing) such security reasons from the herder community—that their own agrarian conception of well-being is overly pacific or naive, or anyway too prone to a blind and defenseless form of trust.[13]

These considerations lead to a third and final point about imposing our conception of well-being on others. While I said that the threat of sanctions against the herders looks, in some cases, like a justifiable imposition, it is a good question whether any behavior can in fact be *ethically* justified here, given the restrictions on the type of 'external' validation under

---

13 The point here is not to make an empirical prediction about the likelihood of convergence between initially differing conceptions of well-being, but rather to highlight its rational possibility.

discussion. This is an attempt, recall, to "derive" a universal set of virtues from a subjective conception of well-being "that makes no reference to virtue" (Prinz 2009, 134). In that case, though, if the agrarian conception of well-being is "substantive" in Prinz's sense, in the sense of being articulable without making any reference to virtue, then the threat of sanctions can only apparently be justifiable in this pragmatic sense: because such activity promotes agrarian well-being. In that case, though, *any* action that genuinely promotes the well-being of the agrarians will turn out to be, in that pragmatic sense, justifiable. The problem here is not, as Prinz says, that since the agrarians consider their own conception of well-being to be better than that of the herders, this means that they will "inevitably" impose their conception of well-being on others. Nor is the problem here, as I argued above, that the attitude of superiority amounts to a form of cultural chauvinism. The problem is rather that without the giving and the taking of reasons—without the rational exchange of practical considerations between the agrarian and herder communities—an insulated and culture-bound conception of well-being provides a recipe for *justifiable* cultural imperialism. This consequence, though, is not a problem for eudaimonistic versions of virtue ethics, but rather for Prinz's understanding of them.[14]

## 5. Conclusion: Giving and Taking Reasons

The discussion so far would seem to leave an 'internal' validation of the ethical virtues as the remaining strategy for answering Prinz's "Normativity Challenge."[15] Such a validation, as I said, would be an attempt to demonstrate that possession of the ethical virtues is necessary in order to secure some good, or to prevent some harm, where the good in question, or the harm, is recognizable as such only from within the evaluative outlook provided by possession of the virtues themselves. Thus, the good to be achieved by possession of the virtues will rather obviously not be characterizable without any (even implicit) reference to them. But the outlook in question can also be shared by people who, like most of us, never manage to proceed

---

14 Nor is it the case that Aristotelian versions of eudaimonism fall prey to the charge under discussion, of imposing a specific conception of the good life on others. Julia Annas (2008, 217) provides some of the reasons why not.
15 The main aim of this section is to characterize further the basic shape of an 'internal' validation of the virtues, not to deploy, let alone to deliver, such a validation. An internal validation would provide an alternative strategy for answering the "Normativity Challenge," *if* answering that challenge seemed philosophically urgent to one, perhaps because of a standing desire (this is just one possibility) to demonstrate that other ways of living are "wrong," "defective," even "vicious." While I do not myself have such a standing desire, I do have a bit more to say about these issues in Birondo (2015a, 2015b). For rewarding and philosophically patient discussions that address the issue of normativity head-on, see e.g. FitzPatrick (2008) and, again, Nussbaum (1995).

further than Aristotelian continence. And the possibility of shared overlap amongst differing ethical conceptions makes theoretical and ethical progress possible. An appreciation of the kind of giving and taking of reasons that I am advocating requires, as I suggested above, a kind of modesty that allows for an open-ended rational exchange with others, with those who hold different ethical conceptions than our own. And this modesty, when actually embodied, ought to mitigate familiar worries about circularity,[16] or about the inevitability of imposing our conception of the good life on others. Moreover, this way of understanding an internal validation of the virtues, by insisting upon the giving and taking of reasons, seems anyway to be required by any version of eudaimonism that hopes to steer clear of the long-standing criticism of virtue ethics.[17]

In order to effect ethical progress, those engaged in ethical reflection need to acknowledge the two reciprocal practices that invoke ethical reasons here—not only the practice of giving reasons for our ethical conceptions, but also the practice of taking the reasons of others into account, even though these others may embrace ethical conceptions that differ radically from our own. Thus, perhaps the Neurathian imagery, at least for eudaimonistic versions of virtue ethics, might emerge as less than fully appropriate, since according to the strategy defended in this paper, the vessel in question—a specific conception of *eudaimonia*—would remain helpfully porous. Or perhaps this dual practice, of giving and taking reasons, needs

---

16 On the worry about circularity, consider a few especially prominent discussions that are not considered or acknowledged in Prinz's paper: Annas (1993), McDowell (1995a, 1995b), and Nussbaum (1995). In dismissing the 'internal' strategies (as I would think of them) deployed in these discussions, it does not seem to me to be sufficient to remark, without any detailed consideration of the discussions themselves, that it is "hard to do this without circularity" (Prinz 2009, 133). Moreover, as I have understood the notion in this paper, the giving and the taking of reasons should mitigate worries from this direction: even if one eventually arrives back at the same point from which one's rational reflection set off, there was no guarantee, in advance of such reflection, that this outcome would eventuate; and of course it may *not* eventuate. The image of circularity here is a bogeyman. Cf. Birondo (2015a, 91).

17 Nevertheless, Christopher Toner has issued the following objection in defense of a broadly MacIntyrean-Thomistic picture of universal human nature: that the sort of naturalism defended by McDowell (e.g., in McDowell 1995a) "seems to give way to a lightly constrained moral relativism, in which morality is multiply, and variably, realized in a diverse assortment of cultures" (Toner 2008, 228; cf. Toner 2011, 457–48). MacIntyre himself maintains quite differently that, "It has often been thought by Thomists . . . that to acknowledge the historically conditioned character of philosophical—or for that matter scientific or historical—inquiry is to make a certain kind of relativism inescapable. And it was one of the several achievements of [Hans-Georg Gadamer's] *Wahrheit und Methode* to have shown that this is not so" (MacIntyre 2002, 158). For McDowell's response to the general charge of relativism, invoking both Gadamer and Donald Davidson, see McDowell (2002). Although I cannot develop this point here, a view like Toner's seems to me to display a version of the prejudice that I have aimed to articulate in this paper; a fuller treatment would be required to show exactly how so.

to invoke a slightly different image: one that involves a 'fusion' of ethical horizons. Regarding this different, Gadamerian image, Charles Taylor has observed that the slogan here might be: "no understanding the other without a changed understanding of self" (2002, 295). Hence, the illiberal prejudice involved in my discussion might also be thought of as an implicit and unjustified rejection of, or at least a resistance to, the idea encapsulated in this slogan, of a changed understanding of our own ethical outlook, and also, one might add, of a changed understanding of ourselves.[18]

## References

Alfano, Mark. 2013. *Character as Moral Fiction*. New York: Cambridge University Press.
Annas, Julia. 1988. "Naturalism in Greek Ethics: Aristotle and After." *Proceedings of the Boston Area Colloquium in Ancient Philosophy* 4: 149–71.
———. 1993. *The Morality of Happiness*. Oxford: Oxford University Press.
———. 2008. "Virtue Ethics and the Charge of Egoism." In *Morality and Self-Interest*, edited by Paul Bloomfield, 205–21. New York: Oxford University Press.
Birondo, Noell. 2015a. "Aristotle and the Virtues of Will Power." *Southwest Philosophy Review* 31 (2): 85–94.
———. 2015b. "Aristotelian Eudaimonism and Patriotism." *Dialogue and Universalism* 25 (2): 68–78.
FitzPatrick, William J. 2008. "Robust Ethical Realism, Non-Naturalism, and Normativity." In *Oxford Studies in Metaethics*, vol. 3, edited by Russ Shafer-Landau, 159–205. New York: Oxford University Press.
Hurka, Thomas. 2001. *Virtue, Vice, and Value*. Oxford: Oxford University Press.
Hursthouse, Rosalind. 1999. *On Virtue Ethics*. New York: Oxford University Press.
MacIntyre, Alasdair. 1984. *After Virtue: A Study in Moral Theory*, 2nd ed. Notre Dame: University of Notre Dame Press.
———. 1999. *Dependent Rational Animals*. La Salle: Open Court.
———. 2002. "On Not Having the Last Word: Thoughts on Our Debts to Gadamer." In *Gadamer's Century: Essays in Honor of Hans-Georg Gadamer*, edited by Jeff Malpas, Ulrich Arnswald, and Jens Kertscher, 157–72. Cambridge: MIT Press.
McDowell, John. 1979. "Virtue and Reason." *The Monist* 62 (3): 331–50.

---

18 This chapter is a revised and mildly expanded version of a paper originally published in *The Monist* (2016). It is reprinted with the permission of Oxford University Press. More distant ancestors of this paper were presented at Australian Catholic University, Melbourne, for the Reasons and Virtues Conference in 2015, at the Mountain-Plains Philosophy Conference in 2016, and at Wichita State University. Thanks are due to the participants on each of these occasions and to the conference organizers, to the students in my History of Ethics (2015) and Contemporary Ethics (2014) courses, and to the anonymous referees who helpfully commented on earlier versions. Special thanks are due to Laura Bernhardt, Robert Feleppa, and David Soles, for their extremely helpful written comments; to Mark Alfano, Lillian Dickerson, Avery Kolers, Kate Phelan, and Kai Spiekermann, for their much-needed encouragement during the paper's development; and to Robert Audi for his generosity and support.

———. 1980. "The Role of *Eudaimonia* in Aristotle's Ethics." In *Essays on Aristotle's Ethics*, edited by Amélie O. Rorty, 359–76. Berkeley: University of California Press.

———. 1995a. "Two Sorts of Naturalism." In *Virtues and Reasons: Philippa Foot and Moral Theory*, edited by Rosalind Hursthouse, Gavin Lawrence, and Warren Quinn, 149–79. New York: Clarendon.

———. 1995b. "Eudaimonism and Realism in Aristotle's Ethics." In *Aristotle and Moral Realism*, edited by Robert Heinaman, 201–18. Boulder: Westview Press.

———. 2002. "Gadamer and Davidson on Understanding and Relativism." In *Gadamer's Century: Essays in Honor of Hans-Georg Gadamer*, edited by Jeff Malpas, Ulrich Arnswald, and Jens Kertscher, 173–93. Cambridge: MIT Press.

Nussbaum, Martha. 1995. "Aristotle on Human Nature and the Foundations of Ethics." In *World, Mind, and Ethics: Essays on the Ethical Philosophy of Bernard Williams*, edited by J. E. J. Altham and Ross Harrison, 86–131. Cambridge: Cambridge University Press.

Prinz, Jesse. 2009. "The Normativity Challenge: Cultural Psychology Provides the Real Threat to Virtue Ethics." *Journal of Ethics* 13: 117–44.

Purcell, Sebastian. 2014. "Natural Goodness and the Normativity Challenge: Happiness across Cultures." *Proceedings of the American Catholic Philosophical Association* 87: 183–94.

Russell, Daniel C. 2009. *Practical Intelligence and the Virtues*. New York: Oxford University Press.

Taylor, Charles. 2002. "Understanding the Other: A Gadamerian View on Conceptual Schemes." In *Gadamer's Century: Essays in Honor of Hans-Georg Gadamer*, edited by Jeff Malpas, Ulrich Arnswald, and Jens Kertscher, 279–98. Cambridge: MIT Press.

———. 2011. "What Does Secularism Mean?" In his *Dilemmas and Connections: Selected Essays*, 303–25. Cambridge: Belknap Press.

Toner, Christopher. 2008. "Sorts of Naturalism: Requirements for a Successful Theory." *Metaphilosophy* 39 (2): 220–50.

———. 2011. "The Virtues (and a Few Vices) of Daniel Russell's *Practical Intelligence and the Virtues*." *Journal of Moral Philosophy* 8: 453–68.

Williams, Bernard. 1985. *Ethics and the Limits of Philosophy*. Cambridge: Harvard University Press.

# Contributors

**Robert Audi** (Ph.D., University of Michigan 1967) is John A. O'Brien Professor of Philosophy at University of Notre Dame. He has written numerous articles, and his books include *Means, Ends, and Persons* (2016), *Moral Perception* (2013), *Democratic Authority and the Separation of Church and State* (2011), *Rationality and Religious Commitment* (2011), *Practical Reasoning and Ethical Decision* (2006), *The Good in the Right: A Theory of Intuition and Intrinsic Value* (2004), *The Architecture of Reason* (2001), and (as Editor) *The Cambridge Dictionary of Philosophy* (3rd ed. 2015). He is a past president of the American Philosophical Association, a former editor of the *Journal of Philosophical Research*, and serves on many journal editorial boards.

**Noell Birondo** (Ph.D., University of Notre Dame 2004) is Associate Professor of Philosophy at Wichita State University. His primary interests lie at the intersection of contemporary ethical theory and ancient Greek philosophy. His articles have appeared in *The Monist*, *Ancient Philosophy*, *Ratio*, the *Journal of Philosophical Research*, and the *Southwest Philosophy Review*. He is also author of the entry "Rationalism in Ethics" in the *International Encyclopedia of Ethics*.

**S. Stewart Braun** (Ph.D., University of Virginia 2012) is Lecturer in the School of Philosophy and a member of the Institute of Religion and Critical Inquiry at Australian Catholic University. He specializes in social and political philosophy and also in normative and applied ethics. His articles have appeared in the *Journal of Applied Philosophy* and *Law and Philosophy*, among others.

**Damian Cox** (Ph.D., University of Melbourne 1992) is Associate Professor of Philosophy at Bond University. He specializes in normative ethics and social and political philosophy and has a research interest in philosophy and film. He has written numerous articles, and his books include *Thinking Through Film* (2011), *Politics Most Unusual* (2009), and *Integrity and the Fragile Self* (2003). He is also author of the entry on "Integrity" in the *Stanford Encyclopedia of Philosophy*.

## Contributors

**Garrett Cullity** (D.Phil, Oxford 1991) is Hughes Professor of Philosophy at the University of Adelaide. In the past, he held positions at Oxford and St. Andrews. Some of his specialties include moral philosophy, metaethics, and normative ethics. He is author of *The Moral Demands of Affluence* (Clarendon Press, 2004), as well as numerous articles and book reviews. He is currently Associate Editor of the journals *Philosophy and Public Affairs* and the *Australasian Journal of Philosophy*.

**Ramon Das** (Ph.D., University of Maryland 1999) is Senior Lecturer at Victoria University of Wellington. His interests include applied ethics, metaethics, philosophy of law, and social and political philosophy, among others. He has written many articles, some of which appear in *Ethical Theory and Moral Practice*, the *Philosophical Quarterly*, and the *Journal of Applied Philosophy*. He is currently working on a book on the ethics of globalization.

**Andrés Luco** (Ph.D., Duke University 2009) is Assistant Professor at Nanyang Technological University. His primary interests lie in moral psychology, metaethics, and normative ethics, especially the relationship between morality and social norms. He has published in the *Journal of Philosophical Research* and *Social Theory and Practice*.

**Justin Oakley** (Ph.D., La Trobe University 1989) is Associate Professor at Monash University and a member of the Monash University Centre for Human Bioethics. His primary interests lie in ethics, virtue ethics, and bioethics. He has written four books, including *Bioethics* (2009) and *Virtue Ethics and Professional Roles* (2001). He is currently working on projects on virtue ethics and medical conflicts of interest, and the moral significance of genetic parenthood and the regulation of assisted reproduction.

**Emer O'Hagan** (Ph.D., University of Toronto 2001) is Associate Professor at the University of Saskatchewan. Her research focuses on Kant, ethics, metaethics, moral psychology, and Buddhist psychology. She has published articles in *Ratio*, *Ethical Theory and Moral Practice*, and *Social Theory and Practice*, among other journals.

**Peter Shiu-Hwa Tsu** (Ph.D., Australian National University 2011) is Assistant Professor at Chung Cheng University. His primary interests include ethics, metaphysics, philosophy of mind, political and legal philosophy, and aesthetics. He has published articles in both English and Chinese, some of which appear in *Philosophical Studies, Acta Analytica*, the *American Journal of Bioethics-Neuroscience*, and the *Australasian Journal of Philosophy*.

# Index

acting virtuously 11–29, 36n7, 49–52, 176–86; 'at will' 91–105, 114–19; *see also* motivating reasons
action guidance 59–62, 68–71, 76, 100–104, 160–66; vs. action assessment 100–104
Adams, Robert M. 3, 22n27, 35–36, 38, 43, 45n
aims of action: as distinct from motives 12–16; *see also* intentional action
akrasia 13–14
Alfano, Mark 22n26, 130n3, 192n5
Annas, Julia 91n1, 130, 192n7, 194, 196, 199n14, 200n16
Anscombe, G. E. M. 13n7, 73, 126
Aquinas, Thomas 137
aretaic advice 19–20; *see also* role modeling
aretaic evaluation: dimensions of 11–16
aretaic properties 16–23, 27–9
Aristotle: on character, determinations of 45; and *eudaimonia* ('flourishing') 130, 142, 189, 192–3; and habituation 127–8; and intellectual virtue 136n, 137n; and modesty 181–2; and practical wisdom 101, 149, 153–4; and self-knowledge 113–14; and teleology 189, 196; and virtue contrasted with continence 25, 191, 199–200; on virtue as 'firm and unchanging' 91; on virtue, perfect 12, 130; on virtue and 'right' response 11–13, 67
Arpaly, Nomy 23n28
Audi, Robert 1n, 4–5, 11n2, 80n22, 91–8, 100, 104, 108, 114–18, 121, 130n5, 133n9, 134n, 141n, 143n, 186n

Backwell, Diana 36n9
Baier, Kurt 151
Baron, Marcia 20n24
Batson, C. D. 120
Battaly, Heather 136n
Benedict, Ruth 79
beneficence 29, 97–9, 127, 129, 141–2
Ben-Ze'ev, Aaron 168, 171–2, 184–5
Birondo, Noell 6, 191n3, 199n15, 200n16
blame 32, 39–42, 45n, 55–6, 98n15
Bodhi, Bhikkhu 122n
Bommarito, Nicolas 168, 170, 174
Bradley, Ben 165n
Brady, Michael 58
Braun, S. Stewart 5
Brennan, Jason 168, 172, 177
Buddhism 122–4

Carey, Ryan 156, 158
Cassam, Quassim 62–3
categorical imperative 73, 79–80
Chang, Ruth 148n
Chappell, Timothy 73n10, 79n20
character: stability of 17n16, 22, 35–6, 62–3, 119–24, 143; transcendence of 4, 91–104; *see also* virtue(s); virtue attribution
charity 60, 149–52, 156–62
chastity 25
Cocking, Dean 42–3, 46
Condon, Paul 108n
Conee, Earl 101n16
consequentialism 33, 42–5, 60, 73, 77n13, 134, 166
counterfactual behavior 33–46
courage 21–7, 28n38, 49, 51–52, 129–32, 142, 187n10; warranted attribution of 34–8; in the workplace 41

# Index

Cox, Damian 3–4, 49n, 58, 59n15
creditworthiness of action 91, 113, 133; in remote scenarios 33–47; *see also* moral worth
Crisp, Roger 77–8, 83
Cullity, Garrett 3, 15n11, 28n39, 28n40, 138n, 143n, 157–8, 183n
cultural chauvinism 195–9
cultural psychology 191–2, 196–9

Dancy, Jonathan 72, 75n
Darley, J. M. 120
Darwall, Stephen 178
Das, Ramon 4–5, 56, 58, 91, 92n3, 101n16, 104
Davidson, Donald 92n4, 133n9, 200n17
Davis, Darin 72
deontic judgments 11–12, 51–3, 62
Doris, John 22n26, 32n2, 36n7, 38, 130n3
Driver, Julia 95n9, 168–71, 175, 177, 184, 186–7

effective altruism 156–64
Egalitarian Account of modesty 5, 168–9, 176–87
epistemic warrant: in virtue attribution 32–47
epistemology 23n30, 62–3, 132, 136n, 139–43; *see also* intellectual virtue(s)
Eshelman, Andrew 91n2
*eudaimonia* 189, 192–3, 200–1; *see also* flourishing
evil action 36–7
Ewin, R. E. 20n24, 27n37
Eylon, Yuval 91n2

fairness 11, 22, 26–9
falsehood: and intellectual virtue 135–6
FitzPatrick, William J. 199n15
Flanagan, Owen 123n15, 168, 170–3
flourishing 130, 142; and luxury 150–1, 156; *see also* eudaimonia; well-being
Foot, Philippa 1n, 20n24, 79n19
forms of life 97, 197–201
friendship 33–4, 42–5, 47; as a non-impartial good 157–9

Gadamer, Hans-Georg 200n17, 201
Gollwitzer, Peter 121
Good Samaritan experiment 32, 120
Greco, John 136n

Harman, Gilbert 22n26, 130n3
harnessing reasons 99–100, 108, 114–24
Hart, H. L. A. 74
Harvey, Peter 123
Herman, Barbara 71n5, 72n8
Hill, Thomas 73n9
honesty 15–20, 29, 43, 50–1; aim of 15–17, 29; as a pro tanto duty 83–84; *see also* Kant, Immanuel: shopkeeper example
Hooker, Brad 77, 134n
Humean account of motivation 98n15
humility 110, 174n; and Christianity 181–2; *see also* modesty
Hurka, Thomas 101n16, 139n, 166n, 194
Hursthouse, Rosalind 1n, 13n5, 18n17, 32n1, 53n3, 53n5, 68, 75–6, 77n14, 91n1, 92n3, 192n7, 196n10

imperialism, cultural 197–9
implicit bias 121
intellectual virtue(s) 95, 126, 128–9, 134–9, 142–3, 153
intentional action 13–15, 98, 131–2, 135
Irwin, Terence 12

Jackson, Frank 57n
Jacobson, Daniel 58
Johnson, Robert 58, 95, 103
justice 21, 24, 26, 46, 54, 73n9, 82, 129, 134

Kahneman, Daniel 14n, 62n18
Kamm, F. M. 77n15
Kant, Immanuel 20n24, 73, 108, 124, 132, 141; on the duty of self-knowledge 111–14; and friendship 33–4, 42; and 'secret incentive' of self-love 33; shopkeeper example 15–18, 29, 50–1, 111, 114–15; and virtue, genuine 33–7, 42, 46–7
Kantian account of virtue 3, 33–37, 46–7, 73–4, 79, 80n21, 111–14
Kawall, Jason 91n1
Keller, Simon 27n37, 59n16
kindness 15–17, 19, 28n, 60, 68–9, 109, 111; role modeling of 126–7
Klein, Gary 14n
Kleinig, John 27n37
Korsgaard, Christine 110
Kripke, Saul 78n17

La Caze, Marguerite 49n
Levine, Michael 49n
Li, Peizhong 121
Lord, Errol 2n
loyalty 24, 27, 79, 110
luck 39, 77, 171, 173, 176, 186
Luco, Andrés 5
luxury 150–1, 156–8

MacAskill, William 150, 160, 163
McDowell, John 1n, 4, 65–79, 81–5, 91n1, 93n6, 95–6, 191n3, 192n7, 193n, 196n10, 196n11, 200n16, 200n17
MacIntyre, Alasdair 79, 189n, 196n10, 200n17
McMullin, Irene 168, 173–4, 185, 187
McNaughton, David 72, 83
Maguire, Barry 2n
Martinez, Joel A. 59n16
Menold, Bill 36
Meyer, Michael 109n2
Milgram experiments 32, 36, 44
Milgram, Stanley 36n9
Mill, J. S. 76, 133–4
Miller, Christian B. 130n3
modesty: and aristocracy 182–3; and envy 171, 173–5, 185, 187; and ethical fallibility 190, 200–1; ignorance account of 168–71, 175–7, 184, 187; and moral equality 178, 180, 185; and practical wisdom 169–71; and social equality 168–9, 176–87; *see also* Egalitarian Account of modesty
Montmarquet, James 136n
Moore, G. E. 134
moral conflicts: between absolute principles 76–7; between pro tanto rules 80–1, 83–4; and unified moral sensitivity 82
moral education 67, 76, 115, 126–8; *see also* role modeling
the moral middle 49–52
moral obligation 4, 11, 51–5, 62, 97, 103, 113, 143, 192
moral worth 23n28, 113, 132–3, 171–3
Moskowitz, Gordon 121
motivational overdetermination 114–22
motivating reasons: and aretaic advice 19–20; and aretaic evaluation 14–19, 22–30, 132–4; and continence 25, 81–5; and counterfactual scenarios 41–2, 44–7; and modesty 174–5, 180–6; and moral development 111–20; and role modeling 127–32; and self-interest 15, 33–4, 50, 113, 115, 141; and vice ethics 50, 54n6, 56–62; and virtue-ethical criterion of right action 91–105; *see also* virtue attribution

Nagel, Thomas 39n, 98n14
Nanamoli, Bhikkhu 122n
Neurathian validation 189–90, 193, 196n10, 200
Nussbaum, Martha 1n, 66, 75, 79n20, 81, 92n7, 189–90, 191n4, 196n11, 199n15, 200n16
Nuyen, A. T. 168, 171, 172

Oakley, Justin 3, 41n17, 46, 73
Oesterly, John A. 137n
O'Hagan, Emer 5, 112n4, 123n15
O'Neill, Onora 66n
'ought implies can' 92–3, 100–4
Override Principle 5, 149, 152–66; and ethical careers 160–5; as maximizing 165–6; as satisficing 164–5

Parfit, Derek 56n, 76, 134n
Pargetter, Robert 57n
Perrine, Timothy 174
Perry, Gina 36, 44
Peters, Julia 2n
Pettigrove, Glen 59n16, 109n2
Pettit, Philip 35, 36n7
phronesis *see* practical wisdom
Pinsent, Andrew 137n
Plato 135, 152
Pogge, Thomas 165
practical wisdom 83n24, 101, 137, 149, 153–4; and conflicts between principles 71, 76–7, 80–1; and silencing 81–4; *see also* Override Principle; sensitivity to reasons; virtue(s): as sensitivity
practices, of community 157–60
prejudice: about ethical outlooks 190, 198, 200n, 201; about rationality 77–9
Prinz, Jesse 190–7, 199, 200n16
prudence 15, 34, 58, 114–16, 119n9, 137
Purcell, Sebastian 193n

racism 45n22
Railton, Peter 42–3
Ramsey, William 16n12
Ransome, William 58
Raterman, Ty 168, 173–4
rationality *see* practical wisdom
Rawling, Piers 83–4
reasons: of cooperation 24, 29; for courage 21–2; impartial 151–2, 155–66; justificatory 139–43, 190–1, 196–201; normative 11–14, 92–105, 115, 138–43, 147–66; prima facie vs. pro tanto 52; of rationally incomparable strengths 148–54; of respect 27n36, 29; self-anchored 151–2; of vice 51–3, 62; *see also* harnessing reasons; motivating reasons
reasons pluralism 148–66
Reeve, C. D. C. 13n4
regret 52, 82–4, 119
relativism 79, 141, 182n8, 200n17
remedial action 103–4
respect 23–4, 27n36, 29, 135–6; appraisal 178–80; recognition 178–9, 184; social 168–9, 176–87
Richardson, Henry 70n
right action, criterion of 18, 32, 35, 37n11, 53–8, 91–105
rigor, intellectual 128, 135–6, 142
Roberts, Robert C. 91n2
role modeling 126–34; and aretaic 'uptake' 129–30
Ross, W. D. 13, 71n6, 80n21, 81, 132
rule-following 4–5, 68–72, 76–9, 82, 138; judgment and sensitivity in 74–6
Russell, Daniel C. 53n3, 61n, 77n14, 92–3, 100–4, 153–4, 196n10
Russell, Luke 44n21

Saul, Jennifer 121n12
Scanlon, T. M. 23n29, 147
Schaal, Bernd 121
Schueler, G. F. 168, 170–3, 182n7
self-assessment 60–1, 110
self-effacement, theoretical 59–62, 134n
self-knowledge 108–14, 119–24, 169–74, 177, 184–7
self-reflexivity 110–11, 117
sensitivity to reasons 14, 17–19, 28–9, 68–9, 82, 95–6, 108–24, 138, 154

Sidgwick, Henry 134, 152
Singer, Peter 60, 150, 156–7, 160–2
Sinha, G. Alex 181n
situationism 2, 17n16, 22n26, 32–47, 62–3, 130, 191, 192n5
Slote, Michael 4, 53n4, 54, 58, 91n2, 101n16, 136n, 164n
Smith, Angela 45
Smith, Michael 97n, 99
Snow, Nancy E. 2n
social deference 179–82; *see also* respect
social ranking 169–87
Socrates 135, 152, 189
Sosa, Ernest 136n
Sreenivasan, Gopal 44n20
Statman, Daniel 170
Stohr, Karen 82n
Sunstein, Cass 62n18
supererogation 51–3, 59
Swanton, Christine 15n10, 16n12, 59n14, 76n

tact 16n14, 18–19, 26
Tännsjö, Torbjörn 56n
taxonomy of moral virtues 20–30, 138n
Taylor, Charles 198, 201
Tiberius, Valerie 4, 66, 95–6, 101
Timpe, Kevin 174
Toner, Christopher 196n10, 200n17
Tsu, Peter Shiu-Hwa 4, 72n7, 76n12
Tversky, Amos 62n18

Upton, Candace 130n3
utilitarianism 60, 73, 77n13; *see also* consequentialism

van Zyl, Liezl 54n7, 101n17, 102
vice epistemology 62–3
vice ethics 53–63; advantages over virtue ethics 58–63; blameworthiness in 55–6; praiseworthiness in 56; wrongdoing in 53–62
virtue(s): absolute conception of 71, 73–9; and codifiability 65–85; cross-over (practical-intellectual) 137, 138n; and development 41, 63, 107–24, 126–43; internal validation of 189–91, 193–4, 199–201; object-categoric 21–2, 24–8, 138n; off-brand conception of 195, 197; particularist conception of 72,

75n12, 81; prima facie conception of 71–2, 81–2; probabilistic account of 33, 37–47; and professional roles 45–7; of proficiency 26–7; pro tanto conception of 71, 80–5; reason-categoric 21–4, 26–7; of relationship-responsiveness 27; response-categoric 21–2, 26–30, 138n; of self-control 25–8; as sensitivity 68–9, 82, 95; social dependence of 35–7; star-crossed 139–42; *see also* Aristotle; Kantian account of virtue; intellectual virtue(s)
virtue attribution 11–30, 51, 129–34; in remote scenarios 32–47
virtue ethics: Aristotelian 65–85, 101–5, 153–4, 189–200; and circularity 193–4, 200; Das's dilemma for 91–3, 104–5; direct (agent-based) 53, 58–9; long-standing criticism of 189, 193–6, 200; maximizing 58–63; normativity challenge to 190–201; and right action 18, 32, 35, 53, 58, 91–105; situationist challenge to 22n26, 32–47, 62–3, 191, 192n5
von Wright, G. H. 25n32
Vranas, Peter B. M. 34n5, 37n10
v-rules 68–73, 76, 82

Wallace, J. D. 20n24
Wallace, R. Jay 77
well-being: subjective conceptions of 191, 193–8; *see also* flourishing
Williams, Bernard 1n, 20n24, 79, 186n, 189n
Winch, Peter 79n18
Wittgenstein, Ludwig 77–9; *see also* forms of life
Wood, Allen W. 113n7
Woodcock, Scott 168, 173–4, 185, 187
wrongdoing: and inadequate reasons 18; and rule-following 68–9, 75–7, 83–4; in vice ethics 53–62

Zagzebski, Linda 101n17, 102, 132, 136n, 142n